much for me. No oth[er] ... [barcode] ... up here. I hardly ... all but there were so many things you did to make it easier and nicer and more comfortable. Everything that was hard. I love my room. It is so nice to open the door and find all my things. Such a wonderful feeling. I want to hug the room! I went to Chapel this morning with E. and walked out arm in arm with someone! It was very nice. Then I went to Seely with Ruth (McBarron) & E. who showed me the note room. Next I

D0484182

BRING ME A UNICORN

BRING ME A UNICORN

*Diaries
and Letters
of
Anne Morrow Lindbergh*

1922-1928

A Helen and Kurt Wolff Book
Harcourt Brace Jovanovich, Inc., New York

Copyright © 1971, 1972 by Anne Morrow Lindbergh

All rights reserved.
No part of this publication may be reproduced
or transmitted in any form
or by any means, electronic or mechanical,
including photocopy, recording,
or any information storage and retrieval system,
without permission in writing
from the publisher.

ISBN 0–15–114180–0
Library of Congress Catalog Card Number: 71–182329
Printed in the United States of America
C   D   E   F

The lines by James Stephens on page 45 are from "The Paps of Dana"
and are reprinted with permission of The Macmillan Company, New
York; Mrs. Iris Wise; Macmillan London and Basingstoke; and The
Macmillan Company of Canada Limited from *Collected Poems* by James
Stephens, copyright 1915 by The Macmillan Company, renewed 1943 by
James Stephens. John Masefield's lines on page 109 are from "The Passing
Strange" and are reprinted with the permission of The Macmillan Com-
pany, New York, and The Society of Authors as the literary representative
of the Estate of John Masefield, from *Poems* by John Masefield, copyright
1920 by John Masefield, renewed 1948 by John Masefield. The lines on
page 110 of Edgar Lee Masters's "Alexander Throckmorton" are from
Spoon River Anthology, copyright 1915, 1916, 1942, 1944 by Edgar Lee
Masters, and are reprinted by permission of Ellen C. Masters.

Everything today has been
heavy and brown.
Bring me a Unicorn
to ride about the town.

A. M. L., 1926

Acknowledgments

I am deeply grateful to my friend and publisher William Jovanovich, whose suggestions sparked this project and whose encouragement throughout has been constant. My special gratitude goes to Helen Wolff who, with her husband, Kurt Wolff, has been my friend and publisher for many years. Without her extraordinary perception, experience, and skill in cutting and editing, long and painstaking hours of work, and above all, without her creative gifts of understanding and intuitive insight, the original diary and letter material could not have been brought to its present form.

I am greatly indebted also to James Holsaert for invaluable advice in cutting and editing and meticulous care in reading, checking, and research involved in the preparation of the manuscript.

In addition, I wish to express my appreciation of their generous assistance in the assembling of material used in this book to the staffs of the following organizations: Harcourt Brace Jovanovich, Inc.; especially to Lisa M. Mayer and Helen Mills. The William Allan Neilson Library, Smith College; especially to Alice T. Hastings and Billie Bozone. The Sophia Smith Collection, Smith College; especially to Mary-Elizabeth Murdock, Winifred S. Brown, and Virginia A. Christenson. The Sterling Memorial Library, Yale University; especially to Judith A. Schiff. The Robert Frost Library, Amherst College; especially to J. Richard Phillips.

For her persevering efforts in tracing and uncovering old letters in voluminous family files of my mother and sister, Constance Morgan, I must thank Ruth Beckham of Vancouver, Washington.

Acknowledgments

For secretarial assistance in the preparation of the manuscript I am particularly grateful for the long hours of careful work of Jean O. Saunders and Joan Amatucci Hutzler.

I cannot end without recording gratefully the time, patience, thought, and tireless effort devoted by my husband to the assembling, reading, and checking of the manuscript.

ANNE MORROW LINDBERGH

Editorial Note

The diary and letter material in this book has been cut for repetition and readability, but has not been rewritten. Spelling has been corrected and punctuation standardized. Since this is a personal rather than a historical record, the footnotes were kept, in general, contemporary with the diary and purposely brief, confined to information essential to understanding the text.

The following abbreviations have been used throughout:

D. W. M.—Dwight Whitney Morrow

E. C. M.—Elizabeth Cutter Morrow (Mrs. Dwight Morrow)

E. R. M.—Elisabeth Reeve Morrow

C. C. M.—Constance Cutter Morrow

A. M. L.—Anne Morrow Lindbergh

C. A. L.—Charles A. Lindbergh

ILLUSTRATIONS

Illustrations

INTRODUCTION

Why do people publish diaries and letters? If they have had interesting lives, they may feel they can add a tiny segment to the history of their times or put a missing fragment of mosaic in the picture. In terms of the individual there is the wish to give testimony to a journey taken by one human being which might amuse, enlighten, or explain other individuals to themselves. In the case of an individual who has lived somewhat in the public eye, there is always the hope of clarifying a record that has been obscured by rumors and blurred by distorted images. And finally, perhaps, the writer seeks some kind of personal summation in order to discover for himself the true essence of a life.

In rereading my material, diaries and letters, for eventual disposition, I was chiefly struck by what an extraordinary life this quite ordinary person led. Some record of it, I felt, was worth publishing. But what form should it take? Since autobiography has always been favorite reading for me, quite naturally I considered using this form. To write an autobiography would mean sifting, picking and choosing, shaping and cutting, and then putting the material into orderly chapters, finished portraits, and polished phrases. There is much to recommend such a process. A more unified literary work certainly results. But there are certain drawbacks. What remains in the end is the point of view of a mature person only. At best—and its "best" is very good indeed—an autobiography reveals a glimpse of life seen at the end of a telescope, from a single stance, that of a woman in the last third of life. At worst, what sometimes emerges can be a glossed-over, retouched picture, mild, pleasant, and perhaps edifying but, on the whole, static.

Once started on the painful journey toward honesty, with the passage of time one has increasingly the desire not to gloss over, not to foster illusions or to create fixed images, inasmuch as this is humanly possible. One wants to be an honest witness to the life one has lived and the struggle one has made to find oneself and one's work, and to relate oneself to others and the world.

So I decided on publishing some of the diaries, along with letters, as a more truthful presentation of these years. There is, naturally, a distinction between diaries and letters. Letters are usually written not only to communicate with the recipient, but also to amuse or please him. So that the truth here is sometimes veiled or colored. Diaries are written for oneself and reveal the writer as he is when alone. My diaries were written primarily, I think, not to preserve the experience but to savor it, to make it even more real, more visible and palpable, than in actual life. For in our family an experience was not finished, not truly experienced, unless written down or shared with another. Much of the sharing was in letters to members of the family, chiefly between the women. The vast majority of my letters in early years are to my mother, the next in number to my sisters, Elisabeth, who was two years older, and Constance, who was younger. There were very few letters to my father, who was considered—and certainly was—too busy to reply. With my younger brother, Dwight, I shared much in conversation when we were together, but there are not so many letters.

Analyzing this preponderance of letters only between the women of a very closely knit family and finding almost the same phenomenon in my own adult family, I come to the conclusion that letters—even good letters—are often concerned with the domestic straws and pebbles of daily life, a realm which, rightly or wrongly, seems traditionally assigned to women. Letters from fathers are apt to be occasions, weighty with advice, congratulation, or information. In return, letters addressed to fathers are often requests for advice, approval, or help in some guise. The starch of self-consciousness tends to stiffen both sides of the correspondence, while letters between mother and daughter, or between sisters, ripple on, trivially perhaps, but totally un-self-conscious.

On the other hand diaries, even honest ones, also have their drawbacks. Some of my early ones, written by a person brought up in the Protestant tradition, without benefit of confessional and before the heyday of analysis, were an attempt both to understand and forgive the blunders and difficulties of the writer. The adolescent diaries in particular, to my embarrassment, are often self-conscious and self-centered, immature and sentimental. But they are, at least, spontaneous, honest, alive, and moving. More important, I detect, even in the adolescent outpourings (much cut to spare the reader), the incipient search for honesty and the early wrestling with illusions, conventions, and conditionings.

In the later diaries, fortunately, there is less self-analysis and more objective description of the people and events around me. But before one can reach that "extraordinary" life that followed the ordinary childhood and youth, one must know something of the background. Here autobiographies have the advantage.

Some hint should be given of the small-town atmosphere in which I was brought up. Englewood, New Jersey, where I was born, was a town, not a suburb, in those days, with generous backyard life and neighbors' children wearing paths through scraggly privet hedges. Some understanding is needed of the close family ties, which extended beyond the immediate family to the preceding generation. My mother's mother, "Grandma Cutter," was an important figure in our youth, making frequent visits and often supervising us—rather strictly, I remember—in our mother's absence. An upright, devout, and gracious old lady, with an unquenchable zest for life, she lived to take her first flight over Mexico City with "Colonel Lindbergh," and to be a great-grandmother to some of my children. My mother's relationship to her two sisters, Annie, who never married and lived with my grandmother in Cleveland, and Edith, who married Sheldon Yates and made her home near us in Englewood, was an unusually close sisterly bond. Both "Aunt Annie," with her wit and knowledge of children's books (she was head of the children's section of the Cleveland Public Library), and Aunt Edith, fourteen years younger than our mother, with a warm spontaneity and vigor that bridged the generations, added sprightliness and gaiety to our lives.

As to my father's side, my mother, with a true matriarchal tenacity, gathered and held together in the larger family circle the great clan of Morrows from Pittsburgh. My Grandfather Morrow died before I was born but I remember my gay and indomitable little Grandmother Morrow, and saw a great deal of my father's older brother, Jay, and his three sisters, Alice, Agnes, and Hilda (who, because of their ample forms, were irreverently called by us "The Larger Aunts" in contrast to the small birdlike "Cutter Aunts").

Summers were a time of family reunions, first in rambling monstrosities of rented houses on Cape Cod, and later in our own white clapboard house built on the quiet rock-bound island of North Haven, Maine. In addition, family celebrations of Thanksgiving, Christmas, and New Year's were not complete without the larger family circle of aunts, uncles, and cousins who joined in our sometimes noisy family jokes, songs, and games at table. These customs, which I have never observed to such a degree in other families, then or since, now seem to me touchingly childish and somewhat inexplicable in a family usually quiet and restrained in behavior. Were these boisterous rites of hand-holding and singing (stimulated by nothing more intoxicating than turkey, fellowship, and sweet cider) introduced by my father or my mother? And were they a substitute for conversation, perhaps become strained among sisters and brothers who had outgrown an earlier relationship? Or were they an outward and tangible expression of family solidarity and a necessary safety valve for the usual seriousness of a generation brought up to be earnest, conscientious, hard-working citizens, with much stress on high morals, good behavior, and self-control?

The strong moral fiber in both parents came from similar

backgrounds in the Middle West. Both families were regular Presbyterian churchgoers, and in both, education was highly prized while money for it was strictly limited. My mother was a pioneer in her passionate desire for a college education. Her years at Smith College under President Seelye were a rich and liberating experience that marked her life and in turn marked ours. My father, the fourth child in the large family of a mathematics professor, scraped his way through college by tutoring and borrowing from an older brother and sister. For him especially, after the constrictive years in Pittsburgh, Amherst College and the beauty of the rural Connecticut Valley were a release for his mind and spirit and a spur to his ambition. In an age of American history when ambition was considered a virtue, and the myth of "Boy-from-small-town-makes-good" was new and valid, both parents were frankly ambitious, with enough energy to match their aspirations. I often think of a remark of my friend Edward Sheldon, the playwright, many years later: "The wonderful thing about the Puritans," he said to me, "was their energy." Our parents obviously had a superabundance of Puritan energy.

Perhaps it was this Puritan energy that made them, by temperament as well as tradition, teachers. My father used to say he was the son of a teacher, brother of a teacher (Alice Morrow), married to a teacher, and the father of a teacher. (My sister Elisabeth later started a nursery school in Englewood.) My mother actually taught school for several years before her marriage, but my father, except for tutoring, never entered the teaching profession. He turned instead, with a poor boy's ambition, first to law, and after successful years in a legal firm, went into banking and international finance, and eventually into diplomacy as Ambassador to Mexico (1927–1929). When he died, in 1931, he was Senator from New Jersey. But throughout his career in the business, financial, and diplomatic worlds, he yearned nostalgically for the academic life—not in mathematics, though he had a mathematician's mind, but as professor of history. Actually, as Harold Nicolson pointed out in the life of my father, in every task he encountered he was continually and incorrigibly a teacher to adults. The reverse, as is often the case, was also true. He was a curious, hungry, and ceaseless learner, an inveterate reader of history, philosophy, economics (Herodotus, Plutarch's *Lives,* and Plato were ranged beside Froude, Bagehot, and Prescott).

With such a propensity for teaching, it is not strange that much stress was put on our education, both moral and intellectual. It started early in the home with nightly prayers and evening reading by our mother from the meritorious *Heidi, The Book of Saints and Friendly Beasts,* and *Little Women,* progressing to the Greek myths and the classics. On Sunday evenings there were Bible stories and sometimes sermons on the green sofa in her bedroom. (This hour was in addition to early morning prayers, kneeling down in a row by our parents' big bed, followed by regular church service.) Our father also occasionally read to us from *The Just So Stories* and *The Jungle Book.* But his teaching was not entirely recreation. Breakfasts were sometimes made horrendous by the public practice of our multiplication tables or questions of addition or subtraction that were shot at us from the head of the table. To this day if someone asks me suddenly: "How much is 7 times 8?" my mind blanks to the child's frozen landscape of panic.

From these worthy efforts we went on to local schools until, when our father became a partner of J. P. Morgan & Co., our life enlarged in scope and we had also an apartment in New York City. I spent four years under the stern but noble eye of Miss Chapin, and went on to Smith College, where I began to grow up under the scholarship, wit, wisdom, and moral grandeur of President Neilson.

There were, of course, vacations, but along with physical recreation our minds were not allowed to idle. If summering in New England, we always had our reading lists and suitcases of books. The communal family reading took on a more relaxed tone in summer, appropriate to wicker armchairs and shady verandas.

Trollope and Jane Austen, I remember, or even something as en-
tertaining as Mark Twain or O. Henry.

Even our trips abroad, which were frequent after my father
joined the firm of J. P. Morgan & Co., were planned instructively.
No doubt these journeys had a business aspect for our father, and
certainly in the hub cities of London, Paris, or Geneva, there were
vital conversations with Morgan partners on finance and loans,
war debts and reparations. Nevertheless, instead of traveling alone
and in peace as they might have done (I think today, in astonished admiration, of their energy and enthusiasm) our parents
elected to take a family of four active children all over the continent of Europe. Travel was considered part of our education and
they were, as usual, thorough about it. We traveled slowly and
deliberately by boat and top-heavy limousine, loaded with mountains of luggage: suitcases, overnight bags, hatboxes, book bags,
and map satchels. Steamer trunks accompanied us on the boat
but were left in Paris or London. Our trips were meticulously
scheduled and documented, and although largely instructive,
they were enlivened by the irrepressible good spirits of our father
on vacation and graced by the new delights of European living.
We stayed at charming small inns and always stopped for leisurely lunches of the local *plat du jour* and *vin du pays*. With my
father's passion for history, we drove across France on Roman
roads. "Look, Anne," my father would lean forward with excitement, pointing to the long line of poplar trees, "see how straight
this is—a fine old Roman road!" So we rumbled on to see the
walls of Aigues-Mortes or the Maison Carrée at Nîmes or the
aqueduct near Avignon. We trouped through the French châ-
teaux, our father reading to us appropriate passages from Henry
James' *A Little Tour in France*. We visited the French and
British cathedrals with our father carrying Henry Adams' bulky
Mont-Saint-Michel and Chartres under his arm.

In Paris, it was our mother who enthusiastically took charge of
the sightseeing, since she had spent a year here with her family
before her marriage. And in England, led by our mother's love of

poetry, we went to the Lake Country to see Wordsworth's house at Grasmere, taking special detours to Tintern Abbey and the Trossachs, which were the subjects of favorite poems. Even the younger members of the family were encouraged to suggest what literary shrines they would like to visit. On an early trip to Scotland, I longed to see where "Black Agnes of Dunbar" defended her castle from the English attack. And my younger sister wanted to mourn at the grave of "Greyfriars' Bobby."

The children of our family were certainly given the best education available. But our parents' belief in education reached far beyond their own family. My mother's convictions drew her into long service as a trustee of Smith College. She was the first woman Chairman of the Board, and, for a short period, interim President of the college. My father's concern for scholarship led him to hours of work as a trustee and member of the finance and executive committees of Amherst College. Despite his business background, his reputation in the educational world was sufficient to merit him an offer of the presidency of Yale University—an honor he sometimes regretted not having accepted. In fact, with our mother's crusading for women's education, and our father's devotion to Amherst, and our sister's pioneering for nursery schools, this stress on education became somewhat of a local joke. A prospective son-in-law, chatting in a train with a stranger, who learned of his impending visit to the Morrow family, was startled by the frank comment, "They're a fine family, but nuts on education."

With all this education and travel, how can one explain the haze of insulation which permeated our early years, our indefinable sense of isolation from the real world? It is clear that no matter what we read or where we traveled we were enclosed in the familial circle, confined, although also enriched, by the strong family bonds and strictly defined child-parent roles. The great bulldozers of twentieth-century society: Freud, Marx, Henry Ford, and—I might add—Charles Lindbergh, had not yet cut their way through the brambled hedges that surrounded the sleeping princesses. Only in college did I begin to realize how much I resembled the "sheltered Emelye" of Chaucer's Knight's Tale, enclosed in a walled garden.

But the world—or the world of the average American family in the early 1900's—was not unlike a walled garden. World War I rolled by, but to children growing up at the time it appeared chiefly in popular songs ("Over There" and "Pack Up Your Troubles in Your Old Kit Bag") and patriotic recruiting posters ("Uncle Sam Needs YOU"), in drives for war-savings stamps, and bandage-rolling sessions, and pictures in the rotogravure section of newspapers. It is true that during the war my father served under General Pershing in London on the Allied Maritime Shipping Council with Sir Arthur Salter, Jean Monnet, and Professor B. D. Attolico. My mother raised money for and visited the Smith College Volunteer Nurses Unit in Grécourt, France. In our quiet lives, these activities were unusual interruptions that brought us a touch of the outside world and a glimpse of what was going on "over there." Later, there were the summer trips abroad but always enclosed in the secure and happy phalanx of the family.

The menacing cloud of the atom bomb had not yet darkened our skies. And we had not heard of concentration camps, pogroms, genocide, or wholesale slaughters. If they existed (and they have always existed in some place or form) they were part of the uncivilized past or the barbaric hinterland. They were not served up for our daily consumption along with our orange juice and oatmeal. Radio and television had not yet brought the sufferings of the world into our parlors. During my youth, outside of his regular job, my father worked with his usual intensity for prison reform in New Jersey, and my mother, for the Y.W.C.A. But though we were aware of certain neglected areas in our social structure, there was a general confidence that these blotches on our national record would soon be erased.

There was, in fact, great hope in the world when we were growing up. People were stirred by Woodrow Wilson's optimistic promise of "a war to end war" and the plans for a League of Nations with its hopes for national self-determination and the peaceful arbitration of disputes, with "open covenants, openly arrived at." Even "the Russian experiment" was discussed with interest and some excitement by my parents and their friends. My father wrote a book called *The Society of Free States* on the history and steps toward international co-operation. My mother campaigned for equal education for women. "Good works" were prevalent and indiscriminate. No one questioned their value or the inevitable progress to the millennium. It was the era of Coué: "Everyday in every way [we were] getting better and better."

This, of course, was the world of the "grownups." I am astonished—on the evidence in these early diaries—at how long the younger members of our family were looked upon, and looked upon themselves, as children. As far back as I can remember, we children always sat at table with our parents and their friends. (And such friends: Chester and Amey Aldrich, the Vernon Munroes, Dean Woodbridge, Judge Hand, Jean Monnet, Ernest Barker, the Thomas Lamonts, etc.) But we were not supposed to speak, only to listen. To be "seen and not heard" was still the rule—or at least the habit—even up to the time I was married.

Our tight family circle and behavior were perhaps unusual for the period. The post-World War I era has been romantically called a time of "Flaming Youth." These were the days of Prohibition, speak-easies, free love (or, in a milder form, "necking"), flappers, the Charleston, and smuggled copies of Elinor Glyn's *It*. The wave of these intoxicating possibilities never lapped the shores of our serene and respectable island. Our mother stayed up waiting for my sister and me if we went out to dance (only with the well-brought-up sons of old family friends) and we were made to feel black remorse if we returned home later than midnight.

In fact, I can well understand the remark made to me by a sophisticated Chilean after a few minutes of conversation at an

Embassy tea in Mexico City (I was then just out of college and seriously considering marriage):

"You have a seester *younger* than *you?*" she asked with suppressed mirth. "Eet ees not *poss*eeble!"

It was not possible, and even as the remark hit home I recognized its truth. I was the youngest, shiest, most self-conscious adolescent that—I believe—ever lived. In addition, I have to confess that my adolescence lasted a phenomenally long time. Dare I say I have outgrown that period even now?

But if one eliminates adolescence from life and records, how much is suppressed: youth, hope, dreams, impractical ideals, falling in love with countless "not impossible He's," gaiety that spurts up for no reason, despair that is gone the next morning, and a foretaste of the inevitable tragedies of life along with one's early confused attempts to understand or meet them.

Without giving a glimpse of the walled garden how can one appreciate the unwalled world into which this "sheltered Emelye" emerged? How understand, to quote my diary of the time, "the bomb" dropped by "Colonel Lindbergh" into our "college-bred, forever book-reading, introspective family?"

Besides, I have a certain respect for the early efforts of this struggling adolescent, who now seems so many lives removed from the self of today. I can laugh at her and am often embarrassed by her, but I do not want to betray her. Let her speak for herself.

1922

Bradbury Private Hotel
North Berwick, Scotland
Sunday, August 20, 1922

Dear Grandma:[1]

We have all just gotten Aunt Annie's[2] lovely letters and it has been wonderful hearing about everything at home. Her description of the garden made me long for it. There are some beautiful gardens here in North Berwick but you only can get a glimpse of them if you are lucky through a half-opened gate. And then, it makes you want to see more of it. Are there any roses in our garden, I wonder? All the gardens here have roses peeking over the high stone walls, and if you can see inside there are red ramblers growing propped up on sticks, and pink and white and yellow tea roses growing in the neat little beds, and all kinds of pinks and sweet-smelling low flowers growing below the roses. We are seeing a lot of the country around here, we children more than Mother and Daddy because we see a great deal on horseback.

We love Edinburgh and went there yesterday to shop and see Harry Lauder,[3] but Elisabeth was to tell about that. We had great fun in Romaine and Paterson's woolen store getting woolen stockings and sweaters and plaid scarfs. I got a red woolen sweater with green stripes on it! Mother would say that it was pink or rose, with a dark border—but I prefer to call it red with green stripes. Daddy bought some more books. We have a whole roomful now. Mr. Campbell[4] says that we will have to charter a

---

[1] Mrs. Charles L. Cutter.

[2] Annie Cutter, E. C. M.'s sister, librarian, lived with her mother in Cleveland.

[3] Sir Harry Lauder (1870–1950), an enormously popular singer of Scotch ballads and songs.

[4] Hotel manager, breeder and judge of West Highland white terriers.

steamer to take them all back. Daddy doesn't do anything but read and play golf and visit bookstores. And Mother reads (to her children) and plays golf and visits antique shops. You can see what a fine time we are having, and we children read and play golf and visit alternately bookstores and antique shops. But we ride horseback and play with the dogs and on the beach and climb up the "Law," too. We have bought a West Highland terrier for Aunt Amey.[1] You know her dog "Coolin" was run over and Mother wanted to get another for her. He is called "Tinker" and he is a dear little ten-months-old puppy with a gentle, loving face. *We* think he is much nicer than "Coolin," who used to howl and creep under my skirts when he heard thunder and howl in the night, too. Do you remember, Grandma?

Dwight is getting on awfully well with his arithmetic as Daddy is helping him, and if anyone can teach arithmetic Daddy ought to be able to.

Con has become a teacher, too. She has been teaching Daddy the Hundred and Twenty-first Psalm. Daddy says that to ensure success in teaching, the teacher (among other things) must be inspired with a love of her pupil. We think that Con satisfies the requirement.

We are going home on the *Adriatic,* you know. I wonder if the purser and the captain will be surprised to see us returning with books enough to fill two cabins, coats, hats, dresses, suits, stockings, golf clubs, shawls, scarfs, prints, pictures (portraits), tables, furniture, an old mantelpiece (maybe), a dog, and we might even have brought along two lovebirds but we left them in Paris with Mme Dubost.[2] I have forgotten, even now, china, antiques galore. I may be exaggerating a little as all these things won't go with us but we will get them in the end.

---

[1] Amey Aldrich, college friend of E. C. M., sister of Chester Aldrich; both were close friends of the Morrow family.

[2] Girlhood friend of E. C. M.'s.

DIARY   *Englewood, N. J., Sunday, September 17, 1922*
Our last Sunday all together. Elisabeth is going back to college
and Dwight to Groton for the first time.

We all went to church together. Sermon was about being able
"to burn one's bridges behind one, to follow a dream." *To dare!*

Mother had us all on the green sofa in her room and talked to
us and she said to us, "Whatever thy hand findeth to do, do it
with thy might." Mother was almost crying and told us always to
remember that wherever we went in the world, "Whatever thy
hand findeth to do, do it with thy might."

TO E. R. M.   [*Late September, 1922*]
Dear Linda:
Thanks loads for taking any of your precious time to write me.
But you'll have to take some more of your "precious time" to
advise me. And don't get too shocked when I utter a statement to
you that will knock you cold!

I want to go to Vassar!

Of course I have been bred and born in a Smith family. I have
been taught to look up to it and have met more Smith people
than any other kind and have been up there and seen it and love
it—the college and grounds and all. And I love it because you do,
and Mother does, and Daddy and Aunt Edith, and "Aunt"
Maud[1] and, oh, *millions* of people, and because I have sort of felt
myself promised to the college ever since I can remember and I
don't know Vassar graduates and I'm not connected with it at all.

But when you went to Smith you knew girls who were going.
Now *I* don't know a single girl going to Smith in my class. *All*
the girls I like are going to Vassar. *All* of them. It's hard to be
left out, but it isn't all. You've gone to Smith and love it. But
listen, although they (everybody) says, "How nice it will be to go
to college and have your sister there," well, that's true, but that's
why I don't want to go!

[1] "Aunt" Maud Hulst, Englewood friend of E. C. M.

You're popular, clever, pretty, attractive, capable, and will be a *big bug!* And I don't want to go with *you* ahead of me. With *you* to live up to, *you* and *Mother!!* And besides, I don't want to go just because you're going, and Mother went, and nothing else.

I want to do something different. I want to start somewhere else. I want to do something entirely independent. It would be hard to have all of you, you and Mother and Aunt Edith and the whole family, against me and all the womenfolk reuning at Smith and going around having lots of fun and me left out. I can see everybody shocked at *me,* "Bess Cutter's daughter, going to *Vassar!!!!*" I caught a sort of spirit of the place that is hard to resist, but still I have thought it over and over and I would like better to go somewhere else. Preferably Vassar. I am *not* disappointed in Smith but *I want something else.* I've only hinted it to Mother but that was last spring. This is what I gathered from her. Vassar is a worthy rival of Smith. Vassar is a splendid college. Vassar is the best college next to Smith. She would not disinherit me if I went to Vassar but would like very much to have one daughter in Smith and one in Vassar if both could not be at Smith.

Oh dear, I know *you don't understand,* you think, "Just because she knows a few nice girls that are going to Vassar she is going to break away from all traditions, all natural instincts, all the feeling and attitude for Smith that she has got in her, she is going to dash away from family influence and wishes and friends' influence and wishes to go to *Vassar!!!*" But isn't it enough to have *two* illustrious people out of our family go to Smith? They might at least let *me try* Vassar and not laugh at me.

I honestly believe that Smith girls are no better than Vassar girls and Smith graduates no better than Vassar graduates and the Smith education no better than the Vassar education. In fact I think they are very much alike but I want to go to a different place from you and Mother and I want to bring back a different view of things to our family, and that plus all my friends and the

Vassar influence in school is pulling me to my opinion. After all *what* do you go to college for?

An *education*, yes, but you can get that at either college.

The *experience*, yes, *very much so*, and that is why I want to go away to get more experience, something apart from what I've been brought up to worship.

The *training, of course.* And you will get trained for life at any big college, but isn't an experiment the best training you can get? I want to experiment. I want to go to Vassar, where I have nobody to "emulate," at least, nothing ahead of me. To try what I can do without knowing about it beforehand. Do you see?

The *companionship. Of course* I think that I could get this at Smith, but the fact that all my friends, everybody I like and admire is going to Vassar makes me feel that Vassar must be made up of such girls, that you *would* get the companionship there that everybody likes. Do you see? I am weak. I have always been weak. It will take courage to break away from *everything* I have been brought up to love (Smith and Smith people, and the place and customs and *everything*) to go and start out somewhere new and against everybody's expectations. Oh, I wish to Heaven they'd let me do something *strong, let* me show that I can stand up alone. Do you see? Of course I'd be homesick, *of course* I'd miss the daughters of Mother's friends that you have. *Of course* it would be hard and seem strange to everyone, but— oh gosh—I wish I *could!*

P.S. *Please* don't write back and say, "All I know is that you'll miss an awful lot if you don't come up to Smith!" That's not going to help me *at all.* Write what you'd do if you were me!

1923

Dear Mother,

This green paper is to cheer you up—I hope you won't need it—or it is to cheer me up. If you write any poems in Nassau about Nassau, won't you send them to me. And I'll try to write some from the window sill. Which is the best place to write poetry. (Here's one borrowed from you.)

> All day at work in musty books,
>   My mind has bread.
> At night upon the window sill
>   My soul is fed!

which is very dumb because if you hadn't worked during the day your soul wouldn't have anything to feed on at night on the window sill.

And here is another one and I don't know why I wrote it as it doesn't apply to me. As Sara Teasdale said, "I write of sorrow, I have no sorrow, I only borrow from some tomorrow."

> COR. 13 (?)
> A trust in you through life and death
>   and this is Faith
> Your soul and mine, Eternity's scope
>   and this is Hope
> And Faith and Hope and God Above
>   And this is Love.

1923

1924

My darling Mother!

The end of the first day! You were so lovely, dear, to leave me the books under the pillow. I found them the next morning when I was making my bed and it made me so happy, especially the lovely "sentiment" in the beginning. I read the first lesson,[1] right away.

The room looked so beautifully neat and tidied and fixed when I came back. How adorable of you to empty the trunk and put away all my things for me. You did so much for me, Mother, when you were up here. I hardly thanked you at all but there were so many things you did to make it easier and nicer and more comfortable. Everything that was hard. I love my room. It is so nice to open the door and find all my things. Such a wonderful feeling. I want to *hug* the room! I went to chapel this morning with Elisabeth and walked out arm in arm with someone! It was very nice.

I love the walk past the President's, every morning. I see Paradise [Pond] and Mt. Tom and think of you.

[*Northampton, September 28, 1924*]
Sunday

Mother, darling—

I should like to write you pages and pages but I simply can't. I never knew anything like the rush in college. It is simply terrifying. Every moment I spend *not* rushing I feel that I'm wasting, that I should be rushing to a class or something or studying. At first the whole thing was too terrifying for words—the social as well as the work side—but especially the work side. Not in the

[1] In a book of daily prayers, or "lessons."

day but at night like a perfect demon hanging over me. And I got quite panicky but it is gradually getting better and better although it still seems new and very strange and I feel very shy and young and incapable.

Elisabeth and I went to Vespers today. It was simply beautiful. President Neilson[1] talked wonderfully about opportunity and the responsibility of it. The text was from Kings and a wonderful one I must find, something like this: "I will give thee two thousand horses if thou, on thy part, wilt put men to ride on them."

This is so hurried you won't be able to read it. People are all *so* nice and things are getting better and better. The more I think of it the more I realize what a wonderful thing you've given me. But I am just wondering whether I can ride the two thousand horses!

[1] William Allan Neilson, President of Smith College, 1917–39.

1925

Mother, darling,

I have been doing awfully poor work lately—I don't know why—in everything; an awful slump. I'm beginning to pick up now. Greek in particular has been hard this term but I'm talking it over with Miss Gifford[1] tomorrow. It isn't really serious.

I have one wonderful thing to tell you before the supper bell rings. I handed my first long, worked-over theme in to Miss Kirstein[2] yesterday. Today I met, going to class, a girl from the other half of our section—Miss Kirstein had read my theme in class (that doesn't mean anything for she often reads poor ones for examples)—but *she said she liked it* and the class liked it and she said she had always felt that R. L. Stevenson was smug but she never found anyone else that did. Then she read another Freshman paper and remarked that the Freshmen were setting a rather high standard for the class! Which is, of course, a joke. Then I came to class and she was giving out papers and she handed me mine and said, "That was very nice *indeed*, Miss Morrow," and then handing me two enchanting books of rhymes said, "I thought you might enjoy these—they aren't as good as those others, but you may take them home and read them, if you like." I am so smothered with joy. She hardly ever says anything—a few delightful remarks on the paper and *this* on the outside: "Very nice, indeed, written with insight and taste and the rare ability to choose the right quotations." Oh, *Mother!*

[1] Natalie M. Gifford, instructor of Greek.

[2] Mina Kirstein, teacher of creative writing; author, under her married name, Mina Curtiss.

Mother darling—

I am terribly sorry not to have written for so long but it has been so frantically crowded and I have been very discouraged and I couldn't bear to write "from the depths"!

It is a little better now. The work seems to be piling up frightfully and the coils are tightening. Finals are pushing from the other side and it gives you a permanent hounded feeling.

And I'm *not* doing any outside things. Not a thing! Really. I don't see anyone that isn't in my classes or in my house and all the time that's not spent at classes is spent studying. Perhaps I get stale.

Writing for Miss Kirstein takes *hours*, too. And it needs consecutive hours. I haven't any consecutive hours except at night and on Sunday. Sunday is always one long stretch of work from morning until quite late, without even the break of going to classes.

I do wish I had some alibi for such inefficiency—something like having appendicitis or being in love, or brain fever—but I haven't *any* excuse—I am a healthy contented sane creature but I seem to work like molasses.

I think a great deal of it is because I can't seem able ever to drop it from my mind and get away from it and come back refreshed. That is awfully silly of me, but wherever I go I take it all with me—all the paraphernalia of work—mental paraphernalia. I look at a birch tree through a mist of gym shoes, course cards, alarm clocks, papers due, writtens, laundry boxes, choir practices, bills, long themes, and *exams*—etc. It hounds me doggedly and I think much too much about it and it makes me discouraged, and when I'm discouraged I can't do *anything*. This sounds so much worse than it is. I really shouldn't get discouraged. It is just because I can't see anything outside of college. It is so absorbing that it has loomed all out of proportion and I feel cut off from everything else.

But, Mother, in spite of this torrent of complaints, I love it—I really do—and I wouldn't stop for anything in the world. I've never had anything like it before. It is thrilling and absorbing and wonderful.

I'm not taking any writing course [next year]. Do you think that's awful? Of course there will be a good deal of writing in Eng. 19, and reports to make and write in the History. The reason I'm not taking it is that I won't have time to do them all as fully as I want to, if I do. Besides, I've learned from Miss Kirstein's course that (thrilling as she and it are) I really need more to think about and less to write about. Nothing I write has any backbone to it and it won't have until I absorb more. Do you think it's very silly?

[*Northampton, October 10, 1925*]
[*Beginning of Sophomore year*]

Mother, darling

I can't begin to describe the classes—the Renaissance History, the Elizabethan Literature course with *Miss Dunn!*[1] *She* is taking it this year!! And she is *so* charming—her conversation so *rich* and so *stimulating*. It is the most glorious world—I feel like a Magellan! It is really a Renaissance course, too, and fits in *beautifully* with the History. Also Miss Lewis's[2] theme course, which is a "change" from Miss Kirstein's but so different that I think it will be very nice. Pure description, though, isn't half as intriguing as doing character sketches or criticism. It isn't going to be very easy for me—I *hate* describing country roads and approaches to houses. She is a charming hostess, a gracious lady in all her classes. She never talks louder than she has to, and that is so unusual here—a low, mellow, soothing voice that it is a delight to listen to. She smiles graciously too—the kind of smile that takes you by surprise. I can't describe it but that is what it does. She

---

[1] Esther Cloudman Dunn, professor of English literature, and A. M. L.'s faculty adviser.

[2] Mary Delia Lewis, associate professor of English.

suddenly smiles, with her eyes first, and then—then all of a sudden her whole face is smiling, too. I don't believe she ever hurries, or that abrupt annoying things ever startle her. She is on an island. I have written one description for her. It was a frightful effort—I haven't it back yet.

Physics is going to be very hard. I am the slowest one in the class.

Psychology is like Hygiene, as yet, we haven't gotten to the interesting part.

The Music[1] is going to be *very* interesting. The man is *charming*.

I have to stop, but I have to tell you that the whole spirit of this place is better—it has entirely changed. I feel differently. Some powers have no hold on me as they seemed to have before—I feel like saying, "Let them not have dominion over me!" Then I am more apart. I've gotten out of things—hockey, and Students Christian Association. I feel as though my head were no longer down under the blankets at the bottom of the bed.

> [*Northampton, October 11, 1925*]
> *Special delivery!*

My darling Mother!
I have just finished this poem. I don't care whether it is good or not, but it just had to come, and I am crying for joy—it has been so long:

HEIGHT

When I was young I felt so small
And frightened, for the world was tall.

And even grasses seemed to me
A forest of immensity,

Until I learned that I could grow
A glance would leave them far below.

---

[1] Music Appreciation course given by Professor Roy D. Welch.

Spanning a tree's height with my eye,
Suddenly I soared as high;

And fixing on a star I grew,
I pushed my head against the blue!

Still, like a singing lark, I find
Rapture to leave the grass behind.

And sometimes standing in a crowd
My lips are cool against a cloud.

1926

Dear Daddy,

I haven't had time to get you a birthday present. Perhaps I can bring one down when I come again, but it took time to get unpacked and I spent one day in bed with a cold (it was very nice. I read a whole book). I am so sorry that a birthday letter is the best I can do.

Daddy, you were *perfectly lovely* to come down to the station. When you were busy and working, to come and see me, it made me *so* happy. I do appreciate your doing it, darling, although I hardly had a chance to tell you so. I was shaking hands with everyone else's family. I didn't want to shake hands with everyone else's family. What was the name of the society?—the "what the hell" something society? You must tell me sometime, again. I did *love* so your coming down.

I am sorry if I showed you—at least that I seemed to be so discouraged during Christmas about my work and college. It seems so very ungrateful of me. Really, I am very happy here and I like to work—if only I could push all the trivial little things that bother me out of the way and dive down very deep. But it is worth it when you work and work—and suddenly discover a new continent. Do you remember that sonnet "On First Looking into Chapman's Homer"? One line I love:

> "Then felt I like some watcher of the skies
> When a new planet swims into his ken."

But that happens so seldom, and in the meantime the marks aren't very good, and those are the only things one can go by most of the time. You know, no matter what one says, they *really are* indicative.

I hope you don't need, or haven't missed this week, your

Erasmus. I hope they have sent you another one. Because I very selfishly took it up here to college. I have finished it and liked it very much, although I want to read someone else's book about Erasmus now. I love Erasmus. I really like him better than any man in history that I have read about (although they aren't many). I want to read about him. I want to read a great deal about him—to understand what many people thought about him because there are so many things about him that appeal directly to me that I am sure I must be prejudiced. I am very interested in him but I could not give you a clear outline of his life or a list of his principal works and their influence, or give at all accurately his religious views. Perhaps I have what someone has called "the precious prerogative of youth, which differs from old age in its happy capacity for admiration without understanding." Perhaps that's why I like to hear you talk. I'm sure I don't understand very much of it.

Erasmus had a delicious sense of humor, didn't he? He said somewhere when he was making out his will that he felt like a poor priest who wrote in *his,* "I have nothing; I owe much; the rest I give to the poor."

Well, you see, there is Erasmus, and then it is very beautiful up here sometimes. I am glad it has definitely become cold and snowy. I hate waiting for winter. I can't enjoy warm misty days when I know that blizzards are right on top of us. It is like trying to read *Life* while you sit in the dentist's office.

Also I like "that little Bacon girl" and "that little Sedgwick girl."[1] It is very nice to be with them and know them on a basis of *reading* instead of on a basis of just New York, if that is clear at all.

I am sorry for this long rambling letter that isn't a birthday letter at all but all about me, and why I like college. I hope you kept it to read it when there wasn't anything else important.

[1] Elizabeth Bacon and Edith Sedgwick, classmates and friends of A. M. L.

1926

Mother, darling,

We are out at Sophia Smith Homestead.[1] Apple blossoms are out, *almost,* and cherry blossoms all out—and I found white violets.

It is heavenly! Yesterday I sat in a field of violets for a long long time perfectly still, until I really sank into it—into the rhythm of the place, I mean—then when I got up to go home I couldn't walk quickly or evenly because I was still in time with that field. Do you see what I mean? It is a rather vague thought—I'll follow it through and tell you more when you come up.

I am getting terribly fond of Sue Cabot—she is a very wonderful person. Out at Sophia Smith's, Sedge and Bacon the first evening were running around like very happy colts. Now, spring evenings and low New England valleys and grass and still apple trees don't affect me that way. I am just as happy, but I don't feel coltish, although it has made me disappointed often that I couldn't skip around in the right spirit with either Sedge or Bacon. I've always tried and not been able to.

Well, that evening when Sedge said she wanted to dance around and run and skip, I said, "You know, I don't feel like that at all—I just feel like sitting here very, very still and absorbing it passively." Sue turned and said, "That's *just* the way I feel!" Do you see, Mother? It's such a relief to realize that you don't have to fit yourself to someone else's pattern. Sue, then, gave me a kind of new confidence in my pattern. You see, don't you? I don't mean that I want to sit in a field all my life and never want to *do* things—I do—but at different times.

Here's another discovery. People don't want to be understood—I mean not completely. It's too destructive. Then they haven't anything left. They don't want complete sympathy or complete

[1] Sophia Smith, founder of Smith College. E. C. M. was influential in restoring her homestead, used by students for overnight visits.

understanding. They want to be treated carelessly and taken for granted lots of times. There's more to that, but I haven't worked it out.

Oh, *Mother!* Such a heavenly thing happened in History—a silly little thing but it *did* please me so—so terribly—more than anything that has happened *for ages.*

You know how I've been feeling around bewilderedly after History, feeling as though I *could* grasp it, but always *just* missing somehow, always feeling toward it, never being able to prove that conviction that I *could* grasp the meaning of some of it—a little (a *very* little), the way Daddy does. You know how I adore Mr. Fay[1]—he's like Daddy—and how I have been longing to do History satisfactorily because of Daddy.

I am always too slow—always too hesitant. Always on writtens I sit and think it out before I write anything—I make little pencil jottings down and summings up—I collect the scattered messy scraps in my mind before I can try to answer a question. Then, of course, I *never* finish.

Well, we had a written the other day. As usual, I spent ten of every twenty minutes making jottings down of facts in pencil before I could co-ordinate it. There were three questions. Nothing is perfect. I never got to the last question at all! But almost everyone did. I was very disappointed again.

The day he handed the writtens back he stopped a little to talk about them. He spoke most about the first question, which he said was not as well done as it should have been. It was a question of comparing the results of two wars on Russia, internal and external results. Almost everyone when presented with a question like that, he said, writes out fully the results of one war and then writes out fully the results of the other, with perhaps a short sentence summing them up in comparison. Then he described the way it ought to be done and then said, "I have a question

[1] Sidney B. Fay, professor of history, later wrote *Origins of the World War.*

here that I think is very good, although too brief." Then he read mine!! (You see, I had written out two columns of results in my jottings down—very simple and obvious—and looking at these had written out a comparison.) Please forgive me for telling you—I know it is just a little thing but it did make me *so* happy. It was the only question he read. I felt like telegraphing Daddy— and it is such an ordinary thing, but I've never been able before to have my slow plodding system justified. He put "excellent" after the question on my paper and gave me *B* in spite of my not having touched the third. Oh, Mother! I am so happy.

I have had two tutoring lessons with Mr. W. — the Physics man. He lives in a stuffy little house and looks like MacDonald[1] when he has just come out of the garage. I have *never* seen hands the color of his. It is indescribable! I don't believe he *ever* washes them. I think he is trying to get permanently that color. He has a kind red face and mussy shirts—and I just *worship* him! He has tutored Smith College Physics girls for years and years and knows just what they give on the exams. He expects you to know *nothing* and teaches you more in an hour than the Physics Department in a month. Much against my will he started me on *problems!* I told him I *never* did problems, I *never* would, I always skipped them on the exams, but he said he could give me the principles of all the different kinds, and I *have* really been working out *problems!* He asked me if I got through at midyears and said I was better off than some! I feel so encouraged.

In *Irish Fairy Tales,* Chapter IV, page 266 (James Stephens), there is a description that sounds like my experience in the field: "There is a difference between this world and the world of Faery, but it is not immediately perceptible. Everything that is here is there, but the things that are there are better than those that are here. All things that are bright are there brighter. There is more gold in the sun and more silver in the moon of that land. There is more scent in the flowers and more savour in the fruit. There is

[1] The Morrows' chauffeur.

more comeliness in the men and more tenderness in the women. Everything in Faery is better by this one wonderful degree, and it is by this betterness you will know that you are there if you should ever happen to get there. . . ." It is very nice.

North Haven, Maine [July 9, 1926]

Dear Grandma,[1]

I am writing this for your birthday. The last time, we had our celebration together. It was very, very lovely and I shall always remember my nineteenth birthday and your eightieth.

I am so happy that we will see you in the summertime. I have so many lovely memories of summers or parts of summers with you. Winters, too, of course, but then winters are hurried and busy. Summers are restful and tranquil and sunny. I think of quiet afternoons when "Mrs. Irving" and "Mrs. Rosebride" sat and sewed with you and then sipped orangeade.[2]

Grandma, I have been so happy this spring, this summer, so happy that I feel like singing and singing most of the time. Does spring seem more beautiful to you every year? It is to me.

Not only that, but our family. It is really so wonderful. We are all together here, it is so beautiful, there isn't anything else that I want. We are so happy in ourselves, our family. We are so happy in each other. Mother and Daddy have done it, of course. But you have done it through Mother. How very wide your circle is, dear Grandma, all around you and so far! Our family is due to you, our happiness—because you did it in your family. This is so vague but I do sincerely want to give it to you somehow. I am

[1] Mrs. Charles L. Cutter.

[2] The reference is to sewing lessons started by Mrs. Cutter for Elisabeth and Anne as children during her summer visits. Characteristically, she enticed them at an early age to hemstitch endless bureau and pincushion covers by making a ceremony of the sewing "bee." E. and A. pretended they were ladies at a tea party and adopted make-believe names; E. was "Grace Irving" and A. "Bessie Rosebride." The afternoon was enlivened by Mrs. Cutter's reading and always ended with orangeade "tea." Much stress was put on clean hands and small stitches.

thankful for your birthday so many times. Your own self first and then you in other people, Aunt Annie, Aunt Edith, Mother, Elisabeth. So many things we love are you, I can't seem to explain except by little things, but flowers and beautiful handmade things—small stitches. So much of our reading and thinking—so many sweet customs and so much of our . . . well, our religion. It is all *you*. I hadn't realized it before. This is so vague but do you see a little, dear Grandma? I want to thank you.

DIARY   [*Sail for Europe—August, 1926*]
                               Friday, August 13th

New York and the docks quiet, deserted, hot, an unrestful quiet, though, like a sickroom in which there is a fever.

It seems unreal, all of it. It has seemed unreal since we left North Haven. I felt tonight (exhausted, dazed, troubled) the way I did years ago when as a very small child I was sometimes taken half asleep and protesting from one bed to another in the middle of the night.

The "suite"—crammed with extravagant and useless baskets, packages, Elisabeth's presents, etc.—really revolted me, especially with Banks[1] unctuously presiding over it (unfair—unfair, *nasty*).

Not half as many people as last time—hot and deserted.

P. sent us a telegram—darling! a beauty—it clicked! Just right—like him to send a good one.

We left.

Lights through the mist and over the water and no sound except now and then quite personal impudent horns from tugs. Those lights, paths over the water. The slow ponderous dignity of our turning ship. Elisabeth wistful, looking back.

That rushing sound of water, horns in the distance, feet on the deck.

A letter from P.

I wish I could thank him.

---

[1] Samuel Banks, the Morrows' butler.

Saturday, 14th

A heavenly day: no deck tennis, no unnecessary people, no bores.
I read Gilbert Murray—very beautiful.
And "The Art of Religion" in *The Dance of Life*[1]—wonderful.
And a third of *Tess of the d'Urbervilles*.
Glorious! A whole week of this—no deck tennis, no men.
Reading!!

Sunday, 15th

More of *The Dance of Life*.
My mind feels damp and heavy.

Monday, 16th

Read *Memoir* of Rupert Brooke—most of it. Perfectly delightful.
Some exquisite bits: "Laughter is the very garland on the head of
friendship." But mostly, rippling cool, swift, like foam, with
laughter through it like sun. I'd like to give it to all the people I
love best.
More of *Tess*. Magnificent.
Dancing.
Met Mr. B.—very charming and kind. Easy to talk to. I can't
help thinking of my struggles with embarrassment, self-consciousness, shyness, stupidity etc. last year. It gives me confidence
to feel that I've gained over those demons a little.

Tuesday, 17th

The Dance of Life—I am all mixed up with vague cloak-words
which mean one thing one moment and another the next—
chameleon words.
The rest of the *Memoir*—too lovely. I feel so angry, so indig-
nant, so amazed that he could die. It is impossible and wrong—I
mean wrong as if there were a mistake in a piece of tapestry, a
blunder, something out of proportion, inartistic and *wrong*.

[1] By Havelock Ellis.

"Partir c'est mourir un peu"[1]—that alone would make me love him. I must send that to P.

A fancy-dress "ball"!

Wednesday, 18th

Finished *The Dance of Life*. The Conclusion meant practically nothing to me. I have decided that I've completely missed the main point of the book but other superficial side points I have understood and liked.

Dwight is in a superb, hilarious mood. I wish I could drink his laughter, I love it so.

This afternoon I sat in one of the cubbyholes and looked for a long time at the sea and tried to write a poem which I shall never, never do. Foam is so beautiful and so manifold in its beauty and so transient. And as always, there are no words, no means of satisfying that feeling *"Verweile doch, Du bist so schön."*[2] I watched every curve and twist and fall, intimately; and (foolishly) feeling like a lover watching each careless insignificant gesture, each bearing still (for him) a heavy weight of beauty.

Finished *Tess of the d'Urbervilles*. Magnificent! I expected to (as I did) rush through it in excitement of the story, but *all the other*—! It is too amazing. How superb to have the rest of his works ahead of me!

Saturday, 21st

This morning very early we got up to find we were at Cherbourg in a cold, misty rain. Off the boat very quickly. The fields were thrillingly green, cut to pieces by darker green hedges. Then the water front, lined with solid rich old stone houses, Mansard roofs, an irregular line of warm old buildings—not stiff skyscrapers, monotonous in color. I looked for the little red-sailed boats Con and I saw last year, but they were rocking unfurled in one of the

[1] To leave is to die a little.

[2] Quotation from Goethe's *Faust*: Abide with me, you are so fair.

little harbors. We watched the *Homeric* steam out distantly. Close to the dock we saw Léon [the chauffeur] and waved wildly. Then good-by to Mr. B. and Chester [Aldrich] and we started over the wet cobblestones. It was unbelievably good to see green—soft green—rain-colored willows and thatched houses. At last over a hill we saw the spires of Coutances (after omelettes and coffee given us by the most beautiful, strong, fresh-faced Frenchwoman). We went up to the square and looked up at Coutances Cathedral. It is very straight and very beautiful, the two slim spires in front, each "rising from a nest of little spires." They were so sharp, the two straight front spear ones, that they really *were "flèches."* I liked this, this view from the square, best of all. Of the inside I remember mostly the many apses to all the different saints—even St. Nicholas! And some old green glass.

We stopped at Granville on the top of its hill under a castle and looked out over the wall, over boats dry and tipping over in the sand (it was low tide) and then in the cove the tide coming in, foam reaching inwards, arms of foam reaching inward. Then down the street there were children's voices singing haltingly and high—a little procession of boys and little girls, all in their black smocks. (I wonder if people would think me mad if I dressed my children in black smocks—I love them so on these children here. Their faces look so fresh, so red and white, so washed above the plain black smocks.) They were singing some marching song over and over and it played on in your mind when the echo was gone: *"Marchons tous!"* They were orphans, Léon said, from Paris, on their *"vacances." "Marchons tous!"*

All the people we passed were beautiful—washed faces, and eyes—always rather grave old eyes even in young people.

Old women with white and black caps sweeping in front of flower-windowed houses (geraniums red). We passed so many little two-wheeled yellow carts, shiny ones—I was dying to ride in one.

Then the first view of Mont-Saint-Michel over and between the hills—just an instant. It wasn't meant to be the first view—as usual, I was cheating and looking behind the scenes. Its first authenticated appearance was exquisitely staged. We came around the peak of a high hill and there in front and to the right of us (and far, far below stretched miles of soft-colored sands and in the distance, much further out than I had dreamed) was the traditional castle, ethereal and unreal as though it had just risen from the sea, like an "Arabian Nights" castle, exactly as if someone had just wished it there: "Abracadabra!" Even nearer, as we came up to it, it was not disappointing; "up they go, peak after peak." It climbs so irregularly to its spectacular spire (like the gesture I always feel like making when I hear that second spire of *Le Cygne*). We went into it, millions of cars around and French honeymoon ("*lune de miel*"—what a heavenly word) couples. Into a hotel, "Poulard," where we passed first through the kitchen; an old woman was cooking omelette on a huge fire with a long-handled frying pan. But I noticed first the very brightly polished copper pans hanging in back. The most gleaming copper I have ever seen. (We saw two pretty girls scrubbing it below us in a corner of the street later.)

After a rest we climbed up millions of steps and along stone walks and past little stone houses with flowered windows, up more steps toward St. Michael—who loved high places! Michael, Michael! I love you! We had a wonderful guide, very fat and slow and genial (with much garlic and also "innatebodyodor"). But he had been born there and really knew about it. In very slow French he talked to Daddy as one would to a child and took all Daddy's jokes very good-naturedly, especially when he (Étienne) explained an ancient order of *only* Kings, sons and brothers, explaining that if "Monsieur" were king, Dwight, "*Oui.*" "*Mais Mademoiselle, mais Madame, non.*" Then Daddy in clear pantomime and scornful expression pushed Mother, E., and me from him and patted Dwight on the head. Then a moment later he kissed me. The guide Étienne's face lit up, his mustaches curled, and his eyes twinkled. "*Quand même!*" he said prettily.

I got very mixed up in the different "Salles" until I read the chapter about it in *Mont-Saint-Michel and Chartres*. Very solid granite, sheer cliffs of walls, and here and there through the floor of stone they had left showing the granite rock itself. But what moved me most was the sand—sand and sea, sand and sea, out as far as you could look—warm-colored, honey-colored sand, and that restless tide again, again the arms of foam. But the gleaming sands, with the evening light reflected in them and the evening light on the sea, too, pearl-colored here, and there a gleaming brown—*café-au-lait* brown. To me there is something completely and satisfyingly restful in that stretch of sea and sand, sea and sand and sky—complete peace, complete fulfillment.

Sunday, 22nd

A long day—I haven't time to write about it all. A peaceful deep sleep in feather beds; a peaceful waking up, the little maid with breakfast. Then later Dwight discovered, in the French paper, Mr. Harjes'[1] sudden death, in a polo game. It was shocking and unbelievable. We turned for Paris. We left Mont-Saint-Michel in the sunshine. In color, the roofs were a blue I hadn't noticed before, a deep sea blue, and gleamed like scales of a fish. The sky was blue behind. Green clambered up the sheer clifflike walls—a little turret to the left by the sea, the blue of the sky reflected in the water and sand there—and the shadow of the Mount in the sand. Blue through the three arches of the top tower, and St. Michael high in the blue. On toward Paris—very fast—through miles and miles of country: willow trees, worked fields, towns, stone houses, fruit trees trained against their sides. We passed many people going to church, in black, on foot or in little carts. Old men in smocks, women with black kerchiefs and their caps on their heads. Some younger ones wore incongruous stiff hats.

[1] Herman Harjes, partner in J. P. Morgan & Co. Head of the Paris branch of the firm, then called "Morgan, Harjes & Co."

James Elmore Morrow

Clara Johnson Morrow

Grandparents of Anne Morrow Lindbergh

Charles Long Cutter

Annie Spencer Cutter

*Mrs. Dwight W. {Elizabeth Cutter} Morrow with Anne,
Dwight, Constance, Elisabeth, 1913*

Anne and Elisabeth Morrow, ca. 1914

Anne Morrow, 1915

Palisade Avenue House,
Englewood, N. J.
Anne climbing the arbor,
ca. 1915

Dwight W. Morrow with his children, back garden,
Palisade Avenue house, ca. 1917

Living room, Palisade Avenue house

Anne's room, Palisade Avenue house

Anne, North Haven, Maine, 1920

Anne, ca. 1922

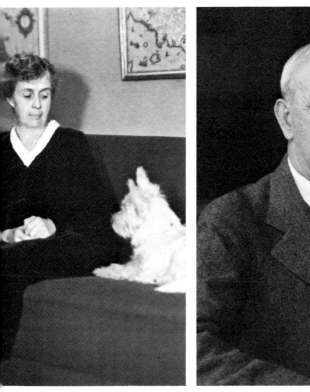

Amey Aldrich
with her dog, Tinker

William Allan Neilson, President,
Smith College

Smith College: Paradise Pond with Mt. Tom
in the distance

PHOTO ERIC ST.

Anne in dance drama East of the Sun, *May 18, 1926*
Smith College, Northampton, Mass.

Morrow family group, North Haven, Maine, summer, 1926

One thing I remember, a man getting off his bicycle to bend over and kiss on both cheeks a little golden-haired child.

On to Paris. Daddy spoke often of "Herman," but we were thinking of Mrs. Harjes.

Past Dreux, I remember the road so vividly. Past Versailles—Saint-Cloud—across the bridge—the Seine! The Eiffel Tower and Paris. Along the river and through the Bois past the "Pré Catelan," then the arch, the chestnut trees, still *triste*, the lights coming on, the horns seesawing—many people running—footsteps.

Monday, 23rd

We walked in the morning by the glittering shops—the near ones—not buying, just glancing in.

We stood outside of Morgan-Harjes today. It was very busy—crowds of people, everything going on just as usual. It was quite shocking. We listened to the remarks about him passed by people to each other in their casual meeting and greeting. From all kinds of people: "Very shocking about poor Herman, isn't it?" and "See, the flag's at half-mast, that's because of Mr. Harjes' death."

Mother and Daddy went to see Mrs. Harjes. Of course she was brave and beautiful.

In the afternoon Elisabeth and I walked past "my boy"[1] ("Home from the Hunt") through the formal gardens and gravel walks into the Garden of the Tuileries. Stepped into a chattering, casual world of sun and children and fountains and hoops. We watched them sail boats in the fountain, then wandered along the chestnut lanes, many leaves, brown and russet and dry, covering the gravel walks. Mothers sewing; children's curls bobbing up and down; hoops. We dropped back into the feeling of hoops and skipping around trees, and being completely

---

[1] Statue in the Tuileries gardens.

occupied, never thinking of older people or anything but that moment and that game. Then on green tables, in the shade, still we ate *chocolat* and *orangeade* and *gâteaux*. Then across to a merry-go-round. The children on horses, tied with ribbon to the horse's neck by a dear old woman. The children "spearing" the rings—the candy-stick prize. (If only I weren't in a hurry I should describe it all.) Why did it make me so happy—so rested, so unconscious of *"le temps s'en va, le temps s'en va, Madame"*? I felt the way a cat must who has purred and sat in the sun an hour. I wonder if P. would ever do as childish a thing as that with me. He might want to but would never find the time.

That evening Chester called up and wanted to take Elisabeth and me out to some restaurant (he had a young friend with him). *Terribly* nice of him. We felt very much complimented. Great fuss about clothes. Finally Elisabeth went in a flowered chiffon of Mother's and her big beige hat with velvet ribbon. (I love her in that hat.) I wore the "rose leaves and cream" and my new big black velvet hat, the one Dwight says looks like a dark shadow over my life, from which my face *peers* out. Chester's "young man" proved to be a very attractive New Zealander, a musician. He said immediately that he had met me before at a dance. Of course I remembered the dance but I had only a very vague recollection of him. Gradually I remembered more and more when it came out that he was a musician and a New Zealander. He seemed in very good spirits and took us to a place called "Maisonette Russe," a small room, hazy with smoke and light, painted *Chauve-Souris* fashion, scarlet and vivid blue; the ceiling "had no beginning and no end," no front or back. Little black masks painted on all the orange lamp shades. We sat in a corner; some Russians behind us vigorously kept up a constant inarticulate murmur (many "smashed china" 's). It was crowded. They were playing a scarlet tango as we came in: "A little, and the heart must skip a beat." The black velvet fitted and I might have smoked, but no. "Rose leaves and cream"--and *smoke?*—*No.* My heart throbbed with the flame of it all, and all the glamour of all glamorous instants came back to me.

We talked, although I cannot remember a thing that was said. It was the throbbing music that talked and the lights, the small clatter of forks against plates, smoke and fingers that danced, and eyes.

Caviar.

That *intoxicating* illusion, sometimes present on an evening like this, that I was young and lovely-looking, while in reality I was a very small excited girl with a very large velvet hat. Elisabeth was tired but "most divinely fair."

We were right next to the orchestra—the most spontaneous, all a part-of-the-atmosphere orchestra—Russians. Man with an accordion played with wonderful gusto and, at times, very softly and delicately. (He felt the *physical* height of high notes, holding his accordion high in the air and shaking out the notes.)

That music! Oh, that music! They played all the songs that have always woven and will always weave enchantment for me—*all of them, all of them,* keys to enchanted worlds, worlds I had forgotten and put in the back of my mind prudently to make room for more honest, more earthly, humbler worlds, that it is wise to be satisfied with. And yet that music— Well, I felt, like that line, "I have been faithful to thee, Cynara, in my fashion." (Dear P., if you don't like this—if you don't—! I know it is superficial and trivial, but it *is* in me—it *is* part of me. I had forgotten until then how much a part of me, and I must have it once in a while even though most of the time contentedly

> I who so love scarlet
>> Wear a gown of black,
> Quaintly fitted tunic
>> Buttoned up the back.)

A woman sang in a whiny voice, a tango ("Florida"!), they sang the Volga Boat Song—distant, unfathomable, unsatisfied

("Chaliapin!"). They played that lilting, wistful Russian thing Mary Walker remembered and played for me. G. [Chester's friend] knew all the singers and the tunes and they laughed together and he asked for favorites, and felt, I think, just as *"touché"* as I did. It was quite thrilling, that word *"frisson."* Also he likes the taste of words, as we do. The caviar was "delectable." He was most sensitive to it all—all the color of it. He had discovered that place. Each color, each tune was to him (a connoisseur) a rare jewel that he fingered delicately and with especial fondness. I hardly dared look at him because all my enthusiasm showed in my eyes, my enthusiasm showed for just exactly those things that he was fingering, but it was only for those things and might be misunderstood. Enthusiasm is so heady. They played and sang Russian folk songs: a wonderful baritone, the light played on his face and the music molded it—beautiful beyond words. G. had seen it too, and we flared up excitedly about it, talking disjointedly and impatiently across the table. Some jaunty airs from opera. The "Chanson Hindoue" ("Mandarin red"—"Think of me when you hear 'Chanson Hindoue'") and "Schéhérazade"; some lilting songs Schipa sang (that evening! that golden evening I heard Schipa!); "Ai, Ai, Ai." When the Russian women sang it reminded me of that thin, faraway, unsatisfied voice of the Russian woman in "The Russian Swan." And they loved singing. They ate and sang and laughed and smiled and clapped each other and joined in when they wanted to—grew intense over their songs—the lightest Italian dance tunes grew remote and unexplainably sad. They were unanswered songs—remote, untouched and untouchable. Still that thick, unintelligible monotone of Russian voices behind us. The windows looked like Columbine's skirt. Then a girl danced, boots flashed, quick deft hands (like Raquel's[1]), red sash, laughing eyes. She did the Charleston too—*even* the Charleston was beautiful, swift, and deft.

[1] The Spanish dancer, Raquel Meller.

Then the man with the accordion played that most wistful of all songs, and most haunting, "la Gitana." It trembles with longing and a *triste* shy wistfulness. I have played it so many times in winter in my little room at college looking at my "Rouge de Chine" shawl and dreaming of things like this:

> "Dreamed it, dreamed it in a dream
> And waked to find it true."

Then a ride in a taxi through the dark, quiet streets—home, where I sat up all night to write P.—*idiot, mille fois* idiot! That mood can't be sustained across an ocean in a midnight letter with pen and paper. It will cool and seem absurd and boring to him. And I paid for it the next day.

Tuesday, 24th

Lunch at Voisin. Across to the Left Bank after lunch. Felt ill with exhaustion in spite of its being my favorite place in the world: the Luxembourg Gardens, the little old streets, Mother's enthusiasm, the bookstalls along the Quai. Bought two enchanting fashion prints of little girls. But it was all spoiled for me—I was too tired even to smile or speak or say how I loved it.

General Pershing to supper. That same fat foreign violinist played bewitchingly. It was all the same: the garden, the light thrown up against the trees, the pink geraniums, the sound of water falling, and the violin, drawn out into melting ribbons of molasses. He played all last year's most intriguing, Junelike tunes—"Indian Love Call," "Rose Marie," "Marcheta," "The Chocolate Soldier Waltz," lingering on the sweetest notes. For us "Cavalleria Rusticana," familiar part. I think he plays very badly, sickish-sweetly, but it is effective in that atmosphere—perfect for those songs.

Thursday, 26th

Felt *miserably*—heavy, dull, listless—*nothing*, nothing, *nothing* would ever interest me again—that feeling: stupid, dull, uninteresting. On days like this I feel with *complete and final certainty* that *never, never, never* will I let myself fool myself that *I* could marry *anyone*.

At night, went again with Mr. Strong[1] to "Maisonette Russe," but the glamour had departed.

Sunday, 29th

Left Paris. Glad to go. This whole week has been one of revolting waste, of numbing artificialities—everything done for us, an impassable wall of Ritz "service."

I want to lie in North Haven fields and drink milk and feel wind.

> "If ever I said, in grief or pride,
> I tired of honest things, I lied."
> [EDNA ST. VINCENT MILLAY]

Oh, I am so tired—so tired of all this. I hate motor trips and I hate hotels and I hate staring up at architecture I don't understand, and I hate guidebooks—and I do so hate and dread this horrible creeping inertia that has drugged me so that I am always tired and always heavy and dull and *never* interested in *anything*. I feel only half alive. Will it *always* be this way? Is it just laziness? What is it? I feel as though I missed most of living through timidity and the thing that lies behind *"Ce n'est pas la peine."*

I am so tired—I wish I were home. I want to go home right away. I don't want to go to Geneva or London—just home. I haven't any time to sit and look at things or think, or read, or write—always too tired at night.

To Auxerre. The twilight part of the ride was heavenly. I am thinking of a poem with the line in it somewhere, "I hold you in the twilight of my heart." Russet roofs; old street lamps at Auxerre.

[1] Benjamin Strong, Governor of the Federal Reserve Bank of N. Y. from 1914.

Monday, 30th

To Dijon: followed rivers, many willows, hills, poplars—lovely country. To Geneva in the morning. Over the mountain— Geneva and the lake in mist far, far below us. It was cool at last and very fresh, the air was simply . . . virginal.

Lots of people on the promenade by the lake under the trees. Kissed Elisabeth good-by.[1]

Wednesday, September 1st—Grenoble

Elisabeth and Connie[2] to classes early. Later Daddy, Mother, Dwight, and I went over to the University. I got quite a thrill out of the cool stone corridors, the quiet, the atmosphere of class-rooms and work. Then to the old building in "Rue du Vieux Temple," where the courses for language for foreigners were. Busy people of all nationalities—very inspiring. Elisabeth and Connie very excited.

Late in the afternoon we took a drive up above Grenoble into the mountains:

> "Up they go—peak after peak . . .
> Into the clouds— Still I mark
> That a linnet, or lark,
> Soaring just as high, can sing
> As if he'd not done anything!
> I think the mountains ought to be
> Taught a little modesty!"
>
> [JAMES STEPHENS]

Glorious sweep of the valley—the wide winding river, the city and poplars and great blue mountains overshadowing it all. Up and up, through very green valleys, red-roofed cottages, cows in the fields, mountains close about. Up further through straight,

[1] Elisabeth Morrow, together with a friend, was to remain in France for a term of language studies at the University of Grenoble.

[2] Constance Chilton, college friend of Elisabeth Morrow.

tall—so tall—pines. The shadows were very blue, the pines very green, the fields vivid green, cool and fresh, and the mountains steep overhanging all about. So fresh, so fresh, the air was cool and blessed to feel on one's face. Up further, finally we reached in the very crest of the peaks a community of mighty buildings, staunch and gray and with peaked roofs—impressive. "La Grande Chartreuse."[1] It was cool evening, and no sound. Into the court—massive, evenly cut buildings. The roof was slated blue, a hard gray blue like the sheer rocks of the mountain cliffs just above. It was austere, deserted, magnificent. We walked through mighty halls of these Carthusian monks, down cloisters. It was cold and shadowed.

We saw a monk's "cell," or apartment. Each monk had *two* rooms and a chapel *and* a *garden!* A bookcase, a desk, windows out into his garden where an apple tree was brushing against the window. He was by himself for five days and on the sixth with the thirty-five other monks. What a heavenly life! All your books, quiet, your own garden, an apple tree, no interruptions, the gray peaks above you, and that air—that fresh, cool, newborn air. Elisabeth and I leaned out of the window and there was no sound except the quiet tinkle of cows coming in somewhere. And in the distance the two fountains splashed in the great court. What austere peace.

Down again—a tortuous road under those great peaks. It was almost dark, the shadows deepened, lights here and there in the little valleys, down, down, down, until Grenoble lay stretched far below us like scattered diamonds on the floor.

My last night with Elisabeth. We are so near, so very, very near. A year *can't,* mustn't, make any difference. I only numbly realize how lost I will be without her. I don't realize—I don't realize.

[1] Monastery founded by St. Bruno, the chief house of the Carthusians, now a museum.

This morning we went to one of Elisabeth's classes in the big amphitheater. Saw all the Smith [College] girls. It was very nice to see them. Good-by to E. out in the court—her green sleeve through Connie's and her head turned back smiling, going to class. We left.

Shopping for Elisabeth and we left things in her room at "Les Genêts."

At Valence for lunch. Daddy wanted to buy the coffeepot, a very ingenious arrangement. Dwight in hysterics.

Over hills in the afternoon—a twisting, uphill climb; rugged country—wild, steep. Chestnut trees, the sheen and sparkle on their rich green leaves, heather, little steep streams, poor stone houses—and always steep hills.

Then into wilder country, wild physiognomy; uneven peaks of igneous rock—an unnatural, fierce country, volcanolike cones, hills of tumbled-down rock, lavalike. I must look it up, geological formation, when I get to college again.

To Le Puy. On two of these steep cones, a church and a cathedral and town. A little like Mont-Saint-Michel. Startling. This seems miles away, distant, in this fierce, wild country. We are only a day's motor ride from Geneva.

We walked up steep, twisted, narrow streets, cobblestoned, to the Cathedral—many, many steps; a stiff Roman exterior. But once up the steps from the top of them one looks through the great arch down the steps, down the cobblestoned twisted street, at red roofs and hills beyond and sky beyond. It was glorious!

If one could only look out on the world like that once a day—before one went down into it.

It was dark and people were having supper. In a dimly lighted shop, the walls hung with sabots, I bought the smallest pair of wooden sabots for children.

Bless Elisabeth.

[*Geneva*] *Saturday, September 4th*

Went over to the Reformation Statue. Superb, moving monument. Austere and stern and magnificent. I don't believe, as Daddy remarked, that that movement stood for the opposite of what the League of Nations now stands for. Separatism was *not* their *end* but only the path necessary, because of the age, to take to reach an end which was in its essence *not* divided. I feel, anyway, as though the pendulum had to swing through separatism to get to a broader internationalism.

Geneva, Sunday, September 5, 1926

Elisabeth darling,

I thought of you so, coming back to the Beau Rivage, and missed you so. I listened to the music in the bright little dining room and looked out at the fountain and the lights along the Quai reflected in the lake, and thought of last year when we were here together and last week, which seems almost as far away.

After lunch the Indian delegation pushed us out of our rooms at the Beau Rivage. So you see all is evened up in this world. But *we,* unimportant in the affairs of state, pushed the Spanish delegation out to get rooms here (Hôtel de la Paix)! It did seem so amusing. If Spain decides to stay we are homeless. Daddy has not had a meal with us. He is very busy seeing "Monnet"[1] and "Salter"[2] and lots of other interesting people. This morning at breakfast he was perfectly thrilling telling us about Czechoslovakia and Beneš.[3] Daddy, also, wanting to talk to "Geeb"[4] and

[1] Jean Monnet, French political economist. Deputy Secretary General, League of Nations (1919–23). Worked with D. W. M. on the Allied Maritime Shipping Council. Later responsible for the Monnet Plan and the European Common Market.

[2] Sir James Arthur Salter, English economist. Director of economic and finance section, League of Nations (1919–20, 1922–31). Worked with D. W. M. on the Allied Maritime Shipping Council.

[3] Eduard Beneš, Czechoslovak statesman; member of Council of League of Nations (1923–27). Later President of Czechoslovakia.

[4] Seymour Parker Gilbert, American lawyer and financier. Agent-general

thinking it would be nice for Mrs. "Geeb," wanted us all to motor over to Hôtel Royal at Evian. But they are coming here, instead, for supper tonight with "Monnet" and "Salter." I wonder if we will eat with them. It will be great fun watching. If only you were here, how delightful it would be, "true to Morrow fashion," hashing it over afterwards "in the pantry" (metaphorically speaking).

DIARY   *Sunday, September 5th*

Felt fat and wasteful and dull—so wasteful of everything— time, and money, and beauty. Sitting around and eating. My books aren't here and there is no hard exercise. One can't just walk the streets forever. I have so little initiative, I feel lame and dependent on everything else. Oh, this precious time that is going!

At least I had a lovely talk with Dwight—that is, *he* talked, about his last year at school. He was very fine and clear-headed about it—very big.

We walked down along the Quai at twilight into "Le Parc de Mon Repos" where we found *le repos* and cool green dusk and periwinkle-blue flowers in the shadow and opalescent colors on the lake.

Monday, September 6th

Went this morning to the opening of the League. Mother and I sat together at the back of an immense hall. There were only three or four rows on the floor for audience, three crowded balconies, and ahead a stage and three or four rows of seats. Beneš spoke—or read—in French. The seats ahead of us were full of delegates. There was a little business done. It was smotheringly hot and close. Then it was over. Crowds outside and in. Pader-

---

for reparation payments in Germany (1924–30). Later partner in J. P. Morgan & Co.

ewski[1] sat just ahead of us. Mother introduced me to him. A great, kind-looking, shaggy man.

Lunch at the International Club. Miss Morgan[2] took us. They were all older people and I felt very out of place. I sat at a little table where they discussed "Reparations" and other League questions. Mr. P. on my right with kind nervousness asked me about my trip. I wish people wouldn't feel they had to talk to me. I'm perfectly happy listening. "Your father is a staunch Leaguer, isn't he?" etc. Then we moved into the big room. Not more than thirty people altogether—Mr. Austen Chamberlain[3] and Manley Hudson[4] at one end. Mr. Austen Chamberlain began to speak about Locarno.[5] A gray, distinguished-looking man with a dry smile and a monocle. He spoke intimately, simply, amusingly, telling the charming, vivid details that accompany great events unnoticed. He spoke as though the room were full of women—as though he were a woman—and yet his conversation did not become trivial and gossipy. Somehow the great significance of Locarno became more realizable, more living, framed in the vividness of the little mortal incidents. He was a consummate artist—tact, grace, finesse, charm. He gave explicit descriptions of details: how he left his card at the German's[6] lodgings, looked

[1] Ignace Paderewski, Polish pianist and statesman. Polish Prime Minister, 1919–21.

[2] Anne Morgan, daughter of J. Pierpont Morgan. Director, American Relief for France.

[3] Sir Austen Chamberlain, British statesman. Foreign Secretary (1924–29).

[4] Manley O. Hudson, American jurist. Member of legal section, Secretariat of League of Nations (1919–23). Later Judge, Permanent Court of International Justice (1936–46).

[5] Scene of signing of Locarno Pact (Dec. 1, 1925), treaties between seven European nations, designed to guarantee existing territorial boundaries and preserve peace.

[6] The reference is to Gustav Stresemann, German Minister of Foreign Affairs (1923–29); negotiated Locarno Pact and Germany's admission to the League of Nations.

for a round table, the shape of the room where they sat, how it progressed from day to day. The delicacy with which they handled it—his talks with Briand,[1] jokes, charming little quips and incidents.

Yet through all these trivialities he gave us a feeling of what he called "the spirit of Locarno." He held our attention, breathless.

But still through it all I felt that somehow he was particularly gratifying the women—all women—who delightedly were saying to themselves, "There! We always knew it was like that!"

Mother couldn't go to tea at Admiral Smith's[2] so Daddy took me. I was a little bit stiff and frightened about going but it was very nice. The girl talked to me and she was very bright and frank and informal and I felt happy and at ease. Mrs. Aubrey Smith was sweet and gracious. I told her Mother "collapsed" after lunch with her cold, and Daddy said afterwards that I "lied like an ambassador"!

Mr. Monnet was sweet and kind talking a little to me in the afternoon while he waited for Daddy. He is dear and embarrassed (a little) when you thank him for something: "Oh, that was nothing."

And when I said I didn't feel educated enough to deserve to listen to the League he said with quiet humor, "But no, you have no reason to think that. Do you think some of the delegates are as educated as you? Believe me, no— [At entrance of D. W. M.] Ah, my dear Morrow!"

We left on the train to Paris and found (most Morrowesque of incidents) when we had gotten on the train that No.'s 7, 8, and 9 meant only three beds, while we—Morrow fashion—had counted on *three rooms*. Mr. Monnet, though, who came to see us off, helped us out of that.

[1] Aristide Briand, French statesman; delegate to League of Nations (1924); instrumental as Foreign Minister in policy of rapprochement with Germany as marked by the Locarno treaties.

[2] Admiral Sir Aubrey Smith, British Naval Representative, League of Nations, 1926–27.

Good-by to dear Mr. Monnet.
"My dear Monnet!"

Wednesday, September 8th

Left for London.

Tea on the London train. How they spoil you here. Imagine tea on the four o'clock to Northampton!

Very tired, we drove through the lighted London streets to the Berkeley.

Thursday, September 9th

Mother and I walked down Piccadilly. It was all brass, shiny and gay, the shops more tempting than Paris. Elisabeth, though, should have been here.

In the afternoon Mother and I went to the Lowestoft shop. A wonderfully rosy and proud-chested man showed us his treasures, tenderly brought out all his favorite children—they were *all* favorites. I loved it and him. It really appeals strongly to me, that china and much old china. We saw "Emma's"[1] Lowestoft set— "Nelson's Emma"! He knew the history of each piece and led us around with smiling simple pride.

I could imagine getting quite drunk with the sight of that china.

Friday, September 10th

Met Ruth [McBarron] at the National Gallery. I saw St. Michael; some ghostly and wonderful El Grecos. Then to tea at the Savoy, where we sat at a little table and ate little cucumber sandwiches and watched dowdy people dance and talked. It was all too lovely, even though I couldn't leap with her.

Professor Barker,[2] his two daughters, and Mr. and Mrs. Har-

[1] Emma Hamilton, wife of Sir William Hamilton and mistress of Lord Nelson.

[2] Professor Ernest Barker, English educationalist.

court Malcolm[1] came for supper, downstairs at a big table—roses and lights and lots of shiny knives and forks and lots of shiny wit from Mr. Barker—I hadn't remembered that. Mr. and Mrs. Olds[2] too—I forgot. She was *so* sweet. I hadn't remembered her as so cordial. And he is very dear and twinkly.

Talking to Mrs. Harcourt Malcolm, I wonder why I bother to tell the truth when people ask me what I think of this and that and how I feel about this and that. I get so complicated and introspective that people often don't understand and are frankly puzzled and (naturally enough) bored. So why bother! It would be so much easier to say what they expected you to, and everything would be easy and pleasant.

Saturday, September 11th

Lunch and out to "Wall Hall," Mr. Morgan's[3] place, with Uncle Tom.[4] In the middle of fields, an old Gothic house, vine-covered and green-walled, almost like a chapel; wide lawns and great cedars, old trees. He greeted us at the door: a great, massive, overpowering sort of man. Shaggy eyebrows, almost a fierce face. A hearty and generous host—very much a host. We walked across the lawn, down walks and through the garden. He took great pride in it all and showed it off with a kind of formal playfulness—the walk, the cedars, the box bushes—a door cut through an enormous one to the rose garden. The green garden: just grass and a pool and a little temple. Then the walls and through gates to hothouses—figs and peaches. He knows a great deal about the growing of flowers.

Then tea on the lawn. I felt quite overawed, and even Tom

[1] Nassau friends of the Morrows.

[2] George D. Olds, professor of mathematics at Amherst, 1891–1927; acting president and president, 1923–27. Teacher of D. W. M.

[3] John Pierpont Morgan, banker and financier.

[4] Thomas Cochran, president Liberty National Bank, N. Y., 1914–17; Morgan partner from 1917; friend of D. W. M.

and Daddy were a little subdued, not exactly at their ease. Just subdued a little, not in high spirits.

It gave me a little shock to see *J. P. M.* on something, the silver or something, and a letter addressed to "J. P. Morgan." A little like the geographical thrill when you see *LONDON* on the signs or advertisements and you realize that you are actually in that familiar dot on the map.

The house was full of lovely things, prints, Lowestoft bowls (full of rose leaves), tapestries. The front hall mantelpiece is lined with "Toby's."[1] Fur pelts in front of all doors. I had a sweet little room—lots of pink under lace. Perfect comfort—a fur rug under my bed, statuettes on the mantelpiece, old prints.

A very nice dinner, at which I sat silent. I say nothing.

The most enchanting Chinese flowered wallpaper on the walls of one room: gay climbing flowers and birds, delicate colors—entrancing—and blue china in cabinets against it.

Sat in a large chair by the fire and listened to the men talk. He is most obstinate and determined in his remarks. Very impressive —very quick, too. I think Dr. Johnson must have silenced his opponents in argument just as Mr. Morgan would.

I sat perfectly silent.

One good remark was to Mother: "I see you are afflicted with that feminine vice, 'personal application.'" That's *good!* Very good. But not for her.

The atmosphere, although of perfect comfort, luxury, is somehow cold and lonely—empty. It lacks a kind of warm glowing ease which perhaps Mrs. Morgan gave it.

Sunday, September 12th

An English breakfast and then to church. It is very cold. I kept thinking—I couldn't help wandering in church—I couldn't help thinking with something of a leap of heart, "Next Sunday on the boat, and *next* Sunday after—Englewood!"

After lunch (at which I was again silent. I say *nothing*) we

---

[1] Mugs in the shape of a stout man, once used for ale.

walked around the place—through the woods, tame old woods, old mossy trees, across a field and a stile, across a stream where there were swans and lilies. Then back through a wooded path, through hedges, up a hill—view across gentle fields to a town, rooks flying—up through parklike woods to the place and across the lawn back to the house.

Tea, poured by the Lion, and then we left.

He must be very lonely.

The Lindleys[1] for supper. They arrived in North Haven the day we left. They talked about it and made me homesick for it. It sounded realer.

I listened with my heart in my eyes until Mrs. Lindley asked me if there were lots of young people up there, and I said, "Why—a—yes," and then Mr. Lindley with a winking kind of smile said, "Now this is the story we heard about your buying property—that you children were having such a good time all together down there that you couldn't bear to think of leaving it for anywhere else and that it was you who really made your father buy the land—at least that's the story." And I, for no reason, got red and had nothing to say. Concentration on peas and duck, after that.

Then Uncle Charlie[2] came in. He is just the same and pressed a fat envelope into my hand with a dear, shy twinkle. It was a fragment of pottery, a bowl, and it was not out of politeness that I gasped at it. Relief work carved on it: delicate, graceful, Greek, flowing. "Victory presenting a laurel wreath to an athlete. Part of Samian bowl, 3rd century, found in London, 1926. Each holds a strigil." There they are safe in that fragment of red clay: Victory, quick-footed, flowing robe, and her arm uplifted holding a wreath; there the athlete, his sinews, his carven strength. It al-

---

[1] Mr. and Mrs. Alan Lindley, Englewood friends of the Morrows.

[2] Charles Sherborn, friend of E. C. M., for more than forty years in the Natural History Department of the British Museum; author of *Index Animalium*.

most made me cry. I thought of "Thou still unravished bride of quietness." Uncle Charlie—I love him—I love his old clothes, his ring holding his tie, his gray beard, scraggly, his twinkle, his trembling hand. I love his devotion, his pride in his work. I love his gruffness, his sincerity. His work—his classification of all animals used in books—will be done by 1927. His work will be finished then, he says—thirty-eight years of it. In the meantime in his spare time he picks up these gems, these coins and fragments, beads and strange rich-with-age things. He gives them away. "All" he has to give or save for a gift for himself—

"Thou still unravished bride of quietness"!

Monday, September 13th

The afternoon I completely wasted waiting in a car while Mother did silver and clock shopping with Mrs. Bliss.[1] Four wretched men whined out sentimental tunes, horrible, screeching, catlike tunes, below in the street. But supper in the room with Mother and a nice fire. I am entranced with *The Revolt of the Angels*.[2] But I am just conscious enough to resent his (Anatole's) serene, almighty contempt.

Tuesday, September 14th

Went to the National Gallery again. So little of it is visible to me, but I enjoy it more each time.

We went to Lord Amherst's for lunch. They have the most stirring portraits of famous ancestors all over the walls. They were cordial and unaffected. It always surprises me pleasantly. There were very few awkward pauses, and that is so exhilarating. When any occasion like this passes off honorably I feel proud and serene. "Well! They didn't find me out there!" Or as if I had gracefully steered a large Packard around a corner.

[1] The wife of Cornelius N. Bliss. The Blisses were New York friends of the Morrows and lived in the same apartment house.

[2] Novel by Anatole France.

To Hampton Court.

The moat, the arches, the courts, Wolsey's apartments, paneling.

A Zuccaro painting of Queen Elizabeth; two Holbeins of Erasmus.

Window seats.

The little formal gardens; shade and lawn and fountains; little gardens—royalty at ease. Roses and the smell of heliotrope. Box hedges. Gravel walks and heliotrope.

The back like Versailles.

Thursday, September 16th

We went down this morning in pursuit of Elizabethan London: Chancery Lane, Holborn, and Fleet Street. Out of the rush of cars, trams, crowding, hurrying men and business, into Lincoln's Inn, a court, a city—almost a college. Old stone buildings, squares, stone walks, gardens, with quiet grown over it like moss.

Friday, September 17th

A day of shopping—especially to Franks on Camomile Street, where I walked through rooms of dust and idols dreaming in aloof supercilious peace. *Subtle, suave, sophisticated.* I wish I had bought one to have with me always. Stones, too, and painted figures and bowls—far, clear colors, but old, so old, as if they had come from the bottom of the sea. Up the spiral staircase to the room of silks where I bought a glorious "rouge-de-Chine" mandarin coat, to hold "against the winter's cold." More shopping, to the Lowestoft place.

I want so to get home—I feel as though I would never get there.

Tomorrow we sail!

Sunday, September 19th

A huge boat but not luxurious, not aggressively marble-tiled-bathroomy.

Read Chesterton's *St. Francis:* extremely beautiful. It gives me such a wonderful satisfaction to really love a book (*the books*) that P. has given me.

TO E. R. M.   *September 24, 1926*
I wanted to tell you that one day—one evening [September 16th] —we went out to Mr. Montagu Norman's[1] for dinner. It is a strange, strange house, quite a little out of London. We went there by dark and it was very still. The house is perfectly bare and austere. He has played with it and done just as he wanted and it has turned out all in keeping with itself and him but very strange. The only decoration is the material out of which it is made—that is, the wood which he has put on the walls and floors, smooth polished clear surfaces everywhere, smooth clear wood. It is quite bare. His dining room *does* look like the inside of a prairie wagon. And you walk out of his hall into a still black garden—it seemed like Lob's wood in *Dear Brutus*.[2] The atmosphere was like that and *he* was Lob. What would he do to us? In one bare little room you got a strange eerie start to see a whole wall covered with an immense peacock, embroidered on white silk—all those eyes! It was the only decoration in the room.

He seemed, though very preoccupied, very much the man of politics, pulling the strings. He was stern and austere—not at all the charming visitor of Château Basque. They were all busy and preoccupied (Daddy and Mr. Strong and he). The air has been electrified. Even steady Mr. Whigham[3] has seemed fidgety and excited—"This Belgian Situation."[4]

[1] Montagu C. Norman, Governor of the Bank of England, 1920–44.

[2] Play by James Barrie.

[3] Charles Whigham, partner of Morgan, Grenfell & Co., London.

[4] The reference is to the Belgian stabilization loan, negotiated in 1926.

1 9 2 6

TO E. C. M. [*Northampton, November 4, 1926*]
[*Junior year*]

My darling—
I am so sorry I left, so hopelessly sunk, for Northampton. Some tea and toast near New Haven, and a long time to think and look at the oak leaves and the brown grass, brought me very quickly to the conclusion that:

> ". . . My dear, my dear,
> It is not so dreadful here."
> [EDNA ST. VINCENT MILLAY]

And I did have such an exciting, full time. Thank you, darling, for everything. It was quite glorious, from the moment I jumped off the train to the Masefield reading, to the moment I jumped on again.

Also it seems that Miss Kirstein liked my second theme, which was read in class. It was very strange and subjective and I thought she would make fun of it. But the girl here in the house who was there has told me very encouraging things said about it, although "it seems a little overdone."

I don't dare ever show it to you, for you will think me crazy.

I went right to bed last night. Today I must work very hard for those two writtens.

[*Northampton*], *November 12, 1926*

Elisabeth, my darling
College (to get this out of the way) is easier on the whole, at least as far as work is concerned. All except the writing. I feel (in regard to that, both in Miss Kirstein's course and *Monthly*[1]) just like the cow who was hopefully first named "Daisy" but later renamed "Sahara" for obvious reasons.

But, Elisabeth, dearest, as for the personal side of it, it is still very hard. I really don't see anyone and then, again, I really see

[1] Smith College literary magazine.

59

more people than I ever have before because I'm so much freer—
but not very deeply.

It is a very new strange feeling—of touching many people
(many more than before) superficially and no one's touching me.
And loneliness is most lovely and most desirable here—I really
love it—all except a kind of physical loneliness that I have never
experienced before. I never understood before that mad (so it
seemed) wish of some people, just to have humans—any humans—near them. *Spiritual* loneliness is hardly possible, and I
never understood that there is another perfectly reasonable kind,
although I do not feel it much.

There are two people who are lovely and I am just getting to
know who are beautiful surprises. One is Laura Brandt,[1] who
talks to me sometimes about Paris and loves music; she sits
sometimes in my room and listens to *Tristan and Isolde* or (!)
"Fleurs d'amour."

Then there is Connie Kelton[2] who is too *wonderful!* It is such
heaven to run in and talk with her about books or people.
Sometimes she shows me things she's found, and sometimes
I show her something, often a bit of your letter or pictures of
Raquel. What strength and depth she has—restraint, and thoughts
that she has worked out with pain. She seems to me quite mellow
and mature in understanding and strength. And what delicacy
in that strength.

So except for those two I think most of the dear people I like
are out of college.

Last week I went home for the first time. Corliss[3] telegraphed
me to save the night. I jumped from the train (12:17) to the

[1] Laura Brandt roomed next door to A. M. L., Junior year, at Smith
College.

[2] Constance Kelton, recent graduate of Smith College, friend of E. R. M.,
worked in the Hampshire Bookshop.

[3] Corliss Lamont, son of Thomas W. Lamont, partner of J. P. Morgan
& Co. The Lamonts were old friends and neighbors of the Morrows in
Englewood and North Haven.

Town Hall where Masefield was reading: *Enslaved* and *King Cole*. There he was with Mrs. Lamont sitting up in the balcony. Mother took me to meet him. And he leaned forward and was kind and dear and shy, and rather far away—a little lost, I felt. He read beautifully—a low voice and sad, and far away—and with such simplicity and quiet that you (and everyone else) were transformed into wondering believing children, listening for the first time, believing for the first time very simple sublime (now platitudinal) truths.

[*Northampton, December 7, 1926*]

Mother darling—

I must tell you about the service for Allan,[1] sometime—not in this hurried letter (and I sent flowers from you and me to Mrs. Neilson—right at first because I *had* to do something).

It was very simple and quite German. But to see them come down in deep black—somehow it is such a shock—to have such a visible sign of sorrow. They sang that glorious old German hymn "Ein' Feste Burg" and then—*heartbreaking*—"Silent Night"— Oh, Mother.

I wanted to write you Sunday but it seemed so terrible, and I couldn't.

[1] The only son of President and Mrs. Neilson, died after a long illness.

1 9 2 7

Mother—I really have done so wretchedly on these exams. It sometimes seems to me such a frightful waste of money and everything to try to give me an education. I have done so badly here in college, scholastically, which is the main thing, of course. It is so frightful—and there doesn't seem any explanation. You and Daddy are brilliant, and got all sorts of distinctions. And Elisabeth did well—Dean's List and Honors in English—and Dwight and Con head of their classes. It is so appalling, my not succeeding at all. And I thought I had been working so hard. Everything seems to have gone. The thing I spent all my time on—*writing*—was just like throwing sand into a pit. I didn't get enough done, didn't do anything remarkable, and naturally, she says marks are very low.

Then in Bible, in which I *have* been doing good work all year: *A* work, and I like Mr. Bixler[1] so *very* much, and he admires Daddy so and expects me to work well and has been pleased with my work, and likes me. In Bible I *completely* failed. And there wasn't really any excuse. I had an exam the afternoon before, came home rather tired, and worked. I thought I would *have* to know the facts. So I worked much too late that night. Rushed to the exam at nine, and went all to pieces over it. I just couldn't co-ordinate at all. It was quite long, and I lost complete control of my mind and my fear. I got very panicky and handed in about two pages of incoherent, senseless phrases. It was sickening. I went home miserable.

The next morning as I was studying for another (in the afternoon) I was called to the telephone—I was in the cold fear of a nightmare stage when the person said, "This is Mr. Bixler, Miss

---

[1] Julius Seelye Bixler, professor of Biblical literature, 1924–33.

Morrow. I called you up because I have just come across your paper—" I didn't let him go on and told him yes, that I knew how *frightful* it had been and that I felt *terribly* about it, and he said, "Well, yes, Miss Morrow, I simply *couldn't* understand. The work was . . . a . . . simply not up to the standard of your other work *at all*. I . . . a . . . simply *couldn't* understand. I wanted . . . to find out if there were any unusual circumstances —a lot of examinations together or something like that." I told him that I had no excuse at all (for one examination a day isn't unusual), that I had stayed up much too late and just gone to pieces over the paper—had gotten panicky. "Well, yes, I thought something like that *must* have happened. It was *so*—well, not at all what I expected from you." Then I told him how terribly sorry I was because it was an interesting paper and I would have liked to do well. "Well, yes, Miss Morrow—I thought . . . you would like it. I saved your paper for the end, thinking that, Well, *here* I'll have a treat! I don't really know what to do about it, Miss Morrow. I don't like to mark you on it," etc., etc.

Well, it was frightful—although *very* nice of him to call up and be so fair and kind about it. Still, it rather unnerved me. I've never really done that before.

Then French, which wasn't hard but I didn't do well—I had to go so fast to get done.

This morning, Shakespeare. Oh, dear, I will feel so much happier when everyone on the Faculty realizes that I have a slow, thick mind! I never never *never* work fast enough, really. I never finish, I never even get *enough* done. Why why *why* can't I keep up to other people? I am so tired of always saying, "I only did half."

I think I failed this morning's paper because I only did two out of four questions, and half of a third.

I thought this year *at least* I was doing well in my work, but there *It* is—baffling.

I'm going to bed early tonight—my worst exam is on Wednesday at four (to six) because I haven't done any work for it, all year.

Then—*home!*

Mother, darling—

I haven't written you for ages, but I have been working very hard.

I wanted to speak to you *last* week before you went to Groton, I had so much to tell you. I am *so* glad I went. It made me very happy—especially the things I heard and saw about Dwight. He is *very much* loved by everyone and respected. I felt that I saw it better than you or any "grownup" could. Have you read Dwight's theme about Santayana? I think it is *beautiful!* The best thing I have ever seen of his.

I have lots of facts to tell you.

Marks—I was terribly disappointed. *All* my marks were pulled down by my exams. The same *inevitable* "Too slow." Miss Hanscom[1]—in which I have gotten A's and B's in the writtens—gave me a C (I only had time for two out of the four questions on the exam). Music—in which I have gotten A's and B's in the writtens—C (I got a C— on my exam).

That is very annoying—the music—because I have done good work and wrote a good exam. But they suddenly (really, I am not excusing myself without reason) marked the exams *very* hard. There was only one A, a few B's, and quite a lot of C's but *many* D's and even failures. Three girls, *majoring* in music, *failed* the exam.

Mr. Bixler gave me a B— which was nice of him.

I'm afraid these marks spoil any chance of any of the *cum laudes* or honors that Elisabeth got.

Still, they're over—there isn't anything to do.

[1] Elizabeth Deering Hanscom, professor of English, 1894–1932.

I went this week to see Miss S., and found that there is a lovely big room, single, on the top floor! She said, "Of course, I think by some arrangement—the girls doubling up—you can have the little single that So-and-So has now. It's too bad—of course, if *only* you didn't mind the floor above, there is a single there now." I *jumped* at it! "Oh, I don't mind—*really* I don't mind." (All the time really thinking *how much* I'd *prefer* to be a little out of the group—and quieter.) Besides, the room is big and has an enormous closet and three windows! So it is really all settled. I can't still see myself moving, but I shall.

It seems perhaps awfully silly to write you all this. But I wanted to show you that things are really settling down and that I feel very happy about this year and next year.

My work is going well, really. I feel quite secure and unharassed, although of course one never gets done what one wants to get done. I have this weekend, for a theme for Miss Kirstein, one I am *very* interested in, and I am so happy at the thought of working at it. It is (of course) the eighteenth century in France: another literary lady of the time of Zélide and Mme du Deffand etc. It is "Spring" dance weekend. There are many boys. I might "stag" at 30 Belmont but I am so much more interested in writing this theme. B. wants to see me tomorrow— Sunday. I am *so* sick of mediocre boys—I mean nice boys who don't interest me very much—"middling" boys. It seems to me that I have seen one every weekend for ages. I *am* so tired of them.

I forgot to tell you that A. asked very tenderly about you and your poetry. He is charming and interesting but I have an inveterate prejudice against good-looking men, especially when they are supposed to be "lady-killers."

Oh, dear, I want to see you and talk to you. I wish I could talk to you about this theme. I wish we could shop for Lowestoft china—I think so often of you and London, having you and London all to myself. I have forgotten all about those neck-tiring expedition for grandfather clocks—I only remember the Lowestoft shops and gardenias in the street being sold and all the shiny brass shops.

My music course is perfectly heavenly. Now we hear so *much* music. It is so lovely. There is a concert Sunday evening.

I am very happy.

TO E. R. M.   [*Northampton, March, 1927*]
My darling darling,

I haven't told you about Groton and *dear* Dwight. He was so sweet and dear and such fun. I went for the Washington's Birthday dance. I stayed at Mrs. Tuttle's.[1] She is young and charming and has an enchanting house—lots of prints and flowers and a great many rare and beautiful books—*and* a baby, an enchanting baby! She is so happy, and so lovely. Don't you often wish this marrying business were all over? I would be willing to sacrifice "falling in love," and all that—honeymoon, etc.—if I could just jump into an everyday life like hers. A home, a nice husband (if necessary), and a baby—everything settled and everyday, no romance but a kind of humdrum divinity.

As for Dwight—he was all courtesy, quite proud and a little distracted ("Durrie") to have me up there. He had a card all made out. A. H. had what the boys called his "passion flower" up for the dance. She had pink cheeks and lisped. A. H. sent her a corsage of *six* gardenias!!! All the boys were sweet—a little shy, *very polite,* and *anxious to please.* Mr. Jacomb[2] came up to me glowing and "the Rector" liked my dress, so I was fixed for the evening—the approved stamp of those veterans upon me. I *love* boys that age and the atmosphere of a boys' school is—there is *nothing* quite like it. There is something (don't laugh) virginal

[1] Wife of Henry E. Tuttle, etcher, teacher of English, also football coach at Groton School.

[2] William J. Jacomb, physical-education director at Groton School.

about it. It is fresh and ruddy and very fleeting. The only flaw of the evening was that A. P.—very charming and interesting and the only eligible gentleman there—paid very little attention to me. That annoyed me because I made such an effort not to pay any attention to him, 1—because he is disgracefully nice-looking; 2—because he is a beau of L.'s; 3—because Dwight, A. H. etc. are always telling me that he is such a "lady-killer."

Everyone loves Dwight—everyone—I was *superbly* proud and happy. All the teachers. And *all* the boys. He is loved and respected. Dwight brought up slews of boys and introduced them (and it was a card dance) and said naïvely afterwards, "I didn't introduce anyone who didn't ask to meet you!" The exhibition came first—lines and lines of sweet earnest little boys, countermarching. Lots of fond mothers and a great many old Boston-Groton-Peabody-Lawrence relations leaning over the balcony. (What a family conspiracy Groton is!)

In the middle of the dance they played some old waltzes. Out stepped Mr. and Mrs. Peabody[1] and "trod them a measure," just like "old Fuzziwig"—do you remember? I love them.

[*Northampton, March 5, 1927*]
(Please return theme)

Mother darling

Forgive me for writing you this right away but it was so exciting I wanted to tell you. You know how long—how terribly long—I work over themes: hours and hours and *hours*. I have been working for *weeks* on this paper about the B's, not trying to write down what happened but just trying to crystallize in some form, artificial or not, some kernel of the feeling I have about them. After writing pages and pages and rejecting them, after shaking it up and putting it in a thousand different molds, I

---

[1] Endicott Peabody, Episcopal clergyman, a founder and the first headmaster of Groton School, Groton, Mass.

finally reached this. It is not true at all—the form isn't, or the incident that happened to fit what I wanted—but I have at last to my own satisfaction at least crystallized something. Now I shall be *very* conceited about it: Miss Kirstein read it in class today. She said things about it that she has *never* before said about *anything* I have written! She said that it was (it seems so crass to put this down) *very* difficult to do, that this was very successfully done, that it shows a great deal of work (I'm glad it shows!) and care, that she rarely came across anything that was as well done as it could possibly be done apparently. And that, really, for *its kind*—for the kind of thing it was—she had in the years she had been teaching never had anything better and she noticed all the threads in it that I had worked over and I had *slaved* so over it. I am not as conceited as I sound, I am just very happy. Praise like that is so rare.

Then after class she called for me and said, "Really, Anne, this is *excellent*. I was really very excited about it. I wish you would send it away. I think you could send it to some magazine," etc. Of course I wouldn't think of that but it was quite intoxicating, and balances for my C in Miss Hanscom.

Oh, Mother, Mother, how heart-warming that is—praise like that—even if it doesn't point to anything lasting, even if you know it "just happened" and will not happen again.

Good night, darling. Do you feel this way when they read your poems? But that happens so often!

[*Northampton, March 8, 1927*]

Dear Mother,

I have something nice to tell you, which I hadn't mentioned before. I tried out for *Monthly* two or three weeks ago—I never have before—and this morning they took me in, which made me very happy, mostly because you did it, although I am just a minor member of the board and you were head. Still, it is something of a justification. I have done nothing else in college. There are, too, awfully nice people on the board. People I have always wanted to know.

I have a "problem" to decide—B. wants me to go with him to his Junior Prom.

Arguments vs.

1. Although he writes charming letters and loves *Alice in Wonderland,* and is a very nice boy, and I like him, in the abstract, it's hard to talk to him and I get bored almost immediately.
2. I'd probably stay at an approved hotel all alone. I'd hate that.
3. I've only three nights left until the end of the year. One, at least, I'll spend seeing you home in May (the end of May or June).

That makes me have no other night left. The Prom is before vacation. Then from the beginning of April to the end of May (about two months) I'd have no chance to go away.

But it will be hard to say no because I have consistently refused invitations of his for two years, all for about the same reasons and always putting forward some excuse about work or authorities. I've already this year used the "seven-nights-only" plea, so I shall have to tell a frightful lie to get out of it.

DIARY   *[North Haven], Tuesday, July 12, 1927*
The day thick and blowy, as if a thin, almost transparent coat of white paint had been washed over everything.

Gulls are gray on top, wings tipped with white. Their small bodies are white, beaks red. They flutter several times before they sail. Their wings are not straight: they curve, even when sailing.

Life today was positive—an assertive reality—in everything: myself, the stir of leaves, the sound of motorboats, gulls, trees against the sky, buttercups.

Wednesday, July 13th
Nasturtiums—vivid, firelike colors, so that one can almost warm one's hands at them. Or shutting one's eyes one sees bright spots

everywhere, as from looking at the sun. It is strange to see such static brilliance, such cool brilliance: poised, detached flames on their smooth green stems—a green white. I love the leaves too—flat, radiating veins from the center. They would float on water—flatly.

Thursday, July 14th (Quatorze Juillet—Bastille Day!)
Inside, "house-machinery noises": a door slamming, a knob turning, the rattling of silver in a tray, the clicking of the latch on cupboard doors, the dull knock of plates being placed on a table, dishes in the sink, the sound of water running. The tinkling of silver in someone's hand, Binns's high shaky voice singing in the pantry, the brassy reverberation of a tray (a tin tray) that has been knocked, the squeak of a door, footsteps—not the definite footsteps of persons going from one place to another, as of a mistress of the house walking from one room to another, but the soft sound of feet walking back and forth, back and forth: kitchen to pantry, dining room to kitchen, maids' dining room to pantry. The creak and rumble of the carpet sweeper over rugs, laughter in the distance, the guttural laughter of the Swedish maid. The chug-chug of the ice pick.

Friday, July 15th
Fog—let-down backdrop dividing the foreground of trees from their usual background, making them stand out as all-important. Everything under this covering partook of the same substance, all seemed part of the earth, the form of a sheep on a slope; the head and shoulders of a man going through a field of grass; a barn looming up over a hill. Grass too, on a hilltop, since it had nothing behind it but this thick backdrop, stood out etched in the mist. By the side of the road wild roses wet and puckered-up, the pink petals clinging together. Birds huddled on the telephone wires. Here a cobweb on a fence, glistening with silver mist-drops.

Dear Corliss,[1]

The butterflies are beautiful—especially a small shiny blue one in the second or third group. But they are not as beautiful as the real fluttering ones that mean summer and leisure. Do you know that poem of [W. H.] Davies that has the line

> "What is this life if, full of care,
> We have no time to stand and stare."

Oh, I have had so much to say to you and now there is a kind of wall made of the paper and the pen and the scratchy noise of the two; a wall between my thoughts and wishes and their expression. Perhaps this is what "Zélide" (or Geoffrey Scott) meant by the "friction of correspondence." I would have written before but there have been duty letters. Imagine *twenty-one* absolutely necessary ones! I have written ten now and there are eleven left. I write about two "unpleasant" letters a day and what a struggle it is! Of course I suppose if I devoted the *whole* day to it I could get almost all done at once. But there is your philosophy that I have hardly had a chance to start on—and then, there are so many things I have been saving up—lots of off-side eighteenth-century memoirs and things—a life of Rousseau—a memoir—some French—some modern writers ("the stream-of-consciousness writers" or whatever they call them that started with Proust etc.). Some Russian stories of Chekhov, *The Brothers,* etc., etc. It is so tantalizing. I can't read fast enough. Then it is so beautiful. I must be out some of the time. The fields are really white with daisies. There are so many lovely white things, clouds and gulls and daisies and the white caps of waves—I saw them all from your garden. Then exercise—one must have some. I take it in the most condensed form—swimming. It is so cold that you exercise

---

[1] Corliss Lamont, philosophy student at Columbia University, later teacher of philosophy and author.

long after you come out just getting warm. Then it makes you feel both like a holy martyr and a god. Today it was warm—yes, really—warm for North Haven. I could have stayed in hours. I wish sometimes I were a seal. I would like to slip in and out of the water and have a glossy slippery coat. Swimming with nothing on gives you the feeling, too, it is delicious in warm water. I like to just slither around hardly moving my legs—like a mermaid and the water so completely holding you up and around you. I love it. Diving is glorious too—though I never learned how to cut through air and water—swiftly and slimly; it is intoxicating.

I meant to talk about the reading but I'm afraid I'm too sleepy—I read the introduction of Royce. I think it is very fine and clear. I loved the part where he describes the philosopher as a "professional musician of reflective thought"—all of it is very fine. It gave me a very inspiring and enlightening view of what you wanted to do and be (in some small way, I mean, I grasped a *little* of your point of view) as enlightening as a sonnet you once read me of Santayana's, beginning, I think, with "Deem not because you see me . . ." etc. Then I read the *Apology* and *Crito*. It gave me a very odd feeling for I had worked them both out painstakingly in detail, in Greek, and hadn't grasped the true sense at all. Yet it was all minutely familiar. I read it, though, at a kind of heat of admiration that I never had before—overcome with the sweep and height of it—especially the *Apology*. I shall read *Phaedo* tomorrow. Thank you, Corliss, so much.

The other day I went on a picnic, we went around Vinal Haven and through the islands; I saw the end of *Hurricane,* with the two little knobs. I thought of last year, those "blue days at sea." There was so much sky in those days—clouds—little white ones along the edge of the horizon or big piling sunset ones— Then the wind and the big four-masters in the distance and our white sail above next to the sky, and the sound of rushing water. Will we have it again—something like it? This year perhaps.

Elisabeth, I know, has asked you if you could come up for a

weekend. You could bring up books. We do nothing else. And we would keep quiet and not disturb you and let you work.

DIARY   *Saturday, July 16th*

Supper on board *Corsair*.[1] It was like suddenly being transported to Paris or Biarritz. An indescribable world of romance. It meant evenings when everything turned suddenly glistening and party and anything was around the corner: music in the distance, lights, candles, lights on the plates and glasses, smoke, the low murmur and laughter of men's voices. The joy of being there almost invisible in this sparkling world, able to watch and listen to the most brilliant, charming men in the world, and a sense of the utmost fairy-tale luxury—everything done in exciting, magnificent style, so much grander than a party of young people. It was as if as a child when watching all the long-legged black coats and stiff fronts, all the gleaming, glistening, gowned ladies radiant with powder and laughter and little jeweled bags—as if suddenly from watching at the cloakroom door one was allowed downstairs into the dining room, invisible but present. And so much more comfortable than a young people's party, so much more *secure*—one could safely stay in one's shell; one did not need to talk, one had only to smile and watch. Then the food: the joy in the many strange, twisted, and sauced dishes—odd shapes, colors, tastes, textures: castles of whipped cream, tarts, toast at the wrong places—and all those glasses, short and tall, full of melted gems one could not taste.

That was the world we were back in. We were transported very swiftly in a closed-in motorboat to the great steamer—portholes sending out flickering lines of light. We stepped out onto the steps, the gangplank, and at the top stood Mr. Morgan—great, gruff, cordial, always with his "superb" manner, large smile, large gestures, large, hearty "How do you do"—his round full voice, English accent.

[1] J. P. Morgan's yacht.

[*North Haven, late summer*]

A walk through the woods on the way to a picnic with Mr. Locke.[1] There was no underbrush, just brown shiny needles, tall pine trunks, and the light coming through as though from a long way off, as if through cathedral windows. It was filtered and strained, somehow, rarefied, as though it had come in a straight shaft through leagues of the sea, and this was a drowned forest.

A day at Helen's:[2] a big, summery, chintzy house, empty and still and cool. And Helen playing Brahms and César Franck. A still, perfect moment, framed neither by time nor by space but high apart, above these. Still, caught—the drop of water from the eaves, swelling, about to fall, but now whole, crystalline, perfect. Those moments are so rare, so few, for anyone—those moments of perfection. Music seems to make mine, to make things stand still, at the Binghams'[3] and at the Lockes'. I kept looking at the flowers in a vase near me: lavender sweet peas, fragile winged and yet so still, so perfectly poised, apart, and complete. They are self-sufficient, a world in themselves, a whole—perfect. Is that, then, perfection? Is what those sweet peas had what I have, occasionally, in moments like that? But flowers *always* have it— poise, completion, fulfillment, perfection; I, only occasionally, like that moment. For that moment I and the sweet peas had an understanding.

I thought then, too, of the summer—so baffling, wasted, slipping by in such petty day-to-day things, and my fear, my deadly fear, that my life will do that too. But then that line, *"Il n'y a pas de vie heureuse; il y a seulement des jours heureux"*[4]—perhaps that is it. These *jours heureux,* these moments make up for the

---

[1] Professor of music at Smith College; lived in Vinal Haven.

[2] Helen Choate; lived in North Haven.

[3] Senator Hiram Bingham. A. M. L. made frequent visits to the Bingham family.

[4] There is no happy life; there are only happy days.

other—at least they are worth the other. Should one marry for those, I wonder, or for the other—the other great majority of the time?

When one looks back over a period of time and says, "I have had a happy (or an unhappy) summer," what one says depends quite often on the mood in which one is at the time. If one is happy—if it is sunny and there is the smell of cut grass and the hum of bees—that moment acts as the door to other moments akin to it. It opens a long vista of sunny afternoons with the smell of cut grass and the hum of bees. That moment touches hands with all its little sisters. One can see nothing else but those moments. But if one is unhappy at the moment when one considers, one is inevitably reminded of all the times one has felt just that way. They seem interminable, stretching back as far as one can see, leering at one with exactly the same face down long aisles, as in reflected mirrors.

These two vistas seem absolutely unconnected—sealed passages with no cross doors, and only one entrance.

[Englewood]

Always when I have lain awake at night or in the morning on the porch, I have looked into those two treetops that brush against the side of the house. They are almost the first thing I remember, and they are not trees at all but a world made up of sights and sounds and smells, imperceptible parts of countless mornings and evenings. This world of treetops and associated, pieced-together memories is as unrelated to the world below of trunks and grass—the world of the swing, of back-yard games, of the clothes-line and of piles of burning leaves, of those round, prickly brown balls (seeds) that fell from above—the treetop world was as unrelated to the world below its trunk as the world Jack of the Beanstalk found in the sky was unrelated to the Beanstalk that he climbed up to reach it.

The physical good-by so seldom coincides with the spiritual—good-bys are unreal either physically or spiritually. Mother [is going] to Mexico.[1]

[*Northampton, September 28, 1927*]
[*Start of Senior year*]

Mother darling—

Even after the second day I am too weary to write you all I want to. But I am well *and* very happy so I wanted just to scribble something to you.

Your dear note I found and gloated over (unopened) that night. I read it in the cool of the first morning, looking out on my garden.

Mother, darling, I did think of you in chapel, singing that thrilling hymn, "From Hand to Hand the Greeting Goes." You have been so wonderful about all of this (Mexico), I think, really, that we children have spoken more of you than of Daddy when we have discussed it. I can't talk more of it, I'm too sleepy.

I walk down the walks under these beautiful trees and think of you. I am so glad I am here where you were.

I walked last night up to see some Freshmen in Gardiner and afterwards to *Morrow*. It was quiet and the rooms were lit and lovely. I tiptoed about a little guiltily (I always feel like some sort of unofficial guardian angel) and sat down in your *own* warm little poetry room.[2] It was so comforting. I feel very near you here.

[*Northampton, October 2, 1927*]

Mother, darling,

It was so hectic over the telephone. I couldn't hear very well, people were making a lot of noise and I was hurried.

[1] In July, 1927, President Coolidge asked Dwight Morrow to accept the post of Ambassador to Mexico.

[2] Elizabeth Cutter Morrow Poetry Library at Morrow House, Smith College.

It must be simply *inconceivable* at home—worse than twenty conventions or drives! You having to decide so many things—moving always means that—a *thousand* decisions, thousands of things to tie up.

Please, please don't make it any harder for yourself, worrying about your children. I, at least, don't need any worrying. The fruit was—*is* (for there is still lots in spite of my giving so much away) simply luscious, only I felt like the Queen of Roumania about to sail, with such a grand and enormous basket. The Lowestoft bowl is a joy sitting here before me, and the flower pictures are very soothing. All my classes are exciting, especially Miss Dunn, and Mlle Delpit[1] is so sweet and charming and kind to me that I think the French will work out all right. It is quite beautiful here now—the leaves beginning to turn yellow. Bitta [Laura Fay] and I are going out for a walk soon—we had tea together yesterday.

That sweet Mrs. Smith (Amherst) has a daughter, a Freshman here.[2] She has asked us to come to Amherst for Thanksgiving, Dwight motoring down with St. John [Smith]. Wasn't it lovely of her?

Darling Mother, I don't see how you can *possibly* get up here. Please don't make it any harder by doing it and breaking down your health. You will see me as a Senior in the spring! And I don't feel much like a Senior now, anyway. Perhaps I could go down (and back the same day). It would be lots of fun. Or if you want just to go to Groton I could motor over there. I really don't see how you *can* possibly come—those nights on the sleeper, the long trip, the heat. What did you say—that you hadn't slept? I couldn't understand. Was it that? Why was it? Has Daddy felt ill again, or have you just been thinking and thinking so hard? Or the heat? Please do save your strength, Mother. I am well and

---

[1] Louise Delpit, associate professor of French.

[2] Mrs. St. John Smith. Her daughter, Frances Smith, plays a major role in the diary and letters.

contented here and amble around the campus with the happy-go-lucky carelessness of someone who feels *completely* at home!

Mlle Delpit was so *sweet* about you. She adores you and said such lovely things I wanted to kiss her. I said you were coming, but she raised her hands with that inexpressibly charming French gesture and said, "Ah, but your mother—she is like some shooting star!"

[*Northampton, October 18, 1927*]

Mother, I haven't had time to write you a long "going-away" letter,[1] and this will have to do. But I have had so many things to tell you. How happy your visit made me—that we had that quiet lunch and a time in the gay little library fixing books. I will go there often, for it is so connected with you. That we could walk arm in arm through the campus and under those trees. That you have seen my room as it is this year. That you saw Northampton at its loveliest time (except the spring, *when you will see it again with me!*).

Mother, I must stop now. This may not even get in the mail and get to you. I shall write often to you, darling, and think of you. You have been so wonderful about it all, so young in the way you have accepted such a tremendous challenge (that sounds sentimental but it *is* a tremendous challenge and so many people realize that and what you are doing, and send their love with you). I shall write you often, even very little things—once a week, anyway—and I do look forward so to Christmas. You know I was telling Con that I think, as far as seeing each other goes (and that is the most important thing), that this vacation may be *much* more satisfactory than they usually are, with none of the distractions of New York and different engagements. Won't that be glorious!

Darling, I am sorry that you left me crying. It is not that I am not happy—you must know—but because, for once, your leaving

[1] Mr. and Mrs. Morrow, accompanied by their daughter Constance, left for Mexico City on October 19th.

and the *realization* of your leaving came to me *at the same* moment and I could not help feeling how far you were going and how much we have together that we like to appreciate together, and that for a while we could not do that as directly. And I would rather feel badly (for that reason) than not feel that way. It is really such a cause of happiness to me.

DIARY   [*Northampton*], *October 23, 1927*
Today was lovely—not only for the outward, apparent beauty. A still, clear, autumn day. The trees, hills, flaming gold—red russet —and all *still,* caught by the frost, ready to fall and blow and swirl, but now for a moment held in a spell.

But it had more than this. It wore, somehow, an extra and divine "bloom," that glowing fruits sometimes have.

A still day with a wind high, high above—a tearing wind up there somewhere, so that one hears a distant roaring all the time. As though we here were sunk in a deep sea and far above our heads great ships passed slowly.

To the oculist. Small child sat opposite me, with enormous glasses on, lenses magnified many times. She looked with these large pensive eyes—unnaturally large, like cow's eyes—all over the room, and *me* (feeling very uncomfortable). I felt as if the cow had licked me all over with her large tongue.

I want to write—I want to write—I want to write and I never never never will. I know it and I am so unhappy and it seems as though nothing else mattered. Whatever I'm doing, it's always there, an ultimate longing there saying, "Write this—write that— write—" and I *can't.* Lack ability, time, strength, and duration of vision. I wish someone would tell me brutally, "You can *never* write *anything.* Take up home gardening!"

[*Northampton, November 7, 1927*]
Mother darling—
Your first letter! It was so wonderful, from the outside "Embassy of the United States" to the *"Diplomatic Mail Free,"* and all that

precious, precious news about your first days. I chortled over it, every bit of it, and tried to picture myself there. The confusion sounded *terrific.* It was all summed up in that scattered sentence of yours: "Daddy going in full dress and high hat at eleven in the morning to exchange compliments with the Minister of Foreign Affairs. The best *Carpenter* in town is *Jesus!* (we are having a bookcase made). The coiffeur makes ice cream in the mornings. I have fourteen servants and I'm not allowed to pick up anything!" Poor Mother! Are they all very tall with twirly mustachios?

I can't wait to get Elisabeth's letter. I wish I were there. What *are* your diplomatic duties? Do *you* have to eat "ham and eggs" with some official wife? I did relish that clipping so: "Calles[1] and Morrow eat Ham and Eggs." I can just *see* Daddy with fork and knife slashing across his two poached eggs absent-mindedly yet firmly, as he always did in the breakfast room!

I am trying to think of news for you. Elisabeth and I had such a *lovely* weekend. We slept together and had meals together and nice talks and planned another weekend, and it was such beautiful weather! She looked *so* well and *so* happy—better than I have seen her for ages, since before college.

The other night I had dinner in Amherst with Mrs. St. John Smith. President and Mrs. Olds were there and President and Mrs. Lowell[2] (for the inauguration). I hope I "did you proud," inasmuch as I could. I sat next to President Lowell, who was very interesting and interested in Special Honors system and the tutorial system at Smith and Harvard. He has a nice sense of humor. He asked me so many questions—I felt as though Daddy were talking to me. You know the intelligent, penetrating questions which demand an intelligent and accurate answer.

I have seen an *awful* picture of you, Daddy, and Con arriving with Daffin[3]—the only recognizable one.

[1] Plutarco Elías Calles, President of Mexico 1924–28.

[2] Abbott Lawrence Lowell, President of Harvard 1909–33.

[3] The Morrows' West Highland white terrier.

I didn't get a chance to talk to President Olds. But it was so "warming" to see them both. They do love you so and spoke with such love and pride and interest of you and **Daddy**.

DIARY *November 26th*

Today I was having my clothes fitted by sweet, bright-eyed little Miss A. She was so rushed. A chance word of sympathy, and she was sitting down on the couch wiping her eyes and telling me everything. I was so appalled. She is twenty-one—my age—her father dead, her mother having slaved for them. An older sister (dreamer), a boy (thoughtless and egotistical), and Miss A. working for all of them ever since fourteen. Her position as under-sewer. Finally striking out alone, helped by one friend. She had to "make good." She had to take all work, at lower price, work every night, she and her mother: work badly done by helpers. She undid it rather than scold them, and redid it herself, late at night, so tired. Even Sundays, worked to keep the house nice so people would come: beaux, like other homes, but so tired. Thoughtlessness of [college] girls: must have it by Friday, leaving it Thursday, and then don't come for it. Wants her brother to have education she couldn't have. She has had no youth, loves pretty clothes—reds—loves tangos, Spain and Mexico.

I felt somehow not at all embarrassed at this stream, I was so moved, so amazed at her courage and her accomplishments. It was so thrilling but so sad—heartbreaking—and unbelievable. The tragedy—no, but the sadness of such struggle.

Then up to tea with R.'s mother. A hard woman and rather superficial; brilliant, at least witty, and charming, but she has put all life from her, pushed it away with fastidious hands, fearing to be hurt. (She was hurt—divorced etc.) She goes to movies and theater to be moved, she admits frankly.

I couldn't help feeling rather shocked at the contrast: Miss A. so much realer. I love her.

I saw the most beautiful cat today. It was sitting by the side of the road, its two front feet neatly and graciously together. Then it gravely swished around its tail to completely and snugly encircle itself. It was so *fit* and beautifully neat, that gesture, and so self-satisfied—so complacent.

A tearing wind last night. I woke up and it was roaring down—I heard it coming like a great wave or a river breaking over its banks, and in a panic closed one window. Felt I should bow my head like a tree to let it go over me.

How odious are closet sweeps and chapped rough hands and hairs on the dressing table and powder on the edges of the drawers and clothes that slide off hangers and dirty handkerchiefs—and combs.

I hate making a bed from the beginning up: that horrible cold bare look when you have just fastened in the first crisp clean sheet.

Clouds today—great archangel wings across the sky.

[*Concert at Smith College*]

Bach, played by Harold Samuel.

Absolute perfection—transporting, pure, clear, unearthly, untouched, and untouchable; escape into a world unbelievably perfect, apart; unattainable perfection caught and held there crystallized. Lucid, faultless, chaste.

Such escape, after all the failures and imperfections of everyday things: of work for Mr. Patch,[1] of papers for Miss Dunn, of poor expression in writing. We are always compromising, taking the imperfect.

Here, here at last, perfection—absolute, cool, instantaneous—and its intangibility. Its beauty slipping liquidly away, while one listened in rapture and in tears.

It doesn't matter that it can't last, that we don't find it more often. To know that there is such perfection, that there has been

[1] Howard R. Patch, Chairman, English Department.

such perfection—it is worth living for. It *exists*. It *has been—it is.*
One can contemplate it and feel a complete peace.

The "wholeness," the completeness of such moments—I can
stumble in imperfections for years to make up for it.

I had all "the imperfections" in one day today, beginning with
a complete failure (from my point of view) in my Chaucer
written.

[*On train to Mexico, December 19, 1927, traveling with
E. R. M.*] All day we have been traveling through this monotonous country. Laredo this morning: nothing as far as one can see
but this gray-greenish-brown sand, and sagebrush and cactus (low
kind), with here and there one of those grotesque deformed cactus finger trees springing up fantastically from the sagebrush. It is
cold—a penetrating, damp, pervading cold. We stop at little
stations; mud-built houses, sticks and stones; standing outside, a
man, dark, savage-looking, a blanket around him, covering his
nose and mouth, showing just those sullen dark eyes. Pigs and
thin, tail-lowered dogs run in and out of his house. A woman in
the door—a great blanket around her, too—her eyes only showing
above the rim. It is so cold.

There is nowhere any color. It is all just the same, this dull
gray green: the sand, the bushes, the sky even—cold and cloudy—
seemed washed with the same color; no reds, no yellows or tans,
just this cold enveloping dry gray. It is terribly depressing. We
have traveled three days seeing nothing lovely: flat fields first, of
cornstalks, then of cotton, now today *nothing* but this gray cactus.
It looks like one vast mildew!

It would be so terrible to have something happen and find
oneself left behind here in this desolateness. It is worse at the
stations. It doesn't seem real when one goes by it—the train
rattles and convinces one that it (the train) is the only reality, but
when we stop and it is still for a minute and one looks out and
sees and hears a pig scratching around, that little bit of motion, of
external motion and sound, shocks one with the horrible realiza-

tion that this place is real! That it exists, that it was there before you steamed into it and (desolate thought) that *it will be there still when we have left it far behind*. That pig scratching in front of the mud house . . .

Tonight we went by a "hacienda," a ranch. Over the wall of the house climbed a brilliant red-purple bougainvillaea! It made one cry out for joy, just to see that flaming bit of color.

Felt like *Outward Bound*[1] tonight, all of us shut in together, any former life so inevitably gone, past, and untouchable. No lights outside, just blank. We rush by—just blank darkness outside.

Where have we come from? Where are we going?

It is like dying.

[*December 20th*]

Now I know what the Children of Israel felt like when they came to the "Promised Land." I woke this morning to green trees—real trees—dripping with strings of red berries off them and canyons—a river brown and sandy winding along. Hills, too, covered with cactus, but at least hills. And cornfields. Little mud huts with women kneeling in front in gay skirts on yellow straw. Red tiles on the roofs, and red flowers against the walls. The houses are painted as a child might paint them. Blue with red around the door and windows, or white with red.

Suddenly, through the canyon and over the hills the mist melted. We were in bright sun. We got out at a station. A woman held up a basket of oranges and limes, brilliant with the sun on it. It was warm—deliciously, unbelievably warm; that delicious Nassau smell of clay roads drying after a night's shower. You could take your coat off and the sun turned you inside out.

Miracle of warmth and sun and color.

We are in a new land now: great plains, still, of cactus and

---

[1] A play (1923) by Sutton Vane in which passengers on a ship come to realize that they have died and are now bound for heaven or hell.

century plants, but they roll up to a great irregular sky, mountains—fantastic and unreal—shadows of clouds upon them.

Men with their great straw hats and sullen eyes, immovable, watch us.

Little donkeys draw carts through the fields, the corn and the cactus growing as high as they.

[Mexico City]

This was to be an objective diary. It stops here! I don't care how much I rave if only I could get down to keep *a little* the feeling of what has happened this last week. I wish to heavens I had written it down as it happened, but I was too moved—and too ashamed of my emotion. It has to be written down, though. I must—I must remember. The trouble is that for the first time in my life I was not conscious of wanting to write it down—I have never felt so *completely* inarticulate. So often I have felt: I cannot express this delicate thing, my instruments are too clumsy, too thick. But here, now, all I can feel is: my instruments are too small, too inadequate, I have *nothing* to express this, no way to deal with it.

The best I can do is to piece together painstakingly the small superficial details, all—everything I can remember, everything no matter how little—and rather blindly hope that a miracle will happen, that this conglomerate, patched collection of fragments may ignite somehow—at least for me—and that some glimmering of the indescribable feeling may be relit in me.

Wednesday [December 21st]

After a day of plains and great sweeping valleys—tremendous mountains. It was dark. Suddenly there were lights, close streets, and in a minute we slid into the station. It was indescribably swift, finding ourselves there on the back platform, Con jumping over the tracks from behind another car, and then we fell out into each other's arms. Daddy went off with a secretary and we jammed into another car, through streets lighted, walled, like

France. Choppy conversation: Did we have all the things? How glad they were to see us! What it was like at first. Were we safe and well? Were we really there? They were *so* lonely at first. How they were arranging rooms.

"Colonel Lindbergh was there[1]—a very nice boy, very nice, but he and Daddy were going out tonight." We hardly took it in, or at least were a little annoyed—all this public-hero stuff breaking into our family party. What did I expect? A regular newspaper hero, the baseball-player type—a nice man, perhaps, but not at all "intellectual" and not of my world at all, so I wouldn't be interested. I certainly was *not* going to worship "Lindy" (that *odious name,* anyway). We drove through the streets and honked loudly before an iron gate with eagles above on the crest; the gates opened; we drew up. A wall covered with geraniums to our right, a great movie-scene door and staircase to the left, stone steps, red "velvet" rolling up, like a wedding, in between palms. Officers stood on the steps at attention. We tumbled out dazed and peered up the red plush stairs between "lines" of officers. What a movie! How ridiculous, was all I could say. Elisabeth sat down on the steps exhausted. We went up at last.

At the top another line of celebrities. Elisabeth went first. Mother hurried up: "Colonel Lindbergh, this is my oldest daughter, Elisabeth." I saw standing against the great stone pillar—on *more* red plush—a tall, slim boy in evening dress—so much slimmer, so much taller, so much more poised than I expected. A very refined face, not at all like those grinning "Lindy" pictures— a firm mouth, clear, straight blue eyes, fair hair, and nice color. Then I went down the line, very confused and overwhelmed by it all. He did not smile—just bowed and shook hands.

A bright fire in the fireplace, great calla lilies on the stone mantelpiece, red tapestry on the stone walls, rich priest's robes,

---

[1] Colonel Lindbergh had flown the *Spirit of St. Louis* nonstop from Washington, D. C., to Mexico City, on December 13–14, 1927. The flight was planned at the suggestion of Ambassador Morrow and made in response to an invitation issued by President Calles.

and the intoxicating scent of something. Chinese lilies? Gardenias? They were tuberoses.

It was all unreal.

Supper that night in a regular baronial hall: stone pillars, stone mantelpiece, etc.

We explored the rooms—high-ceilinged and Nassau-ish. I felt in Nassau, or Panama. I had to run in to Mother every three seconds to feel sure it was true. Daddy, I realized, belonged to so many people now. I was utterly confused. Later Daddy came home, with Colonel L. Daddy told us to come into the little sitting room. "Is there anyone there?" (With *great* pride, restrained.) "Oh no, just Colonel Lindbergh." Elisabeth and I went out. Why is it that attractive men stimulate Elisabeth to her best and always terrify me and put me at my worst!? We sat around the fire stiffly. Colonel L. stood awkwardly by the desk, shifting from one foot to another. Elisabeth talked.

He is very, very young and was terribly shy—looked straight ahead and talked in short direct sentences which came out abruptly and clipped. You could not meet his sentences: they were statements of fact, presented with such honest directness; not trying to please, just bare simple answers and statements, not trying to help a conversation along. It was amazing—breathtaking. I could not speak. What kind of boy was this?

"How did he like the bullfight?" He blushed a little and shifted his position. "Well, I have seen things I enjoyed more," he blurted out abruptly. "Would he show us the cape and hat—Mexican—presented to him?" "I would be very glad to," and he wheeled out of the room (with evident relief), returned with richly embroidered cape and sombrero, which he passed around with dry impersonality. It did not touch him, all this, and neither did we. It embarrassed him to have to talk to us. He was asked a question about the crowds here and in London. They were not half as bad here as in Paris and London, he said with a dry, simple-statement-of-fact statement. Suddenly the picture of that mad crowd, that whole *nation* surging around his plane in Paris, came into my mind. And it was this *boy*—this shy, cool boy—and he describes that tremendous mad scene in a few dry matter-of-fact words. My Lord!

Daddy said we must go to bed. Abruptly, the Colonel announced, "Well, as the Ambassador's orders are such, I will say good night," and he shook hands quickly without looking at us (girls) and wheeled out of the room, leaving a perfectly amazed stillness inside of me.

High ceilings—slat shutters that curl up as at Nassau, keeping out the morning sun. We didn't sleep well, tried to comprehend, to analyze, the popularity of this man. I think it is not what he has done—other men could have done the same thing. It seems as though it must be either that he is the symbol of the most beautiful, most stupendous achievement of our age—as typical and as beautiful an expression as the cathedral was of the Middle Ages—or is it just personal magnetism? For everyone does feel immediately, I think, silenced and amazed at this man.

In the garden with Mother and Elisabeth. Warm; picked roses, red carnations, heliotrope, and crunched over the paths. English daisies. It was so calm and warm and apart, in the Embassy garden behind walls.

Colonel L. had gone to the Pyramids. After lunch we jumped into the Embassy cars, and preceded by motorcycles we speeded through the streets of Mexico City (full of stalls on the streets—one continual street fair!) to the flying field. Mrs. Lindbergh[1] was to arrive from San Antonio in the Ford plane. Colonel L. had gone out to meet her and the five escort planes.

A great crowd by the hangars. We walked alongside of Daddy and had our pictures taken—hard to talk—excited—then the whir, the motor of an airplane. The five escort planes—like birds high up, like geese in a V—then the big Ford plane. They came down nearer—the thrill, the tremendous excitement as of a strong

[1] Mrs. Evangeline Lodge Land Lindbergh, C. A. L.'s mother. She taught chemistry at Cass Technical High School, Detroit, Michigan.

electric current going through you when the throb of their engines runs through you. I felt tremendously excited and understood for the first time anyone's devotion to it. The planes swooped close over our heads. I felt—almost—I could die for this. I don't care if I *do* have my head knocked off if it's for the cause!

The big Ford plane was down—no longer a bird but a great monster dragonfly. It touched ground, stirring dust, and drove furiously towards us (Con and "Sandy"[1] ran out to take pictures). It stopped. The crowd pushed madly around it—we were squashed—people fought to get in. Commander Hamilton[2] was driving people off. The door of the plane opened and out stepped a small, sweet-faced, shy little woman—Mrs. Lindbergh. She turned to Mother and Daddy and to Elisabeth. They forced a way through the crowd to the car. They tried to jam a giant poinsettia plant in with her!

Colonel L. was still in the air—afraid of crowd when landing. We drove back.

I saw the snow-capped mountains Sleeping Lady[3] and Popo-catepetl.

The whir of planes still in my ears—

Back to the Embassy. Met Mrs. Lindbergh and party—Mr. and Mrs. Stout[4] (*just* like Aunt Em and Uncle Henry in *Wizard of Oz!*). Elisabeth with marvelous executiveness had tea and poured and passed like a Lady of the White House. Crowds of fierce reporters, photographers, of all heights and sizes, out on the porch. Mrs. Lindbergh finally spoke to them. Then Cito came to say that the Colonel was at the door. She jumped up and Elisa-

[1] Colonel Alexander MacNab, U.S. Military Attaché in Mexico.

[2] Lieutenant-Commander Donald W. Hamilton, Naval Attaché.

[3] Ixtacihuatl, a volcano.

[4] William B. Stout, Ford aeronautical engineer, 1920–30, and his wife had accompanied Mrs. Lindbergh on her flight to Mexico.

beth with her. I did not see them meet. Then they walked into the little library. I was to follow with some tea for her. I stumbled in. "I am *so* sorry to disturb you, but my sister sent this—" and I held out the tea, dropping the spoon on the ground nervously. They were so sweet. And he thanked me with that simply disarming smile of his—lines wrinkle from his eyes way back.

I felt: There is no use trying to analyze this—I can see how they all worship him. He came back into the room—you knew he was there without turning—then when he is there everyone turns to him, everyone is conscious of his corner of the room. You hear his voice, and listen for it. There is a silence about the things he says: islands of words, surrounded by the stillness of an audience's admiration.

They went out onto the porch to have their pictures taken. He is taller than anyone else—you see his head in a moving crowd and you notice his glance, where it turns, as though it were keener, clearer, and brighter than anyone else's, lit with a more intense fire. From Daddy's window and from the porch we watched the picture on the steps.

Mrs. Schoenfeld's[1] reception: I met Mrs. Lindbergh in the hall as we waited to go. The grownups got into the cars first, leaving Elisabeth, Colonel L., and me at the door with Mrs. Sills.[2] Outside the gates were crowds shouting, peering, jumping. He stood retiringly to the side behind the door—not seen. "Oh, do give them a thrill!" said Mrs. Sills, but he blushed and said, "They've had enough thrill." Then we jumped into the car, Elisabeth, I, and Colonel L., and drove out. Shouts, cries, cheers—people rushing at the car. "Viva Coronel Lindbergh." "Viva Lindbergh!" etc. I said in a low voice, "I *never* felt so out of place in all my

---

[1] Wife of H. F. Arthur Schoenfeld, counselor, member of the staff of the U. S. Embassy in Mexico.

[2] Catherine Sills, E. C. M.'s Embassy secretary.

life. I know, it's right for you and for Daddy, all this, but . . . somehow it doesn't seem as though I had any right at all, just because I am a daughter . . ." I had to stammer something. "All the right in the world," he blurted out gruffly and kindly. (I forgot to say how delicious it was: as we drove through the crowds he said with a dry smile, "Tomorrow the picture will come out, 'Colonel Lindbergh driving to tea with his mother.'" It was so hysterical. We laughed and added (Elisabeth did), "his two sisters.")

The reception: jams of people—a line crowded past Colonel L. and Mrs. Lindbergh and Mother. I stood in the background, back of the receiving line, and watched—and tried to listen to a flipperty person with braids around her head and tried to talk to "Aunt Em" and her husband about their airplane trip down.

Home.

Supper—Elisabeth next to Colonel L. She talked very well to him.

During supper there was the sound of shouts, murmuring outside the walls, cries of a great crowd in the distance (a student demonstration for Colonel L.—supposedly a *"gallo"*[1]). It was ominous and terrifying, like the crowds at the palace door at the time of the French Revolution. It terrified me but he went on unconsciously eating.

Then we went out. I, naïvely (idiot, forgetting the crowds in Paris and London!), murmured to him that I should think he would be frightened, but he didn't look up, just blushed a little and turned away. A delegation of a dozen students came in at the door. They looked so small in front of him. One spoke—a long, carefully planned speech, flowery. He listened simply, courteously, leaning forward a little and respectfully paying the most dignified attention—an attention which dignified them—then, without saying a word, at the finish, he immediately and directly went forward and shook hands with everyone. It was nothing—

[1] A serenade.

another man might have made a speech, expressed his thanks effusively—and yet this was most royal as he did it. The students were glowing with pride.

Then he went to the window—we all went. Down there below us in the streets were crowds of people shouting, pushing, crowding—faces looking up, strangely lit by street lamps—strange costumes, adoring women, jostling men—songs; a strange, monotonous, barbarous song was being repeated over and over, somewhere. Boys were climbing the trees below to get nearer him. He went to the window—one great shout, screams of joy: "Viva Lindbergh!" Mrs. Lindbergh went with him. Some boy climbed up the wall to shake his hand.

To me it was simply terrifying. I had never seen it before—never done anything but read about it. But what could a crowd like this do if it were *angry* or furious? It made one gasp to think. Those crowds! Who has moved men like that before—not with a speech, not intentionally, not trying to move them by any means—just standing there, just existing? What *does* he think about it? What does he suppose he's doing? Why does he move them so? How does he explain that to himself? How does he explain this mad popularity? Does he think (he with his clear, far-seeing mind), does he fool himself into thinking, it is his flight across the ocean that has done this? But men have done it before and will again. Or does he suppose that *aviation* has taken the world by storm? No, he can't—he is too clear-headed to fool himself that way. But how does he explain it? He must be terribly confused (for he doesn't realize anything strange about himself) or else he avoids the issue entirely, does not question, just accepts.

I was simply stunned by it all—so amazed at such a revelation that I could not speak or think, just wonder.

We sat around the fire later—Colonel L. opposite his mother. They talked. In short, clipped sentences—question and answer—showing complete understanding between the two. He listened intently, earnestly, picked up the answers quickly, nodding, with sometimes a quick flash of a smile, then shot another question about the trip.

Friday

Elisabeth, Aunt Alice,[1] and I sat with Mrs. Lindbergh in the sun on the steps. She talked about her trip, and flying, and about him. She is overskeptical of the admiration and praise given her (no wonder).

Shopping; huge crowds chasing the car and crowding around the doors of shops to watch her and touch her.

A big lunch for staff on porch of the Embassy. We went around and looked at the cards and stole nuts.

Mrs. Lindbergh and Aunt Alice get on wonderfully.

Con says he has stiffened up terribly since we came. Isn't natural. He avoids us—at least me—as much as I do him, for I *can't* treat him as an ordinary person (and *will* not treat him as an extraordinary one), so I just avoid him as much as possible.

Saturday, Christmas Eve–Day

Sat in the sun on the steps. It is so sheltered—the secretary's office, facing us across the green court. The walls shutting it all in. The walks around the green center, the roses on the wall, and heliotrope and fuchsia, the orange tree (with oranges) to the left. The great cool pillared porch and long steps. The "White House look" about it all. Sometimes I could see in the office windows men working—silhouettes only—or in the door. Sometimes the door was open out into the street—the hot white street beyond and I inside, in this green garden of trees and flower beds and flowered walls. I felt like sheltered Emelye, in the "Knight's Tale." Over the wall (beyond the palm and orange trees, over the ironwork gate) I could see another wall of another house, and bougainvillaea, crimson bougainvillaea, climbing up. In the street —far away, it seemed—one heard the cries of boys selling turkeys

[1] Alice Morrow, sister of D. W. M.

(they drive them through the streets like sheep!)—nasal cries like those in France (*"Le Petit Journal!"*).

I washed my hair on the roof and walked around and sang and looked at the walled gardens around below. Two little Mexican children (a gardener's) with small serapes playing on one side, a little American boy on the other. The sun makes me happy. We did up packages. Con made fudge for the Colonel. In the afternoon we decorated the tree, strung it with tinsel (great discussion—"Horizontal" or "Perpendicular, like Spanish moss?"—between the boys). Elisabeth threw glowing balls up at Bill[1] on the stepladder.

The staff Christmas party that evening: Commander and Mrs. Hamilton, she bright and red, sparkling; Captain and Mrs. Winslow,[2] she tall and fair, green and cool, like cucumber sandwiches, refreshing. Captain Winslow you notice before anyone else in a room: you feel his sympathy and his generosity. He has a very sensitive face. Mrs. Schoenfeld "a handsome woman." He sparkles too. The tree lit; Captain Winslow kneeling on the sofa teasing Rosamund Winslow. Elisabeth talking to Colonel L. She, lovely in lavender robe-de-style. In to dinner, Colonel L. to Con: "Miss Morrow, can I take you in to dinner?" *"Me?!"* said darling Con with a very natural and modest surprised smile. She went in on his arm! I behind, with Bill. We looked for our places. He looked beside me, thinking, of course, "Well, the older one has sat next to me, I suppose it's the second one's turn. I'll have to sit next to her tonight." But he didn't—thank heavens—and of course in trying to avoid him we bumped into each other and, embarrassed, apologized profusely, and again having found my place quickly and sat down, he made a kind of effort to push my chair in.

I sat between Colonel MacNab and Commander Hamilton. Colonel MacNab told me stories about the desert. The long table

[1] Bill Marvel, friend of Dwight Morrow, Jr.

[2] Alan F. Winslow, First Secretary.

was gay and scarlet—candles and flowers. In the middle Elisabeth and I distributed red-rose caps for ladies and cardboard top hats for men. Someone made a beautiful speech to Daddy. Mother read telegrams.

Then into the Christmas tree room. Mr. Schoenfeld as an urbane, clever, stoutish Santa Claus; presents handed out. Fudge to Colonel L. the first. Mrs. Lindbergh was very embarrassed by the presents.

Then dancing. I loved it, in spite of myself, and felt, for a while, un-self-conscious—blessedly so. Music does that, and dancing. It is so heavenly—I glowed with the pleasure of it. Commander Hamilton danced divinely. *He* didn't dance but stood apart and watched—not with envy, but with a kind of dazed pleasure. Grateful, perhaps, to be a silent spectator for a while. But quite dazed. I did not look at him at all but knew where he was all the time behind the sofa, his hands in his pockets, bending over a table.

The music was gay—Spanish. It sang like Raquel, and the tune lilted.

A Virginia reel.

Then we sat down exhausted in the hall, and Dickie B. and Dick[1] dressed me up in a comb and mantilla and shawl and a red carnation in my hair. I felt glowing and frivolous—until suddenly I saw the Colonel behind me and I took them off, feeling silly, and tore the carnation out of my hair.

"She should have been born in Spain," Richard[2] said, fishing, to him, "shouldn't she?" He said yes a little gruffly and embarrassedly and I shook my head and was quiet for the rest of the time and went to bed with only a nod in the distance.

Sunday, Christmas Day

Breakfast together in the big dining room. I was getting used to getting everything by signs, and the recurrent phrases *"Más café para la señorita," "crema—poco,"* or croissants—*"caliente."*

[1] Richard Bissell and Richard Childs, friends of Dwight Morrow, Jr.
[2] Richard Scandrett, cousin of A. M. L.

Walking, hands on shoulders, from the back hall into Daddy's room. No stockings, no fireplace. Even the chairs full of presents gave me rather a sick feeling—like too much Thanksgiving dinner. Our family and family customs did not seem so all-inclusive, so shutting out the rest of the world. Christmas Day seemed so arbitrary—an arbitrarily set date with very little meaning.

That boy—last Christmas, Elisabeth heard from him—was flying on the air-mail service from St. Louis to Chicago.

The last glimmer of childish excitement at opening Christmas presents was gone. Although Mother gave me some beautiful Spanish earrings, a Lowestoft platter, and a Cartier bag; Con, a Lowestoft cup and saucer; Elisabeth, beautiful books and an illuminated page of St. Francis' words about *courtesy*.

Mrs. Lindbergh gave both Elisabeth and me a fan with Colonel L.'s signature on the card.

We went in to thank her, feeling really so touched at her doing it, at her taking the trouble to get us something. We told her so. She was pleased but afraid of taking too much to herself. She thought we were merely pleased to have his signature and were flattering her. He came across from the chancellery, across the grass, his hand in one pocket, head forward. He saw us, saw that we saw him, but when he came near he lowered his head embarrassedly and went on without looking at us. "Now, what makes him do that?" I wailed. "I haven't been silly." Con explained that the only girls he had ever met before had fallen all over him.

Before lunch we were all sitting on the porch in the sun, on the long board table. He and his mother came out. Elisabeth went up to him, and Con, and then I did, to thank him. "Your mother and you were *very* nice to give us . . . me . . . the fan." He was swinging his leg and smiling in an embarrassed way. "Well, it was my mother. I really . . . couldn't get downtown. I'm . . . glad you like it," gruffly. We told him we didn't want it signed and he grinned and said, "Oh no, don't have it signed." He was pleased. Then Elisabeth brought him presents to see. He was such a little boy—we had to be so careful not to "frighten" him.

We stood around shyly, putting in a word now and then, hoping he might listen and smile—like trying to win a child, trying hard not to say anything to make him stiffen up. It was sunshiny and we did warm up. We tried to be careless and young and simple, not to startle him, not to spoil it.

It was the first good step. In to lunch. I sat next to him and Daddy. I could not talk—what could I say to this boy? Anything I might say would be trivial and superficial, like pink frosting flowers. I felt my whole world before this to be frivolous, superficial, ephemeral, and I was so young, so fuddled, so ignorant. I felt above all that before him I wanted to be completely and simply sincere, and my sincerest feeling was one of great humility. So most of the time we sat side by side in complete silence, or I would ask Daddy something. Sometimes I could ask him something: Wasn't he terribly tired of this? Why did he ever come down? At least, I would feel that way; one or two technical questions that he answered in his direct, attentive way, seriously looking right at me while I in a panic tried to think up another one to ask him when he finished! "He is a beautiful boy," Daddy keeps saying. He adores him—I can understand it.

Then again when I started to say something and stopped, thinking Daddy's conversation would be more interesting to him, "What's that?" he said. Then I stuttered out, "I . . . I'd almost always rather listen than talk," and he nodded and smiled.

Then we had "Ring-around-a-rosy." That was so funny and gay—it broke the ice. Only I, embarrassed, snatched my hand away as soon as I could. Then, laughing, I explained how we used to smash people's fingers getting the upper hand of the unsuspecting guest. "Yes," he said, smiling, "I noticed you let go very quickly!"

Elisabeth is so wonderful and so natural with him. It shows that you are not thinking about yourself when you can do that. She is so much more like him than I am. I don't believe he *ever* thinks about himself. Con is wonderful, too. She is so keen and intelligent, never loses her head—steady and intelligent—more like him than the rest of us.

After lunch we were out in the garden in the sun, and laughing. How much easier it makes everything!

We talked of going to Xochimilco.[1] We all wanted to go—would he go? He wanted to, but then he said he was afraid he might "spoil our day"—a crowd would gather. It was quite pathetic, for he wanted to go. I said, "I feel as though the nicest thing we could do for you would be to leave you alone." He smiled so kindly but said, "No, I'd like very much to go—very much indeed." We were off! That thrilling afternoon, because it was unofficial—the occasion—and he was unofficial too. There was an exciting holiday-escape feeling about it. We were running away, and he, like a prince incognito, was slipping off. It was the spirit of adventure and it loosened everything up.

Mother, Colonel L., and Mrs. Lindbergh in the back seat. Elisabeth, Con, and I in the little seats in front, Dwight up front. The drive was so heavenly. We bubbled over with the first shy excitement of feeling at ease. The ice was broken. The immense relief of it! The strain gone, we laughed and joked and sang, half afraid it might end. He passed Con's fudge around and pointed out the mountains and places to his mother and told different historical things about it. We argued over the pronunciation of Popocatepetl. He stubbornly stuck to his point, but what did it matter—it made us all laugh! (Questions, answers, and arguments, even petty ones—what marvelous "self-starters" they are for difficult conversation, I never realized before.)

He talked on and on that afternoon. I can't remember about what, but I know he felt relieved, too.

He sat a little forward with his hands on the back of the chair in front (tremendous hands, he has, too, and wrists—strong but not clumsy—steady and firm) and said that this was just the

[1] A town near Mexico City famed for its floating gardens.

position he sat in, in his plane, but that his plane was *far* more comfortable!

We were talking, too, about how he beat the sun, came to meet it on his flight (amazing), and I remember his saying abruptly, "I only had about two hours of complete darkness." *Only* two hours of *complete darkness* over the ocean, alone. My God! What lies behind *that* statement.

Only twice as we passed did someone yell, "Viva Lindbergh." We stopped by the canals; very few Americans. He got out, someone saw him, people turned, another and another, and started curiously toward him, pushing, poking, craning. It was disgusting. He turned away, behind the car. We got onto a low, covered barge. The water was covered with them, some small canoes, heaped with carnations, violets, calla lilies. They pulled up to us, Mexican women poling them, and held out violets. Dickie Bissell—the only one of us as tall as the Colonel—was taken for him. A great Mexican with open arms barred his way: "Adored hero, I cannot let you pass without embracing you!" This delighted all of us. We pushed off, laughing, up the stream bordered with poplars, down lagoons, calla lilies growing on the banks. The broad-brim-hatted Mexican stuck his pole in the water and then ran down half the length of our barge. Two flower-sellers climbed on board.

It was almost sunset. Through the poplars we could see the light yellow-gold sky behind some church's dome.

No sound except the swish of the water.

Mexican women and children on the bank washing clothes.

We walked back to the car, down walled streets.

I watched her [Mrs. Lindbergh's] face through the glass. It was, sometimes, so sad. The other day I told her how sorry we were to intrude the first night and she said, "Oh, we're used to that. I don't mind—I just like to be in the room with him, I just like to be there and see him." I felt like saying, "Yes, I know, I feel that way too—just to watch him answering other people, his direct nod, the turn of his head listening, his head a little on one side, his clear-cut profile."

He is going to fly between the two peaks—*Popocatepetl* and *Sleeping Lady*—when he leaves.[1]

Home. We hated to get out. It had been so quiet, so relieving.

Con and I sat next to him again at dinner, Elisabeth directly opposite. We *all* of us talked about aviation, how long it had been going: twenty-five years—half as long as automobiles, and the progress made has been greater. It was quite exciting. But it was almost as bad as at lunch. Elisabeth talked across the table at him. He listened intently (even when I was trying to say something). A discussion about civilization—that our Western civilization lacked something that theirs (Chinese) had, that it was higher spiritually, culturally. He said you couldn't have a high cultural civilization with bad social and physical conditions. He argued firmly, directly, looking at Elisabeth, collecting his points (focusing them, the way he does—"drawing up arms") before speaking; argued with confidence, with singleness of purpose, looking down between each point. "Well, in the first place . . . in the second place . . . I mean by that"—firm, courageous statements, looking squarely at Elisabeth at the end for an answer.

She argued well, but she had no answer. I, fuddle-headed, was floundering around trying to figure out what one meant by "spiritual." But he did not listen—thank goodness—he was listening to Elisabeth. It was very interesting and dinner went well. (But I was sick—miserable—heartbroken, with my *odious* envy again—envy of Elisabeth, envy of her confidence, her forceful charm, her being noticed, her quick wit. I thought I had gotten over it. It seems as though I had been fighting it for so long. But here it was again, that heartbreaking choke of misery inside me, feeling that I was of no use, no value—I had nothing to give him or *anyone* and I envied those who had.) Some dumb remarks of

[1] After his visit to Mexico, Colonel Lindbergh flew southeastward on his trip to Central and South America and the West Indies.

mine about parachutes capped the climax. I felt a worm. My question really was funny, it was so dumb. Con and I laughed about it later. (I thought people were killed by the speed of a high fall. If this were so, parachutes—in use for years—would be absolutely valueless.)

Movies that evening. Con is wonderful—she knows so much about it. He likes her and is not afraid of her. He *should*. She is "the best of the lot."

Then in the hall, as we were going to bed, he addressed Elisabeth, standing with Dwight: "You'll be on the field about eleven tomorrow morning?"

Elisabeth expressed her thrilled gratitude and questioned, "Really?"

"Yes. I'm going to be going up anyway. I'd be very glad to take you up—and (with a smile and nod at Con and me) *that includes everyone.*"

"Won't it be rather a bother for you—there are so many?"

"Bother?" he asked, not understanding.

"I mean, you have to be polite so much. And you don't have to be polite to us."

"Oh, no, I'd like very much to . . ."

Then good night.

It has been so heavenly here—to wake in the morning and hear that intoxicating sound of the motors of airplanes, distant whir and then louder throb. I wake dreaming of them.

This morning we drove to the field; excited faces around of those who had already been up. I kept saying over and over to myself, "God, let me be *conscious* of it! Let me be *conscious* of *what* is happening, *while* it is happening. Let me realize it and feel it vividly. Let not the consciousness of this event (as happens so often) come to me tardily, so that I half miss the experience. Let me be *conscious* of it!"

A crowd around the hangars. The Ford plane shone—silver in the hot field—a group around it. We went over and stepped in. Mother, Aunt Alice, Elisabeth, Con, and I (and Mr. Stout). It was like a train inside: wicker chairs, only slanted back at a *terrific* angle. The plane was nosed upwards. That angle gave me my first and only impression of fear. I looked out of the window and from under the wing could see the crowd and Dwight and the boys (*so* separated from us) taking pictures. Mr. Stout grinned and pointed the movie camera at us, one by one.

Then he came, across from the hangars, with Captain Winslow. He was striding along in his everyday suit and gray felt hat, hand in pocket, head forward a little, talking to Captain Winslow and avoiding the looks of the crowd. He looked up quickly as he approached the plane and saw us and smiled, nodding. Then he stepped in, bending not to hit his head. Mother said "Good morning." "Good morning, good morning," he said and hurried up front to the pilot's seat.

The engine started. It wasn't as terrifically loud as one expected, but it quivered through you. I felt exalted.

He kept looking out of the window at the engines.

"Let me be conscious of this! Let me be conscious!"

The engines whirred; easily, we started to roll—faster, faster. I did not look out—I was too excited, exalted, to watch the wheels. It all happened so quickly. Things whizzed past—trees, the hangars—I did not know when we left the ground. Jo[1] screamed something to me above the engines' roar.

Con, Elisabeth, and I went forward to the front seats just in back of the Colonel and Captain W. (and separated from the rest of the car). Then we were happy—so terribly and ecstatically happy, alone and together and able to watch him. Suddenly I felt the real sensation of going up—a great lift, like a bird, like one's dreams of flying—we soared in layers. That lift that took your breath away—there it was again! I had *real* and intense *consciousness* of flying. I was overjoyed. Then for the first time I looked down. We were high above fields, and there far, far below was a small shadow as of a great bird *tearing* along the neatly

---

[1] Mrs. Graeme, personal secretary to E. C. M.

marked-off fields. It gave me the most tremendous shock to realize for the first time the terrific speed we were going at and that that shadow meant *us—us,* like a mirror! That "bird"—it was *us.* We were over the city now; it looked like a doll's model. The sun gleamed on the gold wings of that great statue in the square. How tiny it looked! The small drops of shadow circling the haystacks in the fields. The fields looked like braided cloth.

It was very smooth and steady now. There was a crack of the window open, and a sharp knife of swift air hissed in, giving the sense of speed.

The others were in back, far away. It was too Pullman-carish back there. Here, in front, we shut out the whole world. We were close against the sky—we were flying!

He was so perfectly at home—all his movements mechanical. He sat easily and quietly, not rigidly, but relaxed, yet alert. One hand on the wheel—one hand! He has the most tremendous hands. I can see him still, and the grasp, the strong wrist, the grip of the thumb, his other hand rubbing his nose or something equally trivial! Looking clearly and calmly ahead, every movement quiet, ordered, easy—and *completely* harmonious. I don't know how I can say that, really, for he moved so *very* little and yet you felt the harmony of it.

Elisabeth opened the door (front) and asked where the Embassy was. He half turned to hear, nodded and looked out, then Captain Winslow pointed it out.

There it was: the little grass court, the steps and shadows clearly marked (shadows are very vivid from the air). He turned around once and smiled at us.

We were pointed towards the mountains—the mountains he would cross.

We saw a lake like quicksilver; a hill (marked with an advertisement) like a mound.

Oh, to go on and on—over the mountains! I could understand why people never can give it up.

Cows and sheep are specks: our shadow tore over them,

peasants looking up—even the hangars looked like cardboard boxes.

The mountains—the mountains looked at us!

The sun on the tinsel wings of the matchstick statue, the minute circling cars—so small, so small—the tiny patch of green, the court of the Embassy, where we would have the garden party that afternoon and he would stand and shake hands with thousands of those black motes in the street.

Now he looked down on it all and rubbed his nose and looked up toward the snow on "The Sleeping Lady."

No wonder he has a disregard for death—and life. This is both.

We were turning. He motioned to us to go back. In a minute we were wheeling around—"banking"—at a terrific angle, over on one wing.

I did not look down until we were almost on the ground. I expected a terrific bounce. I looked out at the wheels: they grazed the ground, a cloud of dust but an imperceptible, balloonlike bounce, then again; we were down, a terrific speed, we rolled in and stopped.

We stepped out, dazed. Con and I watched Colonel L.'s head in the cockpit window, turning and looking out at the engine.

It was a complete and intense experience. I will not be happy till it happens again.

Colonel L. got out and walked away, hand in pocket, head forward, to the hangars to see his *own* plane. We followed. Just inside the door he stopped. Mother, Aunt Alice, and Elisabeth thanked him. He smiled and nodded; he did not notice me thanking him. We walked in to the plane—so small and silver, the hood sort of honeycombed. Two men in overalls were up on a ladder prying into the engine. He stood talking to his mother and others while we looked it over—NX 211, Ryan NYP. A monoplane (like the Ford) but *much* smaller. He sits in a wicker chair. We saw where they had to cut away a groove in the wood above his head, he was so tall. It looks just like an automobile with compasses, meters, etc., set into it. All in front of this in the nose is gasoline, also in the wings on either side. Con asked intelligently, "How does it feed?" We were amazed. Then Commander Hamilton worked the controls for us and we watched the wings. There is an up and down control that works in the tail thing, and a sideways control in tail rudder. For "banking," a control in the side wings—one flap up on one side, one down on the other, a little on the principle of paddling. The flags of the countries he had visited were painted on the side of the nose.

Then we drove back followed and preceded by motorcycles, he behind in the open car, smiling when we passed.

In the back hall, later, Mrs. Lindbergh asked him about something. He said, "I'm more interested in lunch, just now." I went back and got some digestive crackers. With a long stride and reach he ate them by twos! We sat on the table and told him how much we liked it. Just Con, Elisabeth, and I—and the Colonel. We sat and faced him. He grinned like a small, pleased boy, his hands in his pockets, standing with feet apart, nodding. Elisabeth spoke of the shadow, I spoke of how glorious it was—the soaring lift, really the way you dream of it. He grinned and nodded. Then we spoke of learning to fly—could we? I thought Elisabeth meant it in fun, but he took it up quickly and asked us, "Do you all live together, in the States?"

"Do you *really* think we could?"

"I don't see why not." He grinned delightedly and reached for another digestive.

We asked how we could learn. "Well," shifting his stand, "the best thing to do would be to get a pilot to teach you." A discussion followed about the various schools.

It was so lovely sitting there all together, gobbling digestive crackers like twelve-year-old boys planning our adventures: what we were going to do "when we grew up."

[*December 28, 1927*]
The next morning—dark—driving through black, empty streets at 5:30 A.M., escorted by motorcycles, to the field.

The two planes in the dusk nosed up in the same direction, like great monsters ready for flight, spitting fire and roaring.

The throb of the engine through one's body.

Suddenly a tall, stern, helmeted man shaking our hands: goodby.

The engine roared, a cloud of dust and blank gray darkness, then above our heads wings dipping in salute.

And up and out—black wings against the gray of morning, toward that bright star and the mountains!

But these are the outside superficials. I can't tell the others.

The idea of this clear, direct, straight boy—how it has swept out of sight all other men I have ever known, all the pseudo-intellectuals, the sophisticates, the posers—all the "arty" people. All my life, in fact, my world—my little embroidery beribboned world is smashed.

> "But gathering as we stray, a sense
> *Of Life, so lovely and intense,*
> It lingers when we wander hence,
> That those who follow feel behind
> Their backs, when all before is blind,
> Our Joy, a rampart to the mind. . . ."
>
> [JOHN MASEFIELD]

The feeling of exultant joy that there is anyone like that in the world. I shall never see him again, and he did not notice me, or would ever, but there *is such a person* alive, *there is such a life,* and I am here on this earth, in this age, to know it!

> ". . . When first I met
>   Your glance and knew
> That life had found me—
>   —And Death too . . ."

"In youth my wings were strong and tireless
But I did not know the mountains.
In age I knew the mountains
But my weary wings could not follow my vision.
Genius is wisdom and youth."

[EDGAR LEE MASTERS]

I cannot feel envious of Elisabeth now. People give me so much—I couldn't possibly repay them or tell them or measure it. They don't know—it is unconscious—they do not notice me, or speak to me, but they give—they give so much. I am so grateful and feel taller for it.

I remember once, at North Haven, looking at the sky—a great arc—stupendous, and yet with one quick glance you could sweep it all with your eyes, possess it with a glance.

I feel that way now.

I will never look at birds again without a leap of my heart and a keener alertness of my mind and eyes—to look at their wings, the shape as they leave the body, how they soar and glide, wings horizontal, and turn—"bank" like an airplane.

I have never looked so much at the sky, clouds—long horizon ones, and nebulous misty ones, and round packed ones, piling, and a covering of little gray birds-breast-feather (dovetailing) ones.

Clouds and stars and birds—I must have been walking with my head down looking at the puddles for twenty years.

1928

I want so intensely to get this across to people, some people— those who will get "it"—what Colonel L. is. I feel that they should know. I want terribly to enlighten people about him— from the newspaper prejudice.

How can I best tell them, best reach them—how explain? What points can I give?

He is great not because he crossed the ocean alone. He might have shown his genius in some other way. This explains the mad devotion of him. The flight gave him to the world. He is not a *type* of anything, as the newspapers have made him. Keen, intelligent, burning, thinking on all lines— The intensity of life, burning like a bright fire in his eyes. Life focused in him— When he in turn focuses his life, power, force on *anything,* amazing things happen.

He wastes nothing—words, time, thought, emotion.

Impersonality

His tremendous power over people—unconscious, untried for— Every action sincere, spontaneous, direct, full of meaning.

His effect coming into a room, going out. His effect on men— practical, cynical, worldly men—

Dignity—

The harmony of all his movements in the plane—

His youth—

His clean-cutness, freshness—nothing smeared—keen sharpness

Quickness and accuracy of thought and action.

Nothing "grates": never a false note, a hint of smallness—never a tinny sound, as one might expect in a vulgar phrase, or badly kept fingernails—

His cool "knowing what he is about" *all* the time—utter lack of recklessness, an amazing, impersonal kind of courage—

Most of his modesty is not modesty—more selfless than that: impersonality

Tolerant good humor—
The way his smile completely changes his face—
The small-boy-hands-in-pockets looking-straight-at-you attitude.

[*Northampton, January 15, 1928*]
Sunday

Oh, Mother darling—

I cannot write you and yet I must. You must know, of course, by now—Frances Smith.¹ I wish I could feel your hand. Oh, Mother, this is so terrible I can't understand—I can't understand tragedy like this. We feel numb, quite numb, thinking it over and over and over, and gradually realizing it.

There aren't any words to describe this. I shouldn't write you, but of course you will see the papers, and I wanted to touch you and tell you that I am well and alive and that I love you so very, very much—love you all--and am thankful that we have each other.

Oh, Mother, I don't understand. Why are there such things? I have never come so near before. People *dying*—that is terrible sorrow, terrible tragedy sometimes—but *this*—this is unspeakable, unununderstandable—frightful torture.

Mr. and Mrs. Smith are amazingly splendid about it. Courageous and calm and not bitter, facing everything. They do not reproach anyone.

But, Mother, I feel convinced that it was suicide. Of course there is still hope, and they will search for *months and months*. All that agony.

They do not reproach anyone, but she was depressed—terribly depressed about her work and life—and she had so few friends and did not confide in anyone. I had a long talk with her before vacation and tried to help her and we talked *everything* over and I felt I knew so much the way she felt in her difficulties with

¹ See note, p. 80. F. S., a Freshman at Smith College, disappeared in January, 1928. Her body was discovered months later in the Connecticut River.

college, and she seemed happier and was so grateful. I saw her only once after vacation; asked her how she felt and (but it was just in a second) she seemed much better. Joy [Kimball] (in her class) and Edith and I were really her only friends. But, Mother, she had come to me—she had come to me several times in the little worries she had gotten into, and I did try to (and *did,* I think) understand and help her out.

But I hadn't seen her after vacation, except for that moment. Oh, if I *had*—

And, Mother—this is the worst—when they told Mrs. Smith she was lost, over the telephone she said that if Frances confided in anyone she would have confided in me, she would have come to me, for she had before and I had helped and she loved me more than anyone— Oh, Mother, Mother, Mother—forgive me, but it does almost kill me to think of that.

If only I had talked to her after vacation—if only I had gone up to her room—if I could have just caught her in that gust of despair that must have come over her suddenly.

I *wasn't* there—I *didn't* realize—I didn't *go to her.* I was going to see her, but I was so busy, coming back late, and I waited.

Mrs. Smith was *lovely.* She arrived last night at twelve and asked for me this morning, saying again that she knew Frances would have come to me if she had felt troubled about things. Oh, Mother, what a saint she is not to reproach me—*I* should have gone to *Frances.* And, Mother, one of the things I felt happiest about coming back was Frances: I loved her and felt that there, at least, I might be of some use and help.

Oh, that family—Mr. and Mrs. Smith. Mother, was there ever anything so horrible?

Forgive me for this, all this sorrow, but I knew you would see it. I wanted to write you that I was all right—and . . . *this* just came. You see, I cannot talk this way in front of the girls (or *of course* Mrs. Smith) because there is such a terrific strain and suspense on everyone, and we must not give way and make it harder for everyone, especially Joy (Frances's one friend in her class).

The actual realization of what has happened only comes in spasms.

Oh, that wretched, wretched mother and father! *Why* should anyone be so tortured? I cannot understand it, Mother, it takes away one's faith in anything good.

Mother, don't think this letter is absolute weakness—I have not and will not break down. I am strong and well and see clearly. I can work and I will pass all my exams.

I will try hard to be your own daughter and help Joy and Mr. and Mrs. Smith if I can in any way.

I meant to write you before, a happy letter to tell you that I want more than anything to go down again and see you at Easter.

Perhaps she will be found by the time you get this.

DIARY   *[Northampton, February, 1928]*

Three weeks ago—a little more—Frances Smith disappeared. It is like another life, anything before then. There is a huge gulf separating me from anything before that.

The face of everything has been changed. I look out and I do not see the same things. There is no way to describe this new life of the last three weeks.

The indescribable horror, confusion, suspense, inability to think or see or hear—to question the same things over and over and over in a kind of hopeless repetition, till things were meaningless.

The great overwhelming gusts of realization, of remorse, of picturing, imagining—

Remembering that Friday night, what it was like: wind—

Seeing Mr. and Mrs. Smith Sunday morning.

All Sunday afternoon and *evening*. The first snow, like death, coming down.

Our defensive league about Joy: trying to keep calm, to keep ourselves and her calm, quiet—

To work.

Those nights of terror, waking up and waiting for 4:30, when I could distract myself by remembering Mexico, counting 4:30 as the beginning of day: "4:30. Now we are getting up to see Colonel Lindbergh off. Now we are having breakfast. Now we are driving through the streets (at quarter of five a whistle blows, at five the trolleycars start, at 5:30 the milk bottles—two loads). Now the engines have started; now he has gone." Gradually the cold blue light comes in, and *that* awful night is over.

Days in which we walked in a kind of dazed, hideous, solitary nightmare.

The frightful sense of tragedy—not tragedy but a dry, black, despairing horror all the time; not tears, just that dry, black horror everywhere, like a burned and blackened landscape.

It seemed impossible to look at it from any point of view—and there it was, there was nothing else in the world.

Is there *anything* beautiful, is there anything good, anything lovely in this world, if such things can happen?

I said poems over and over every night, frantically, so as not to think.

A nightmare of reporters, papers, reports, clues, detectives, questioning.

The terrifying vague news of Dwight very ill.

Terribly frightened and did not understand. Elisabeth brave over telephone—each night after one of those long nightmare days (a *year* long, a long siege) she and I talked to each other, each after our long day, so much older—

In the midst of this a fresh, warm, healthy letter from V. It was like a breath of April—a smell of flowers when one had forgotten or had ceased to believe in flowers.

[*Northampton, February, 1928*]
Friday

Mother darling—

Last night the President called me up and asked me to come for supper. Of course I went. Mrs. Neilson was ill with a *frightful* tooth but one daughter, the Dean's little girl, and Miss T. were there.

It was quiet and softly lighted and I came in all alone quietly and sat in the living room with him before supper. It was so natural, and no atmosphere of strain or tautness as there has been in college.

He asked me if they had been bothering me—detectives and the warden's office etc. How perfectly *lovely* of him, with all—*all* that he has. I was overcome, really. I did not mean to talk to him about Frances but of course he couldn't think about other things so we did and I just sat quietly while he talked and talked and talked—*went over it all,* in such weariness. He is exhausted, and so old-looking. I ached to do *something* for him, to help at all, but I could only sit there and listen, and talk more freely about Frances than I have to the detective or to them (Mr. and Mrs.). Of course that was a help.

At supper of course we couldn't, and oh, Mother, how grateful I was for the Lindberghs! Miss T., who hardly talks at all, the two shy girls, and tired, tired President Neilson—I could at least talk a little, quietly, about Mexico and you and them, and I think it interested him. At least I drew a few smiles out of him, and he flashed a smile once and almost laughed, saying, "Your mother must be having a time, there!"

It was quiet and calm, though, and homelike. I felt it was too good to believe. After supper he and I sat and he talked again, went on and on the same way. I have, though, never felt so un-self-conscious, so at ease and natural. But oh, Mother, he has had so much. One terrible thing after another. And yet he is so calm and sane, so patient and considerate, so kind, and even has his sense of humor still.

When I was leaving I said I was sorry to have made him talk about it all again. But he said, so kindly, "No," that he had wanted to ask me about it, he had wanted to see if I were getting too tired from it. And he said, "I am very glad to find you are not," and then very kindly he said good-by and, looking out at the snow falling, made me promise to change my shoes and stockings when I got home!

Colonel Lindbergh arriving in Mexico in the Spirit of St. Louis,
December 14, 1927

Parade en route from the airport to Mexico City

*Colonel Lindbergh with Ambassador Morrow being greeted
on his arrival in Mexico City*

P.I.

*Colonel Lindbergh on Embassy balcony, Mexico City,
December, 1927*

*Colonel Lindbergh, President Calles, and Ambassador Morrow
at a banquet given in honor of the aviator*

DE WORLD PHOTOS

The United States Embassy, Mexico City

Charles Lindbergh with Anne and Elisabeth Morrow,
Embassy grounds, Christmas, 1927

Charles Lindbergh, with Ambassador and Mrs. Morrow
and Constance Morrow, Mexico City, 1927

Ford trimotor plane landing at Mexico City with
Mrs. Charles A. {Evangeline Land} Lindbergh, Sr.,
December 22, 1927

Mrs. Lindbergh with Elisabeth, Anne, and Constance Morrow
on the Embassy steps, Mexico City, Christmas, 1927
At right: Mrs. Charles A. Lindbergh, Sr.

Family group, Embassy grounds, Mexico, 1927

*Colonel Lindbergh at controls of Ford trimotor plane before
taking up the Morrow family, December 26, 1927*

U.P.I.

Xochimilco

It did rather adjust things a little for me just to see how wonderful he was. But I couldn't tell him, of course—I stammered something about balance as I went out of the door.

Mother, your letters are wonderful. Do you think we ever, *ever* will be in North Haven all together? Will summer really come again? Exams do not frighten me, or even matter at all. I will sleep and eat and not bother.

DIARY   [*Northampton, February, 1928*]

The long, long siege is, in a way, over—at least having to keep tensely restrained and calm and up to the mark, not to break down during exams. That is over.

I dare to remember now that awful nightmare of fear—fear that my mind would snap somewhere. The obsession that everyone was watching me. In trains, stations, on the streets. When I was thinking so much about Frances—perhaps *because* I was— once or twice people called after me, "There's the girl that is lost"—laughing—and once when I was running a cruel boy shouted in fun, "Oh, Frances Smith, I have you now!" I knew they were just laughing but it was shocking. . . .

There are two things people have said lately that I have turned over in my mind with slow enjoyment. Said by two people who are to me almost the most *vital* in the world. They are, both of them, in a different way, so *vital*—so alive, so tangible—and they have a certain wholeness and completeness about them that is both restful and inspiring.

Amey said of hurry, that not only is it an unpleasant thing in itself, for what it is, but (she realized this since she has been sick) it is very unpleasant for the people around you. Some people came into her room and rushed in and rushed out and even when they were there they were *not* there—they were in the moment ahead or the moment behind. Some people who came in just for a moment were *all* there, completely in that moment. She said the most vicious motto she ever read was one in her home that said "Do ye *next* thing." (Perhaps all this is simple enough to see, but it never occurred to me before when people said to me, "Live from day to day—just live from day to day," that the important thing about doing that was *not* just that you worried less but that you *lived more richly*. If you let yourself be absorbed completely, if you surrender completely to the moments as they pass, you live more richly those moments. Of course there is a danger here too, but I have not thought it out clearly.)

Mrs. Munroe[1] said, "I do not think it is lack of time that keeps me from doing things, it is a lack of vital energy. I do not *want* enough to do them." Still, I think that all the little petty things that crowd one's time sap this "vital energy."

A letter from P. breaking our silence of a month and a half suddenly announcing his engagement, or probable engagement. It shocked me but seemed still unreal after Mexico and this last month. The thought of him seemed terribly sad. I do not want to hear of love—I cannot believe in its reality, except what one feels for one's family.

I hope he marries this girl. She is beautifully "suited" to him. Does one marry people because one is *"suited"* to one another?

[*Northampton, February, 1928*]

Darling Mother—

The other day the Neilsons had me for lunch—just asked me to come up very casually. Wasn't that *lovely* of them. I do love them so. Mrs. Neilson scolded me for not telephoning and asking myself up—*as if I could!* They are so charming and witty and so delightful—I just sat and laughed and appreciated, and didn't talk at all. Mrs. Neilson always leaves me with lots of fresh nice thoughts, like leaves swirling around that I remember at odd

---

[1] Wife of Vernon Munroe, banking consultant; old friends and neighbors of the Morrows in Englewood.

times later, when they blow in. Very often they are just very sensible, quite wise, half comments that strike you as remarkable common sense. She has such serenity and yet that sparkling wit and keen, deep understanding. And aren't they *amazing* together! I loved sitting there, with a deep rich delight, watching them: such interchange, such a relationship is very challenging, very wonderful for a young person to see, and so encouraging. Do you remember how Virginia Woolf, who writes mostly of relationships, deifies (that is not the right word for she does not idealize it so much as she makes it the supreme thing) marriage?

The President disconcerts me sometimes for he always asks me for the student opinion, which I am the *last* one to know! What do they think of the Mississippi Flood Relief work, or of Koffka's[1] lecture, or the *Monthly,* etc., etc.? This time he asked me if they were still *dieting!* It did seem so comical to have the President sit there and ask me if *I* dieted, I was too thin as it was—how much did I weigh? (Like Daddy's inevitable "How-much-do-you-weigh-stripped?") They sat and talked about his speech that night. She was so *delicious* telling him just what he should say to please the alumnae.

Mrs. Neilson said how nice it was when one was married and old. One could show people just how much one liked them without complications following. I laughed—I hope it is true. It does seem impossible now. Certainly I feel now that I want to see no boys of an eligible age at all ever again. I can only be natural with delightful ones, younger than me, like Vernon[2] and Dick [Richard Childs], or else nice "old" married men. It *is* so annoying to be enthusiastic over a person's ideas or conversation and have them take it personally—that is, marriageably.

I have just extricated myself, not really from a complication,

---

[1] Kurt Koffka, research professor of experimental psychology at Smith, 1927–32.

[2] Vernon Munroe, Jr., friend of Dwight Morrow, Jr. Later partner in New York law firm, White & Case.

but it might be one. Y. is at Amherst and *very* nice, very interesting and delightful. We have had several nice talks, but when a person sees you most of Sunday and then calls you up again *Thursday* and every following day—well, I don't want to see *any* man that much. When he suggested coming up to Maine I saw our precious summer threatened at any spot and I said we would probably be living in a little, *minute, cramped,* rented *bungalow* in the town ! (Waiting for our house to be built.)

But it is amazing how rude one has to be, to be effective!

I meant to write you most about the service for Professor Gardiner.[1] If only I could have written it right then— If only you could have been here— The President organized it so splendidly. It was *not* a *funeral* exercise but a true and beautiful commemoration exercise. You would have loved it. The President started it by saying with perfect dignity but courageously, "The occasion which brings us together is *not* one of sorrow." Then he said that it was a congregation of people who had been fortunate enough to know him in some capacity, in some relationship (as friend, teacher, etc.), none of which relationships was a sad one. He then introduced a fellow philosophy teacher who spoke (at great length!) of Professor Gardiner's work and influence as a philosopher. He ended beautifully with a quotation which he said he thought was Professor Gardiner's favorite one from Plato—and it was the prayer from the *Phaedrus* that Daddy loves so! Do you remember: "Let the outward and the inward man be at one"?

I have written for hours, but I had so much to say and there is still more: my marks, which are very lucky on the whole except for Miss Chase's[2] C and she was so nice about that—I flunked the exam. It was the first one and in the middle of all that [Frances Smith tragedy] (though I didn't tell her) I didn't have time to study. I am on the Dean's List in spite of it (only the Dean's List does not prove anything this year! Isn't that ironic). I am quite

[1] Professor of philosophy at Smith College during E. C. M.'s college years.
[2] Mary Ellen Chase, professor of English, author.

amazed, for every mark is at least two points higher than I hoped.

Tomorrow is a holiday. I will try to get some letters written. Oh, Mother, there are so many—so many things to patch up. I go over them in my mind every night and morning. I have about twenty things that are just *vital,* have to be done—twenty accusing fingers. I squirm over them.

I am miserable—but then I think that Dwight is better, we are all well and alive and most of the winter is over, only four more weeks to Easter vacation. You are near—I love my family—I don't care if I don't see anyone else. (I told Y. that!) There are amazingly nice people in the world like the Munroes and Amey and Chester and the Neilsons and the Fays—and there is always the hope of a letter from Con!

DIARY [*Northampton, February, 1928*]
The very thin sharply cut new moon surprised me with a shock at its fine beauty tonight. I had a strange simple feeling of revelation (I was thinking of Frances—once I met her coming up that hill by the willow. There was a new moon, and I asked her to come out with me for supper), a feeling of reconciliation. I was suddenly saying to myself, "Why, there they are together, how strange that I should see them together." I could think of her and see that beauty at the same time, and there was no longer that horrible wrenching at the incongruity.

And yet I could not take the path down the hill by the willow. I went the other way.

Would like to look up Flecker[1]—he has not been *half* appreciated.

The perfection of everything he wrote appeals to me—restraint, economy, musical perfection.

Then his magnificent richness of *color,* which saves his verse from being classically cold.

[1] James Elroy Flecker, 1884–1915, English poet and playwright.

Mad day—simply terrific: one of those days you *completely* and *effectively* spoil for yourself and others.

Cut all my classes to finish the book review, struggled all morning over trite expressions, *writhed* and *agonized* over my inarticulateness, got entirely worn out and in a state where I could not write decent English and didn't know the meaning of words.

All the time a tireless, insistent wind wailing, climbing, keying one up to a state of agonized suspense so that I felt almost a physical pain at my throat.

Spent the afternoon worn out (that stage where you don't know whether you are sick or hungry!), trying to do odds and ends and trying to rest—and reading Flecker.

A tearing wind tonight. The stars and moon are sliding all over the sky and the world is topsy-turvy.

Must have been hungry: a delicious birthday party for Wendy —after ten!

Heard airplanes all day.

I feel like a sick dog that wants to go out and eat nothing but grass—only I would prefer asparagus, green peas, *green* string beans (small kind—no strings), green spinach, Brussels sprouts, broccoli.

What a dearth of vegetables there is in this town!

Someday I shall write my invective on the potato.

"Why potatoes?"

Colonel Lindbergh flew over Northampton Wednesday night. No, Thursday morning.

My general nastiness all weekend [at Englewood].

I wanted to be left alone, not poked or pulled or hurried, or dragged to one thing after another. Everyone is so energetic and able to make quick decisions.

I think one of us will die. It won't be me. It ought to be—I am the complete loss in our family. But the useless people never die!

Nothing must happen to Dwight or Elisabeth or Con. They are and will be so much in the world.

I wish we could be unconscious for more of the time, to be really conscious for the rest of it—vital periods. But this semiconscious stage! If only I could sleep from now till spring—hearing nothing, not the wind especially—and then wake keenly alive.

Perhaps I am a bear, or some hibernating animal, underneath, for the instinct to be half asleep all winter is so strong in me.

Out of the train window I saw a flock of birds dip and wheel and turn, like leaves showing white before a rain wind.

A letter from Daddy, starting "Beloved Anne."
I felt so happy.

Ceaseless wind climbing and crying.

It has always seemed to me that people hear and see when you are talking and laughing at them much oftener than one realizes. I am conscious of their embarrassment, or of that alertness in them that is listening, has just caught the glimmer of a word (as clear as a dog rigid, pricking up its ears).

A very blue, sunny day: the warm, inexpressible divinity of sunshine. When I am out and walking along the street I try not to get in the shadowed parts at all; where a house's shadow comes across my path I try to edge it or hesitate to go into it as we used to edge the waves, dreading to get our feet wet, by the sea.

Today it has snowed a fine driving snow—ceaseless, cold, white, deathlike.
It is numbing.
Everything is numb and white and smoothed over—dead.
Spring seemed so near, yesterday. This puts me back in feeling and spirit into the Middle Ages of this winter.

I have gotten back the book review and I am completely reshaping it. This agony *all* over again—and what does it matter, why all this trouble over a book review?

But anyway, it gives me a rather exultant feeling to be able to see *where* and *how* that first attempt was all wrong—to tear it up and start again.

Y. is very keen and charming—quite rare until he talks about marriage. Why do men want to get married?
Why is everyone so cheerful about it?
Oh, "Get thee to a nunnery, go"!

Still, the wind—

Chaucer speaks of a horse and says,
"And therewithal so *horsly*"!
I love it! The vocabulary says "all that a horse should be."
I have worked for two days steadily on Chaucer—watching the clock, keeping up to record, having the day go by in fifteen minutes in pages.

Today I went out. It smelled, it felt, it sensed spring. I had for the first time faith—not intellectual belief, but a sudden feeling of turning tide. "Yes, there *will be* spring."
I went out and walked by that garden, but nothing is up.
Think of having a garden—to dig and smell and put new slips into and—*garden gloves!* Old grubby ones, but still, what they do suggest!

A letter from Jay[1]—at last touched again. I read it through and the intensity of his personality and the intensity of my feeling for him were so terribly real and terribly painful that I was crying out "Jay!" before the end of it and feeling that I must see him, be with him immediately.
Why is it that you can sometimes feel the reality of people more keenly through a letter than face to face? Is it because the letter is focused spirit while in a conversation the dross of matter is too in evidence? The very body of a person is a barrier. One is distracted by outward things and loses the essence. The very

---

[1] Jay Scandrett, a cousin of A. M. L.

closeness of the person is confusing, blurring, stifling. And you touch through a veil of proximity. I think my feeling for him is more real and more intense than for anyone I know.

I feel like taking my life, everything I ever loved—all little petty silly things, all the trivial world I stand for: bits of flowers and lace and scraps of silver paper and red ribbons—and throwing it all away for someone. Saying, "Nothing I have ever been or done, nothing I stood for, nothing I am is worth the smallest thing in your life. Let me work through you. If I can do *anything* for you, then at least there is a reason for me."

Colonel Lindbergh out to Englewood.

He is coming to North Haven. I don't think I can bear to face it. *Now* I am not envious. I can see things clearly. I do not mind that here is a person I have nothing in common with, to whom I am really antagonistic, I am so far away from—someone whom I cannot talk to or give anything to; someone who is more likely to dislike than like me. Someone who *naturally* would like and get on with Elisabeth and avoid me.

Oh, I know so well just what it will be like. It has happened before. I can see it: He will come. He will turn quite naturally to E., whom he likes and feels at ease with. I will back out more and more, feeling in the way, stupid, useless, and (in the bottom of my vain heart) hoping that perhaps there is a mistake and that I will be missed. But I am not missed. They never notice and become more and more interested in each other and you must be more and more careless and happy, although *you notice* every little thing, and you have long sessions with yourself stamping out the envy, persuading yourself it is only fair and right. You raise yourself painfully for a short time onto a platform of cool spiritual calm and generous detachment—and then at the table, some slight thing and you are down in the mess of it again, and that lump choking in your throat and everything closing in around you: the atmosphere is too close, your face and feelings too bare. You want to get out and you must stay and pretend you feel easy and happy and careless.

Then finally the day comes when you realize that you have shut yourself out entirely and completely, and *they realize it too.*

Of course it is not really going to be like this—I am just remembering. For of course it will not be on this basis—the falling-in-love basis—and it is absurd to talk this way about it. But even on a friendship basis it is terribly trying.

If only I could be a disembodied creature watching, then there would be no striving.

Oh, I don't see how I can face this and fight it all over again. I dread this summer.

Sunday, [March] 18th

This has been an *interminable* day: sleet. Cold, gray. I have counted every half-hour and tried to think ahead to every "preparing time": "Only an hour till four, and then I must get ready for Vespers. Vespers at 4:45. Supper, then . . . etc." I can't wait to get away. I feel as if I had been sitting in a steamer chair for a year.

I have looked over my notes for a "written" all day long and only the retinas of my eyes know it!

It is terribly amusing how many different climates of feeling one can go through in one day.

That numb, slow torpitude after breakfast: "I *cannot* make this bed again!"

Then that chill with Elisabeth's message that she could not go to Mexico with us: Dwight wants her. But I think—after the first pang—that she is happy to make the sacrifice. It is challenging and inspiring to be wanted, to be needed, to be and feel of value to someone. She has answered each challenge this winter courageously and swiftly, unhesitatingly, and no regrets.

But the chill that she will not go down with us . . . It reminds me of what I became very aware of this Christmas: that her presence makes the room warm and alive for me. I want to be where she is. It is not a very conscious feeling—just a vague discontent with the places where she is not. There is more life where she is. I get up and follow her when she moves from one room to another as one might unconsciously follow a moving patch of sunlight in a room.

She is not going to Mexico. It takes all the heart out of it.

That dreadful crying wind that I cannot sit quietly through, all during French. I can only describe it in terms of pain (although I have never had pain like that). It takes you and pins you through, so that you hold your breath while it insists and rises to a pitch, and then it drops suddenly and leaves you exhausted.

At Mrs. Curtiss' [Mina Kirkstein's] class, talk about the Jordan Prize,[1] just after I had successfully stamped out all my vain ambitions to work for it or to expect it. After I had finally disciplined myself to believe: No, you idiot, don't try, don't expect— you haven't any talent like that, you can't do anything like that.

Mrs. Curtiss always excites me to write.

At night a long talk with Y. He is amazingly gentle and keen, with both humor and strength.

And I really think he has a peculiarly sensitive and beautiful face.

It gives me strength and a feeling of *security* to talk and be talked to like that.

I suppose I must be content with my world—the things I love, the things I stand for.

They seem just now utterly worthless compared to the world of Elisabeth and Colonel Lindbergh—that world I cannot touch, those people I cannot be like.

[1] The Mary Augusta Jordan Prize, awarded for the most original piece of literary work in prose or verse.

I must give up trying, I must believe somehow that my world—that I despise now—is of some worth, that there is some essential in it worth working on. That I must find something in myself, peculiar to myself (not like, not up to, the things Elisabeth and he have to give), that I can make and give.

The birds, wheeling round and round that sharp steeple as you turn the hill, lift my heart.

Back in New York—first night.

Dr. Hammer's. It *does* really help to say to yourself when you're having a tooth drilled and the thin pain is climbing—to say, "This is just physical pain, just physical pain." Taking it out by the hand and looking at it, it becomes impersonal.

Anyway, once you get beyond the crust of the first pang it is all the same and you can easily bear it. It is just the transition from painlessness to pain that is so terrible.

Besides, it sounded like airplanes some of the time, and that was exciting!

To the F.s' for supper. Such a boring, platitude-sodden evening I never had. I could not even take the trouble to be superior! But I did not really want to for I kept feeling, "Now, what are *you*? Yes, they *are* stupid and platitudinal but they are honest, unselfish, steady people, kind and good. They have done their work in the world—what have you done?"

But I was too tired to try to be polite and platitudinal too, or sincere and rude. I just slipped back into my "shy-meek-little-girl-with-nothing-to-say" pose.

Still, it was the most terrific effort at times not to scream with impatience at them. I sat and dug my nails into my palm and smiled gently when they noticed me.

Platitudes and Pie and Radio.

Forty Thousand Miles with Colonel Lindbergh.[1] Overwhelming. I sat sick with amazement, realizing it and saying to myself,

[1] Motion picture shown in Northampton.

"Did I ever meet this boy? How could I possibly comprehend him or it? I am much too small."

I must say over and over to myself, *Make your world count*—it is little, but you must find something there. I am trying to work it out. What do I want to do—what *can* I do? The nearest I can get to it is that perhaps I could be useful and happy trying to help people to appreciate (by teaching or some other way—writing, *perhaps*) (and perhaps through a family and children) the things I care most about: the beauty and poise and completion of flowers, or birds, of music, of some writing, of some people— glimpses of perfection in all of these.

Perhaps those very rare moments of stillness and harmony and wholeness that I sometimes have had, looking at flowers or listening to music, could help me. At least these are worth living for.

This sounds very vague and meaningless.

But I cannot dream or hope to do or be anything in that other world.

Such a happy morning. I went down Fifth Avenue in the sunshine with a purple hat, and sang and kept my eyes on the steeples.

Then I bus-rode—very happy just in the bustle and chatter and sunshine, changing crowds and motion, sparkle and light off cars and windows.

Sitting on a bus laughing and singing. No one enjoys New York the way I do—I treat it so flippantly!

[*En route to Mexico on Easter vacation, March, 1928*] The excitement of leaving: bundles, bags, coats, crowded cars, last messages and too many people—trying to be nice to too many people at the same time.

My poem out—very unreal.[1] Too bad it is over. Before, I still could look forward to it. Now it is over and will never happen again.

[1] "Height," published in *Scribner's Magazine*.

The verse about the lark makes me *shudder!*

The whole thing is rather sentimental.

Mother is so sweet about it, generously making too much of it. It is overwhelming to think what she has been through lately.

I watched her tonight, asleep, and tried to comprehend her beauty and strength and life—tried to realize what she felt, what she made about her, what it would be like if she died.

I have taken so for granted this warm, safe, beautiful world she has built around me—the world that is her—that I just sit back in and live on.

I feel as though I were part of the dream she is dreaming (like Alice in the Red King's dream) and that if she should die (if she should wake up) I should go out like a candle.

[*En route to Mexico, late March, 1928*]

Elisabeth darling,

I am sitting in the St. Louis station. Mother and I wanted to go to the Jefferson Museum.[1] If you had been here we would have *insisted!* It closed at 5:30—took half an hour to get there and it was 5:15 when we asked about it. When we go down to Mexico in the fall, we *must* go—we could jump *out* of the train into a taxi, telephone them to keep it open, and ♩ ♩ !

My dear, your letter was so beautiful. I feel just that way about you: that we are not *only* sisters. It is an amazing and sort of doubly strong association to be linked instinctively (and by environment, early life, association, etc.) *and* by one's desire and reason. It is a rare relationship. I feel as though you have leaned down and lifted me up to where you were so many times. At least if we have had things together your having them first or at the same time has helped me to realize and comprehend better what was happening. Having an experience with someone else enriches it *so* much. You feel for them and yourself.

Darling, you have been so marvelous this winter—all I ever

---

[1] The Jefferson Memorial Museum had the Lindbergh collection on exhibit.

thought you could be. Amey said so last night and she doesn't often give such extravagant praise. She said something like this: She was *so* splendid. You never know what wonderful things a person has in them until they are tested like that.

I know, dear, it was hard for you to have us go off, and you were so gay and so pretty and fine about it. It is, though, wonderful to be needed as Dwight needs you.

You have proved yourself as wonderful as Mother. You have handled all this as she would have.

TO E. R. M.   *En route, Pullman Private Car*
                                      [March 25, 1928]
Darling—

We are going through Texas. Yesterday was a dreadful day: we were so sleepy and tired and sunk. I wanted to send a telegram from St. Louis but everything went wrong there. We waited too long and were too tired to get out and see the city. What was my *joy* to see James on the car, quietly taking the roses out of the box and saying, "Yes, ma'am—yes, ma'am," in his slow voice. "And what time do you want dinner, ma'am?" I almost embraced him on the spot! I told him that you and the boys had asked for him and he asked about you and wished you were here. He asked first, "How is Mr. Dwight?" He is so nice and smiles about the telegrams that I want to send to you. The car is *exactly* the same. I am sitting at the little desk in the long room, using that *enormous,* unwieldy red fountain pen. (It gives you the same feeling as riding a horse with too broad a back!) "The General" [a porter] is always trying to help you with the most simple and unceremonious things. He took half an hour filling this pen and getting out the ink.

It seems impossible that you are not in the other room. Of course—as usual—I have made a bad guess and I have taken all my papers, pad, letters, books into the wrong room (where you are not), but I shall move in a moment into the front room where you are. I want to tell you what I thought of last night in the St. Louis station. All the mundaneness of it. The fruit counters, and souvenir places, and soda fountains, etc., etc. And all the mediocre people. I was so glad that ☀️He☀️ never goes anywhere by train. One cannot and one does not have to imagine him there. But that he never sees a train somehow seems to me one of the most *enormous* things separating his world from ours. At least it somehow brings home to me in a practical, realizable way the enormous gap.

TO E. R. M.   *En route, Pullman Private Car*
                              Sunday afternoon [*March 25, 1928*]

My dear—
I have just had a long talk with James. He says you are a most lovely lady—"a very wonderful young lady," so lovely and so mature for your age, "wantin' to go out and do somethin' good," etc., etc. "A most wonderful young lady," on and on for about a half hour.

He has been telling me about Grant and Sheridan (yes, really!), Roosevelt, etc., etc., saying that although he has met a great many heroes, Lindbergh is to him greater than all of them. He was very disappointed not to see him or Mrs. Lindbergh.

He has a box full of souvenirs of all his trips with famous people—which, he says, are a "consolation" to him when he is "downcast." He goes over them and remembers all the wonderful people he has met.

You and Colonel Lindbergh stand highest, though! I have made no objections.

Darling, I hate to think of your going on working for another week. It has been such a long, hard winter for you. Do not worry about social obligations at Southern Pines—just *be rude* and turn them out and say the doctor prescribes a *complete rest*, which you need badly. Let Jo say you're too tired to see anyone.

It is so terribly hot. I cannot move to the desk, even though James has fixed it for me with an indulgent smile, saying, "I know you allus write a lot" (as one might say, "I always knew you had a weakness for peppermints!").

I would like to go to Germany this summer if I thought we could *really* learn to "glide." Garry's[1] pamphlet is thrilling (though complex in spots). But I am afraid it is entirely outside of my world. I have to keep reminding myself (I have finally reconciled myself to it), "This and that are not your world—you must find something in your world, whatever that is."

DIARY   [*March 26, 1928*]

Through Texas.

Peach blossoms (color of raspberry ice) and sprays of white, white cherry. Warm, damp air—trees new green. Sun. I sat and sang to the rhythm of the train.

Middle of day, terribly hot.

Evening, cool—smelled like garden after rain. Saw two hawks —simply beautiful—flutter their great wings three or four times and then sail on the same plane. Their ragged wings are very large in proportion to their bodies. It was terribly exciting to watch them move so easily, so slowly and regularly, great wings straight.

Saw the first plane I have seen since Mexico. I leaped with excitement. Near Austin.

Desert.

Very different from December. Desert not gray now—green— and even the cactus have great bunchy white flowers. There are prickly white poppies with yellow hearts.

In a burning, airtight car we were shot through space in an endless day over an endless desert.

---

[1] Garry Norton. Later Assistant Secretary of State (1947–49) and Assistant Secretary of the Navy for Air (1956–59). The Nortons were old friends of the Morrows in North Haven.

Burning, and dry, and glaring white outside. But I prefer this to numbing cold. It is more conducive to thought! You eat little, you feel thin.

It seems to me—a simple enough thought—but just realized that if you really and sincerely and passionately want to do something (and wholeheartedly, with the whole of your sincerest self) it is by doing *that* that you will be most useful, will be giving the most, will be of most individual value. I am sure Colonel Lindbergh never fussed or gave a thought to where he would be most useful or where he could give the most. He just went ahead and did what he wanted terribly to do—what the whole of him wanted sincerely and in a selfless kind of passion to do.

And, of course—

Another very simple thought! When people take friends who have a great sorrow away—abroad—it is not so much to distract them or try to lighten their hearts by amusing and pleasing them, or even to make them forget, but to give them a kind of peace they can keep while the other is still part of them, a peace that comes (a resignation, perhaps) from seeing the vastness of human life and human sufferings.

Your thing gets swallowed up in it, becomes part of it and you can accept it, knowing that so many are accepting it with you.

I counted the hot hours and watched for long shadows until about six, then we came into Monterrey.

Suddenly it was cooler, the sun hidden behind those high, jagged, tortured mountains (Amey[1] said they looked tortured). The mountains became very dark and clear against the sky, looked unreal and one-faced, like silhouettes, like stage-setting mountains cut out against the sky. Mountains at twilight do look like that: North Haven.

---

[1] Amey and Chester Aldrich were accompanying Mrs. Morrow on this journey to Mexico. Chester Aldrich, of Delano & Aldrich, was the architect of Next Day Hill and Deacon Brown's Point in North Haven.

There were green trees (shadows here), green fields, hedges, little gardens, donkeys taking people home; a cool green valley; many birds with long tails—twice as long as their bodies—did not sail—fluttered their wings and flew swiftly in groups over fields.

The blessed coolness of this place. This evening, a hawk soaring way up slowly, almost without motion, almost in the same spot, turning slowly.

People coming home from fields: men jogging easily on donkeys. Women in the doorways of the little white stone huts.

It makes you think of all the Bible stories and even Greek stories of hospitality. The blessing of a cool evening, after a burning day. A tree's shadow, water from the well to wash dust off the feet, oil to anoint the head, cool wine to drink.

"The shadow of a mighty rock . . ."

Also Baucis and Philemon story.

I do not seem to touch Mother. We have had three days. It is my fault. She has been through so much this winter: any comment I can make is trivial, yet I feel toward her more intense sympathy and understanding than I ever had before, more appreciation of her strength, vitality, unselfishness, broad understanding.

When she is in the room with other people I rather sit back in her amazing personality and admire her, but I am more a helpless part of her than useful, or a thing in myself.

I am still just her child.

We have never talked together the way we have sometimes in letters. Why do I meet people better in letters? Perhaps the dross of me is somewhat purged in letters.

I love Mr. Rublee.[1] He is one of the kindest and gentlest men I have ever known—gentle and patient and a little somber, yet always that sense of the ridiculous . . .

[1] George Rublee, Washington lawyer, legal adviser to the U. S. Embassy in Mexico, 1928–30; traveled on the same train.

And quite humble! He is the kind of man I feel I can sit with for hours and not have to say a word and yet will feel in perfect sympathy.

He intrudes so little that he leaves room for you to intrude. That is, he is the kind of man who, if you were sitting next to him at the theater, would let you have both arms of your chair!

I feel perfectly natural with Mr. Rublee.

I am having the most exhilarating time saying and acting just as I feel and think, lately—speaking when and what I want, and keeping quiet when I want and saying to myself with a daredevil feeling, "Oh, well—that's me. If they don't like it, so much the better to know now!"

Mr. Rublee is the kind of man I can just look at and smile.

This mad, fantastic country: yellow flowers out of cacti. People —short, sullen, wearing bright skirts, living in the glaring white houses painted vividly. Plains and fields plowed by oxen; men with great hats, blue trousers. Then wild gullies, bare cactus-covered and stony hills, canyons—

And then there are people like Professor Woodbridge[1] who say, " 'Justify your existence'? Nonsense! *Life is a gift!*"

[*Mexico City*]

The only way to look at this Maine [North Haven] visit is to look at it quite clearly and brutally. Colonel L. is miles removed from us. He is another world, represents another set of ideals. We cannot possibly be like him, or enter that world at all, or understand it. We must believe in the value of our own world—its *individual* value. On the other hand, we must *not* try to drag him into ours. It is impossible and it will only spoil everything. If *we can just recognize and remember the differences* . . . It is so

[1] F. L. E. Woodbridge, professor of philosophy and Dean of Columbia University.

idiotic to sentimentalize him, to see into his personality things we want to see there—things which could never, *never* be there. Everyone has made that mistake: he has been made a kind of slop bowl for everyone's personal dreams and ideals.

I have got to keep saying this over and over to myself to keep myself from slipping into my *incorrigible* habit of sentimentalizing—seeing, for instance, trying to see in his interest in birds something akin to my interest.

Amey is the most selfless person I know. She is so selfless that when I try to talk about *her*, the essential *her*, I don't know what to turn to at all. Usually you can touch people through their work, or their hobby, or their vanity or loves—*something* with a touch of egotism in it (not always in the bad sense). There is *nothing* egotistical about Amey, and yet she has the most *decided*, the most *positive* and *drawing* personality.

I think most of her is in her vigorous and detached (selfless and yet not cowing) devotion to people.

It is such an intense and deep joy to be with Con again. She is a touchstone: realities spring out of false things when I see through her eyes, and every joy, every feeling, every sensation is intensified when I have them with her.

It is evening. I am sitting on the long, pillared Embassy porch looking across at the offices. The grass of the garden is a gold green. There is no wind—the trees are still and there is no sun. The smell of earth and roses, geraniums red on the wall, and bougainvillaea—a few birds singing and, out in the street beyond, the cries of men selling things. It is noisy there—rattle of carts and horns blowing, people going home—but it is still, here, and cool.

Now, after a long day, I feel calm and quiet and controlled, above myself. I can sit apart and touch things quietly.

Why is it this way? How is it possible that I could have been so frantic and unhappy at noon?

———

I have never in my life felt so restless and so dissatisfied with myself and my life.

I wish terribly to stop reading and ruminating—to spend a year just exercising and using my hands. I would like to run on a beach, and ride and swim, and the rest of the time play the piano, pat little earthenware bowls, dig in a garden, paint. Sleep and bathe a great deal and live on vegetables and fruit.

And dance, too—dance all alone to music and sing.

Then I think I should have poise and control and be able to think and write.

Up very high over a cobblestoned road, up and up over very wild country: cactus and stony hills, men driving loaded donkeys. This is the road Cortez used—treasure carried up from Veracruz. After a long drive we could see down—far, far below us, below the woods we had just come through; spread out and cut up in little green patches, the valley. It was sunny and gold-green down there. It had just rained. We went down. It became suddenly very warm and soft. Great buzzards sailed slowly down the hillside. We passed huts with masses of bougainvillaea tumbling over them. Poinsettia trees. The air was gentle—*douce*. It smelled like Nassau, gentle and soft, and fragrant and of wet clay roads.

Cuernavaca.[1]

Down a little street, stone houses flat against the street, one with bright Zuloaga-blue shutters, pink oleander trees on the outside. We knocked at a gate and opened into Mr. Ovey's[2] house. A patio in the center of this one-storied place. In the middle a fountain—persistent soft splatter—cool. Great terra-cotta pots full of climbing red geraniums against the yellow-pink walls; arches opened into rooms on three sides, so that the room was entirely open on one side. On the fourth side, across an arch climbed an enormous bougainvillaea vine—a tree of bougainvillaea that

[1] Mexican town about fifty miles from Mexico City, and at a lower altitude.
[2] Esmond Ovey, British Minister, later Sir Esmond Ovey.

shaded almost the whole patio. Little flagstones led across the fresh grass of the patio. The heavy sweet scent of tuberoses in a pot. The soft splash of the fountain and clear-toned birds somewhere in the back. Tiles—blue and yellow—set in the cream-yellow walls in places and niches. The doors and windows into the rooms are Zuloaga blue. The roof has terra-cotta tiles, and the floors are cool stone with rag rugs on them. Strange plants with queer red, drippy flowers in the patio. A bush of these and one straight, tall pine. I have described it plainly, regularly, trying to get it all down—but that is not the effect. It is a confusion of shade and sun, of cream wall and flaming color; a sudden turn and here is another court, and stairs up to the roof, and there the garden going down, through an ironwork gate, terrace after terrace. There is the sense of no plan. It is all corners, and every corner is perfect—a geranium plant, tuberoses, bird cages against the wall, a parrot with a red tail—fantastic twisted trunk and branches of the bougainvillaea. And through it all the sound of that splashing fountain.

He [Mr. Ovey] has made an ironwork gate in the cream-yellow wall in the second court—ironwork of Zuloaga blue. Blue plumbago falls over the gate and the wall, and one looks through, down a terrace and another terrace. English grass on the terraces, roses on the walls (first terrace, yellow wall; second terrace, blue wall—plumbago-colored) and crimson bougainvillaea. Strange tropical plants and flowers, two or three great palms shooting up.

After a rest Con and I went out of the gate and walked down the cobbled streets: pink and yellow stone houses flat against the street, children sitting behind the grilled windows. Con bought shoes at a little shoestore. Then we went to the old church gardens: the same pink-yellow walls; above, the graying dome of the church and tops of palms and, beyond, the gray hills. A boy was walking slowly through the garden with two watering cans balanced on a stick over his shoulders. He leaned down and watered the petunia beds. The sun was going down and the garden was shadowed and empty. It had a somber dignity and we walked slowly and reverently. We had no hats on and we did not go into the church, though I suggested we wear handkerchiefs over our heads, and we laughed.

Then we walked to the Bishop's gardens, into the big court, stone steps running up to the left, past the tower to a stone porch with pots of red geraniums on it. In the back of the court an arch covered with rich royal bougainvillaea masses of the red-purple shade. We stood on the upper porch and looked at the town, graying, at the court below, Mexican children playing there, at the Cathedral dome, at the terra-cotta roofs of the town, down to our right the old overgrown garden of the Bishop's ragged fruit trees—vines running all over them—surrounded by an old, tall wall. It was quiet and we were all alone. This whole place—the town seems deserted, gone by, especially the places like the Cathedral gardens and the Bishop's palace which were once royal and bustling and alive. They have still all the dignity but there is no clatter of donkeys' hoofs in the court, only the caretaker's little brown children playing. The big bell in the tower is green and rusty. The bougainvillaea has overrun the big arch and almost hides the door. The gardens are tangled. It isn't sad or gloomy—just the sense of repose, of quiet old age—and it was evening. The time of day corresponded with the time in years for the Bishop's palace.

The air was so soft and gentle, and those great birds slowly, lazily sailing down over the tiled roofs.

I felt so calm, so quiet, and so controlled, able to get every bit of peace and beauty from it. I felt relaxed and opened up, as if it were all pouring into me—this peace, this sun, and the smell and the quiet of old deserted, sun-warmed courts.

We walked lazily and quietly down the still white streets, in harmony with it all. It was like summer evenings—all of them. We walked without coats or hats. And to be with Con—it was so rich. We were so close, and shared it together, and nothing jarred. We talked of how rich, how real, things are to us when we are together and apart from other people. When you are *shown* things by other people, or even with them, you get it secondhand, like looking at postcards. It is not yours. It is not a *pure* sensation—it is blurred and smeared. Katherine Mansfield understood this. When I read that part I wanted to cry out, "Yes—yes, yes!"

Then we walked down to the "Borda Gardens"—an old place, low, yellow stone. A patio, and then down steps and terraces through gardens to a pond. All under mango trees, shaded and cool. Old stone steps and fountains and always that sense of desertion, of old, past grandeur. An old Frenchman built it years ago—before Maximilian—thinking vaguely of Versailles, perhaps. One can see him planning steps and walks and fountains and an esplanade and a pond with swans in it, under the thick shade of mango trees. The smell of orange blossoms, and pink hibiscus on the walls. Fountains going, flower beds. Then Maximilian found it and loved it, with nostalgia, perhaps, for Versailles, a retreat— heaven knows he needed it. Did he walk down the steps and watch the swans and dream?

Now there are no "gardens" left, really—just mango trees, thick shade, and the old stone steps and walks and fountain figures, and at the end of the terraces a small pond where swans splash lazily and swallows dip swiftly like summer flies.

There was no one else in the garden; we walked slowly and stood a long time watching the swans and the dipping swallows, the gold sunset rippling in the water.

I felt so happy and calm and at peace—as though I had woken up from a long, deep sleep.

We walked home through the quiet, still streets—now starting to be lit. The people here are gentle and smile at you. They sit in their doors and hold their sweet children and sing sometimes.

We walked in Mr. Ovey's gate—it was almost dark—and stepped into his patio. The fountain was still, a few birds singing and thick sweet scents in the dark. What was it (one could hardly see)—the tuberoses in the corner? The bougainvillaea was a dark tangle against the sky, and the pine tree black beyond the roof. All the arches were lit, a lantern in each one. A man came around and lit small candles and set them in niches. A table was set under one arch and candles lit. We had supper there, looking out at the sky and the bougainvillaea against it. The fountain and the thick scent, everywhere, of tuberoses. It was so perfect, so magical, so unreal—those small niches lighted, the lanterned arches, the cloudy moon half hid behind the bougainvillaea, and thick, sweet tuberoses.

It was too perfect—everything ready for something. It was so unreal: nowhere could one pierce through unreality or to something familiar and commonplace. And no one to disturb our appreciating it! As though we were invisible, for we were children to Mr. Ovey (Con and I), and we were left blessedly alone, not spoken to. We did not need to talk; we sat back in this and in our dreams. We were not there, for social purposes, and it was all ours!

After supper down the terraces under a straight palm (like a rocket, Amey said) we sat and listened to crickets and cicadas. The white, bell-like lilies hung down and were heavy with scent (only at night). They were white in the darkness. One pushed perfume aside, walking: orange blossoms, and a syringa perfume. Some queer frog whistled like a boy every few minutes. The grass was soft. Con sat in the hammock. It was so dark and so heavy with perfume. Blessed invisibility!

We were soaked with it and heavy with sleep and happiness.

After we got to bed, out in the street some serenaders (soldiers) singing *Nunca!* Heavy, sweet, like tuberoses. *Nunca!* Warm and sweet and haunting.

In the morning a *perfect* breakfast—my dream of all breakfasts—under an arch, looking out into the patio. The leaves were fresh and green, the geraniums flaming against the walls, sun and shade very strongly marked, and it was cool. And in the court beyond birds sang, one with an especially clear, cool, like-drops-of-water song. Con said it was a *robin* in a *cage!* It was almost too fresh, too intense, too real a voice for this dream garden. I thought of Flecker's perfect poem: "A linnet who had lost her way . . ."

Oh, the splotches of sun and shade on the red stone floors, on the grass, on the cream-yellow arches, on the pink and red geraniums; and the fountain and soft grass. And those birds, and breakfast looking out at it from a shaded arch—

And marmalade and toast and orange juice for breakfast!

After breakfast Con and I sat under an orange tree and sketched the ironwork gate in the wall, with the blue plumbago trailing over it. We laughed and were so happy and silly over the ironwork designs (the "embryo" curve) and how to draw plumbago and leaves.

Then "they" went off. We were not noticed or dragged along. We were so happy—so secure and calm and happy. We sat under an arch (it was like walking into *The Enchanted April*[1]) and talked and laughed and could look ahead calmly, and could rejoice in our closeness, our intimacy, the miracle of it and its preciousness—and we were alone! And I felt calm and controlled: that feeling of sitting back like a chess player and moving myself with my hands, as though I were working a chess game. Oh, the joy and completeness of that morning! I can live on it for a long time.

"*Il n'y a pas de vie heureuse. Il y a seulement des jours heureux!*"

All that twenty-four hours: our closeness, the joy of turning and smiling at something lovely or amusing, the joy of quick exchange and quick understanding—and no one else understanding!

Mr. Ovey is like someone in Henry James: charming, cultivated, traveled, attractive-looking; loves puttering around his garden—pride in showing it off like a stage setting—loves to press

[1] Novel (1922) by "Elizabeth" (Countess Elizabeth Mary Russell).

a button and make the fountain go. Very little interest in people as personalities; is painted in clear, flat colors and sees clear, flat colors; likes simple food, knows what he wants, likes a good joke and honest people, and is quite contented with his life.

Colonel Mitford, also typical: more a sporting type, attractive and attracted to pretty women, never opens a book, likes fishing, always running around seeming very busy, but not really; hair slicked back. Con and I watched him that evening pouring cocktails in the lighted arch for "them." As Con said, he was *just* like an Englishman in a play: "Won't you have a cocktail? Oh, do have a cocktail."

Mr. Ovey says the Russians always talk in proverbs. You ask a peasant if it is going to rain and he says, "Make hay while the sun shines!"

I love that! It is so *enraging* to a Britisher.

> *First day on train, alone*
> [*Trip back from Mexico, April 5, 1928*]

A sort of panicky feeling at first, not talking the language and not knowing how to read the money.

But at least this is real. The experiences one has alone are satisfyingly real.

If only Mrs. Schoenfeld had not introduced me to that man. He has a loud voice and inquisitive eyes, is kindhearted, robust, and acquisitive. He knows all the Mexican girls on board already. I had lunch with him. I tried to be polite. He has been in Mexico six days, talks about it fluently, wants to exploit it. Has a vast amount of miscellaneous information and utter assurance. When I asked him how he got so much (information) in so short a time, he laughed his loud (the kind that goes on louder and longer than you expect—uncontrollable) laugh and said, "Oh, I made myself a perfect pest (I can well believe it!) going round asking questions."

The two little porters (Mexican) whom Mother told to look after me eye him with suspicion—think he is a bad character and leading me astray. The little stateroom porter saw him give me a lime and whispered confidingly, "Don't eat it! It's green!"

I tried to get out of having supper with him, but— We pulled up the shade and there was the moon, still and full, hung perfectly motionless and white above some clouds. We both gasped a little. He said, "It looks like it was painted there—don't it?"

Well, he got the idea, anyway!

Any place is lovely in the evening.

I read *Airmen and Aircraft* quite late into the night as a calming influence! All that is a kind of stabilizer to me now. First, of course, because Colonel L. is *"le seul saint devant qui je brûle ma chandelle"*[1] (how incongruous that is!)—the last of the gods. He is unbelievable and it is exhilarating to believe in the unbelievable. Then because all that world is so tremendous, new and foreign to me, I could not get further from myself than in it.

It is so incomprehensible that it gives me a tremendous thrill to comprehend the smallest glimmer of it.

It is, though, amusing to read the requirements—and quite sad—for an aviator. They are comically *so* opposite to anything I have:

"Instantaneous co-ordination between his muscles and thoughts
Good eyesight
The ability to withstand great physical and mental strain
Never become stampeded by unforeseen difficulties
A complete lack of fear while in the air
Readiness to take risks when they are necessary,
but calm and levelheaded at all times"
!   !   !   !   *Dieu!*
To all of which I sigh, *"Rien à faire."* Good eyesight is my only qualification! *"Voilà qui laisse de l'espoir!"*

I managed to miss my Philadelphian at breakfast this morning and had the worst oatmeal I have ever seen—the liquid and solid

[1] "The only saint before whom I light a candle."

not at all amalgamated, brownish-gray lumps swimming in a blue liquid!

3–11:30 in Laredo

Terribly hot, and I felt very sick. Many people shaking my hands and handing me cards and asking me if there was anything they could do for me. I felt like saying, "Yes—a bath and a cool bed, if you please!"

"Philadelphia" knocked on my door when I was nearly prostrate and took me out into Laredo. It was cool and quiet, and gentle. I could not talk, but he was *inexpressibly* kind. I take back all my remarks.

It was terribly comical, though, driving through the streets of Laredo, he wanting to show me how much better Texas was cultivated than Mexico. He smelled onion fields with triumphant delight. I, feeling miles and miles away and quite resigned and helpless.

But he was so kind that I didn't mind what he was talking about—agriculture, criminology.

Lunch *alone!*

We are getting north very rapidly. I have never come into spring this way around. But it is really quite as exhilarating to see the change from hot summer aridness to spring green as it is to see the change from winter aridness to spring green.

The cool, sweet freshness of it.

Fruit blossoms and new green leaves.

And those white—breath-taking white—layers of dogwood.

I realized this quite simple enough consolation prize for Colonel L.'s not liking me—for the impossibility of my touching him in any way. It is just another example of not being able to eat your cake and have it too: if I could not appreciate him, I would be the kind of person that is more sympathetic to him.

One pays for appreciation, and—naturally—it is so great a joy and inspiration.

I am always misjudging people. "Philadelphia" has great vigor, keenness, and sensitivity (one would not guess by his laugh), gentleness, kindness, idealism.

But the sensitivity is rarest. He actually sensed that he might be imposing on me, *that I liked to be alone.* I believe he missed lunch so I could have it alone!

That kind of sensitivity ranks him among the angels (with me).

I found myself talking quite frankly, sincerely, and objectively with him tonight about *everything!*

I cannot keep a reserve with someone who has seen me like a rag—with indigestion or a bad time at a dance.

But I have been so insulting to him. I find him not listening at all to what I'm saying, but just watching me with those little inquisitive eyes and smiling. Then he laughs and says, "You're just precious!" Lord!

Easter [*April 8th*]

No! This is the solution. Don't say meekly and despondently, *"I have nothing in common with Colonel L.,"* but flippantly and arrogantly say, *"Colonel L. has nothing in common with me!"*

"Philadelphia" got his seat in the same car as mine from St. Louis to N. Y. He had some flowers brought me at the station!

I was really overcome—and uncomfortable. I was being perfectly natural and open with him because I felt so safe, so sure that he was not on the beau basis—and look what happens! He wants to come up to Northampton. Oh dear, I hate to be nasty for he has been so kind and is really quite unusual. He "gets" everything, but he expresses it so objectionably, like his noticing the moon, and these flowers for Easter, and it was a heavenly thought. But he buys *white* carnations and puts them in a hideous little vase made to hang on a hook (serviceable and reliable—just like him)!

There is something so pathetically comical about the way his coat whisks kittenishly behind him as he hurries ahead of me opening doors to get to the diner, like a dog frisking his tail.

Yet it is a great pleasure to talk to him—a keen, alert, quick-to-understand mind, and very sound.

Oh, the miles and miles of green Pullman aisles we have galloped through, that whisking coat and I!

Monday

Breakfast riding through Lancaster, Pa. "Richest county in the world," "Philadelphia" says. (He talks just like a prospectus.) "Fine, big farmhouses, all the evidences of prosperity."

"Are you great pals with your brother?"

12 A.M. North Philadelphia

It is cold. The streets are gray. Men walking in and out of banks; lots of sooty roofs as far as one can see, taxis, filling stations. "Philadelphia" has left. He says he has lots of work to do today. ("We own stock all through these towns, all the way up from Laredo!")

I saw his little squat form swinging off down the street, his coat flapping.

Well, he's gone, just like that. It is very strange. We slid away from the station and I watched two gray sparrows walking up and down the gravel by the tracks. In a second they were gone. He, as completely. He has dropped back into (in my mind) a world of generalities and statistics. He has melted into generalities from a personality.

Forsythia is pure joy. There is not an ounce, not a glimmer of sadness or even *knowledge* in forsythia. Pure, undiluted, untouched joy.

Home. I had to go out to Englewood. I didn't need to but I was so dissatisfied and restless in the apartment. I felt I would have to get home—really home—before I could start again, like those games at running where you "touch home" and start away again.

It was good to bump out over that old road. Each familiar place clicked in my mind with a kind of relaxing pleasure: the lights along the river, the white fence, Pierce's Pond. I felt a little more relaxed, a little more rested, sinking back into it at each one.

Then scrunching over the gravel—home. The old rugs, the white woodwork, the comfortable smell of it. That same relaxing process went on: the relief, the quiet restful relief, of walking gently through each room, touching old things, and gradually sinking into it, quiet and rested.

April, Northampton, after [Easter] vacation, 1928

I am trying to think of some gesture—some gesture delicate, beautiful, graceful, and slight as a sigh or breath, some gesture to describe or compare with the exquisite breath-taking grace of these trailing elm branches resting so gently on the air. Some gesture of a beautiful and gentle woman.

I love *The Book of the Duchesse;* it is spring compared with the rich summer of *The Canterbury Tales.* It is the fresh, pale, gold-green of spring grass and leaves. Some of it like Elisabeth:

> "Therwith hir liste so wel to live,
> That dulnesse was of hir a-drad.
>
> . . .
>
> "That she was lyk to torche bright,
> That every man may take of light
> Ynogh, and hit hath never the lesse.
>
> . . .
>
> "Me thoghte the felawship as naked
> Withouten hir, that I saw ones,
> As a coroune withoute stones."

I love the valentine quality. But there is much more besides—a kind of light shining through the paper lace.

Strange: I think I am nearer (understand better, have more in common with, touch more directly), I am nearer to the man who digs ditches, or the man who sells papers, or the fruit-store man, or my Italian dressmaker—or "Philadelphia"—nearer, *far* nearer the last two than I am to Colonel L.

I have more in common with . . . *anyone*—the most distant of distant people—than with him. Isn't it funny. It is hard to even contemplate a person so different, whose whole outlook, way of thinking, looking, reacting to things, is utterly and completely opposed to mine—not even as near as being *opposed*—in another plane that I can hardly believe exists.

Daffodils and hyacinths out along the bank where the afternoon sun hits them slantwise if you look back.

[*After a reading at Smith College*]
Robert Frost. He is a simplifying genius. It was superb tonight, like walking through a wood and seeing a road always following ahead, opening up simply, where you could not see before.

If I could only see him often! It is the view from the mountain-top that you need more than just once in a while.

Chaucer describes his first flight (held in talons of an eagle, high above world):

> "And therwith I
> Gan for to wondren in my minde.
> *'O God,' thoughte I, 'that madest kinde,*
> *Shal I non other weyes dye?'* "

Have lived in a dream, a nightmare, for days now.
Struggle over *The Trembling Veil*,[1] trying to write book review, took me days. Couldn't sift it, shake it into form; felt my

[1] William Butler Yeats, *The Trembling of the Veil*.

mind leaving me. Have no control over my mind—can't analyze, can't sift, can't see things whole, can't develop logical thoughts.

Tore things up, started over again.

Words meant nothing. Only discovered mistakes.

Can't write.

The agony of trying to.

During the "struggle," one period of enlightenment. Must write it down later:

What I can do— Where my world joins the other.

April—still

Out in the car after Mrs. Curtiss' class—anywhere, to get away. We stopped at the flying field, got out. Man in overcoat tying airplane struts? wires? together with ribbon! We walked across green wet field. The planes (two blue ones) nosed up. The sky blue. Man in overcoat still busy over tying plane together. I started asking questions—all the technical questions I could think of: Make of plane? Angle of gliding? Slope of wing? How plane is made —wings? Streamline? Commercial aviation? etc., etc., etc. He thought me mad, but he was gentle and went on tying ribbons. He seemed pleased and told us we could get into front cockpit. I worked the controls and asked questions! Funny, gentle-eyed little man in brown overcoat, tying wires with ribbons. Bright blue little open biplane. F. D. [Florence Dorothy Bill] and I squeezed in front cockpit feeling like "The Motorboat Girls at Play" or the cover of some *Popular Aviation* magazine. But I was so excited, so proud (secretly) that I had been interested, that he knew I was interested. It was so close and thrilling, and he talked so calmly of it. I was so foolishly, childishly proud of flaunting those technical terms that I could not possibly have spoken of to Colonel L. (and did not know at all).

But it was like a child handling great swords or guns that he could not use and yet knew had some great and it seemed magical power—some tremendously strong and dangerous explosive.

———

Colonel L. took serum up to try to save Bennett's[1] life. New York to Quebec in snowstorms, by air—the only person who could have gone there that fast. It is strange and gratifying to think of his being indispensable in such a practical way. Like him to go immediately and then to turn around and come back immediately after he had finished his job, not staying to get in the way.

Thought they were going to Montreal but he went on to Quebec, a hundred miles further north. Man with white mice (never been up before—shaken) gets out. Colonel L.: "This is Quebec," in matter-of-fact tone. Man with white mice: "Oh! I thought this was Montreal!" Colonel L.: "No, this is Quebec."

Took my driving test. My gentle, soft-toned, anything-we-can-do-for-you garage man has the air of a family dentist toward me. Does *everything* for me, and so quietly.

He talks of the test as though he were a doctor, saying, "Well now, don't worry, you have nothing to worry about, I am quite sure it won't take long. It won't hurt much."

He is *so* polite, vanishes and appears when wanted. Wears gray spats and talks in a soft-toned, completely efficient voice. He treats me *just* as all those railroad agents did in Laredo.

Saw white birches on way to Deerfield. They have the same breath-taking whiteness that white dogwood has. I can't think of anything else quite the same.

After all, I don't see why I am always asking for private, individual, selfish miracles when every year there are miracles like white dogwood.

April

Such an exciting day. I went to Miss Sturm's[2] for tea. She is unbelievable.

[1] Floyd Bennett, Commander Byrd's pilot on the first airplane flight to the North Pole, died of pneumonia in a Quebec hospital.

[2] Marthe Sturm, assistant professor of French at Smith College, 1926–28.

Two goldfish on the wall: a Japanese print, heavenly, done with one sweep, as though blown glass. All one piece—great beauty and calm in the composition.

Reds in the room—she loves red. That made me happy. I did not tell her what scarlet means to me, but it is so exciting to find someone whom scarlet affects that way.

"A little—and the heart must skip a beat!"

Nice red in curtains—Canadian—and in a pillow—Swedish work (strange, she thought, that those Northern people had produced it), and in a table cover and red bittersweet in a jar that seemed to catch their gold-red fire from the goldfish on the wall. (She was a little shy, the way I am when I want very much to please someone.)

The room small and neat except for her desk, piled high in disorderly layers of papers and books. (She said she did not tidy up if someone came to see her, for she *was* that way and if her friends could not accept it they could not accept *her*. Besides, she said, she knew just in which layer were the things she wanted!)

Then we talked. We talked and talked. Oh, she is so keen, so quick, so sensitive, and *so* lucid. Her mind is clear and carved. She raced ahead and I clung to the chair from the sheer excitement of it. I was simply trembling from excitement, the way one is on spring days, when anything is around the corner. I could not get the words out fast enough. I struggled to be clear, to seize my thoughts as they exploded in different directions from one sharp touch of her thought.

It was fencing. It was exploring. (*"Touché! Touché!"*)

"You have read Proust?"

"Yes. . . ."

"His construction?"

"He has none."

"That is what I mean. One can have formlessness and yet great genius, great art."

"But I do not feel that he succeeds—he is the pendulum swung too far, he . . ."

One waits so long to find people like that. It is rare and frightening. It is too good to believe.

After months of arid silence one can talk, one soars, one dips and turns like a bird, one has power over one's mind. As if one suddenly found that one had a clean, clear, sharp weapon and could use it. And it glints and shines when one handles it, as if it had been kept polished.

"I think that we . . ."—"*we*," she said, as though her mind was anything like mine—her lucid, brilliant, clear-cut, analytical mind, sharp and keen and piercing—*as if* her mind were like my muddy, illogical one, blowing all directions—as if! "I thought that we should have something in common," she said.

My desk is untidy too!

I have come to believe that you can get along without anyone—that is, without the close contact of any one person. That is a terrible shock to me, but I think it is true. You do need *companionship,* but wherever you go, in whatever new environment, you will find people who, to a large degree, take the place of those you left. That is, you will find as many contacts, they can become as intimately a part of your life as friends before.

If you can get along without friends is it all gone after you leave a person? I don't think so, because when you see them again, or write to them, it all comes back. You can meet and talk with as much intensity and freedom as before, your connection is as strong even though the contact surface is not as great.

Besides, I think that companionship is a static, objective thing. You can have it with anyone and it is relatively the same, while friendship is subjective and multicolored. There are as many different kinds of friendship (for me, at least) as there are friends. The intimate companionship goes, I think, when you leave a friend, but friendship stays. It is an inherent possibility of relationship that, once admitted—well, there it is.

Some papers take hold of you by the teeth and shake you as a dog does a rat. And you feel limp and wilted. The Yeats paper did that to me.

May 1st

It is so good to see the sky again blue: sunshine after two weeks of cold and rain. It was like a heavy blanket and weighed you down. Now that *blue*—I am walking in it! Blue and white clouds. It is too good to believe—I have to keep looking at it from sheer joy. I feel as though I were wearing it.

A glorious storm—great curves of rain, sweeps, people running. The hard beat of it and those heart-lifting breaths of fresh cool when it stops a little.

A rainbow against a black sky (the sun behind me as I looked at it). The sun gleaming on that white birch in Mr. Schintz's[1] garden. Behind the white birch the rainbow and the blue hills and black sky.

The grass a *living, moving* green, so intensely green.

Fuss about writing for Jordan Prize. Oh, these struggles, these ridiculous moral molehills that I stagger over.

This one: that, of course, nothing would make me happier than that prize, and yet it is perfectly clear that not only I *could not* possibly but I *should not* get it. I haven't "original writing" in any sense—I know I haven't, I can't "create" in any sense. My things aren't "out of the whole cloth."

So *not* getting it doesn't make any difference, either. It doesn't change anything. Still, here I am . . .

Joy and I picked bloodroots. They are sweet, fresh little flowers to look at—cup-shaped like anemones, smooth-stemmed. They look pure and sweet when you see them—white-petaled cups with yellow hearts. But you pick them and they have tuby roots, and rust-red juice runs out, and their scent is so *shocking*—poisonous, Joy says, they smell like steel shavings.

They repel me now. I feel quite hurt, too, and annoyed at such deceit.

Witch flowers.

[1] Head of Department of Romance Languages at Smith College.

A warm, still, expanding day; lots of veiling clouds and the elm tree branches hung heavily. I suggested to F. D. *Flying!* In the afternoon! We drove out at three to the field. The two planes but no man; two boys waiting. We asked them; *nothing.* Finally we asked man in filling station. The aviator generally came at five and *had been* taking up passengers!

Back at five (after afternoon of suspense). Plane gone, people standing around. Where was he? Just coming over the mountain.

Down. He got out, looked so funny in flying suit, talked to other people—men—and got his clothes from car and, not noticing us, walked away. We asked a boy if he was taking up passengers. Boy ran after him. He came back and smiled at us, remembered us—me. "I'm afraid I was very impertinent the other day, asking so many questions, but I really was interested . . ." He smiled and said very sincerely, "No, I was glad to tell you, I'm glad to tell anyone who's interested."

He said he *was* taking passengers up and—we gasped (it seemed so simple and matter-of-fact when we had thought about it and waited in suspense for it for so long)—*would take us up.*

He started the engine (first turning the plane around—it is *so* little), twirled the propeller, and a great wind flurried. He helped us in. Thought our bandanas would blow off, said it was "bumpy" over the range, said it was awfully windy "up there."

I said I would let my hair blow. He said it certainly *would* blow. The engine roared. We got in. A heavy belt snapped us both in. He told us to hold on to the bar—it was bumpy over the field. F. D. said faintly, "I think I'd rather not be tied in, so I *could* jump out if anything happened."

The wind from the propeller blew furiously. We started (he in behind us). F. D.: "Is it better *not* to look?" I felt quite sick with excitement.

We started, bumping very fast, clinging to the bar, and terribly, terribly excited and nerved up; very contained and laughing the way frightful excitement makes you. We were up quickly in great intoxicating lifts, as before. I was delirious. Then, below, Mrs. Curtiss' little gray roadster along the highway! And then the river like quicksilver. The wind was strong and the noise terrific. We went up and up. Then, below, fields like pieces of cloth—tweed—in lines, and apple orchards looking like the "manors" we made in the sandbox, sticking twigs in lines. The hills all flattened out. It looked like a clay model in geology—could see oxbows and curved lakes, water in "puddles" all through the flat valley. Paradise like a toy pond with a minute twig on it—a canoe. The observatory. The dormitories, like dolls' houses, neatly proportioned. Cars minutely going, *so* slowly, along a white ribbon. The sun on the quicksilver river and all the little pools—towns up the river.

We went over the Holyoke range, over Mt. Tom. Saw both sides at the same time. Those hills—*so* diminished, yet one did not seem far away from them. Everything so clear: those marked-out fields, green and brown, streaked, the quicksilver river, toy houses, ribbon roads. We went over a factory, an anthill of a sand pile (probably a huge mound of sand for building). He shouted altitudes to us, and smiled, and pointed out things: the shadow of the plane. I saw a rainbow glint that the shiny wing made on a lake. A huge mound of logs looked like a pile of matches.

The country was shining and beautiful spread out suddenly and simply like that under our feet, and I felt, How simple! *This* is the way this valley *really* looks, really is. I see it all now—how clear, how simple! It's such a little place, such a little world, and how neatly and plainly laid out. I can see it all. And I felt like God.

I watched the wings—we hardly seemed to move—yet that terrific wind . . .

It was intense pleasure and *real, so real!* Because I had it *alone,* and it was my own responsibility. It was not handed me on a silver platter and taken for granted. I *made* the effort to get it and it was *mine—my utterly possessed experience.*

We came down suddenly and landed with a bump—not much, but a little.

Hair tangled, ecstatic. He asked us *how we liked it* and was pleased at our answers, helped us out, and *wouldn't take any money!* "No, you are really interested in it, and the people who are really interested in it—I like to take 'em up!" He smiled—the angel.

We had pleased him—I was so happy. We walked off quite wobbly and hysterical. A new sense that it gives you—a fifth dimension, a shock of revelation, as if one suddenly saw the world upside down. He will never know the joy and life it gave me. I *couldn't* thank him.

The cherry trees are a mist of pink, and the magnolia buds cream white against this soft blue—this *"douce"* sky of spring.

Jay *home!* It is too good to believe. I heard his voice. "Jay? Jay! Jay!" I said, incredulous. "Yes, *Jay*—how many Jays do you know?" I will see him, the darling. It is too good. He was *so* far away.

F. from Amherst. *Typical* college boy, but nice. The veneer of culture—touches everything a little, almost hits things, sometimes hits the right thing. Nice, good-natured, agreeable, mediocre, platitudinal.

"The nature lovers": "Lots of fellows will appreciate a sunset if you lead them on."

A little appreciation seems to me even more insidious than a little learning. It taints everything it touches and it touches everything, just the veneer of appreciation. Nothing real or distinctive about him. There are *thousands* of him (thank God for one Colonel L.).

I'd much rather talk to a garage man.

He is a mass of conventions—his talk, his ideas, his clothes, his car.

We went to a conventional movie where a conventionally

pretty girl went through the conventions of sex appeal and love. *Hideous.*

This has been a happy day. I went to bed so early the night before and it has been so happy today—full and rich. I have felt things clearly, sensations and impressions have been clear and real, not blurred with my personal, subjective worryings due to depression or tiredness.

Tomorrow is my off day again! Will I *never* be steady? Is it *just* a matter of sleep?

I know it is superficial and silly, but these spring evenings and long, soft afternoons I don't want to talk complicatedly and consciously with Y. I should like to look pretty, to be thought pretty, and to walk and laugh with a very nice-looking boy and hum sentimental tunes that are all lies—and a different "nice-looking boy" each evening!

The airplanes and the cherry trees and these long evenings will really permanently upset my equilibrium!

Two days with Jay. Beautiful. But he has changed: all his defiance has slipped off and left him rather bare and quiet and dependent. It is best that way but so sad—I felt terribly sad all the time. I could not analyze it, but there was deep inside an unfathomable, hopeless sadness.

Jay—tired, getting a little old, resigned and dependent. And could I help him? Yes, if I were with him more of the time.

And I cannot do that. Oh, it should not have made him so happy—this weekend. There was a wrongness in that—in his being so happy just being with me. I was happy to be with him and at the closeness of our understanding again, but also happy for sun and the gleam on the grass as the wind bent it and the good roads and the motor's hum and singing and fields faintly blue with suspicions of violets—*not just* him.

And underneath was this sadness—that I could not help him more, that this was only temporary, that tomorrow I should be happy again at grass and violets—brutally happy—not caring for anyone. Not that he can't get on without me, or anyone, for he can—more now than before, now he has learned to be quiet and compromise.

But he has been cheated—by his own unyielding and brave and dear and foolish defiance—of what was his due: love and people who loved him, all ties and home. But love, mostly.

He depends on me for that and I am—selfishly—not ready to pour it all out for him. I give, but not as much as he needs—*the whole* of someone's love. I understand him. I could give it if only I would—but can I?

Oh, I felt so selfish, so brutal. I can't look at him, at his life, without that sadness.

And I drove back from Springfield with a reckless exultation at the fast, steady driving—powerful engine—along the road, my head up, singing all the way.

How was that? Why?

H. D.[1]—exquisite.
Eurydice! Lapis lazuli and Ezra Pound.

I have felt really alive tonight—alive and keen and concentrated, as though a great rhythm were running through me.

I have been happy trying to make something out of fragments of poems—or might-be poems.

Is it just being in *wonderful* health—having slept *really* enough and eating not too much or too heavy food and having enough sunshine?

It seems to me we should work for these moments when one is in such perfect physical and mental health. It is a slim state, physically and mentally; all the excess is sloughed off. One's actions and one's mind are pointed, not dull and obscure. The force and energy is concentrated, not frittered away.

One is *fit*—one is ready to feel, to see, to appreciate life very fully and richly.

[1] Hilda Doolittle, Imagist poet.

Apple blossoms *just* before they come out—that pink haze. *No—pink* under a *green* haze.

White dogwood—virginal.

All the asparagus I wanted!

Tomorrow will be different, for I have stayed up too late.

There is too much—too much. Life is so very full now. Riding this morning. The joy of physical exercise—trotting fast uphill, head in the sky, wind blowing against one's face.

The joy of walking around without a coat, the sun warm on one's shoulders and a little wind rippling one's silk dress around the knees and blowing across one's bare throat.

We rode through woods of tender birches—the kind one wants to eat—little ones.

This evening, picnic. Apple trees everywhere, overburdened, heaped over, pouring down pink-white blossoms. That's what has happened to them—May has given them too much beauty, generous pink and white beauty spilled all over them.

They say, "My cup runneth over."

The lilacs are almost out by the *Tarry-a-While.*

> "O Spring, grow slowly,
> Exquisite, holy . . .
> By little skips, by little steps,
> Like a lamb or a child."
> [ALICE MEYNELL]

Men plowing fields, dropping potatoes, onions. Farms spread out greenly beneath us as we came over the hill and the river still, still and flat in the flat green meadows. Feathery trees along the edge doubled in the water—so still that you could not tell the difference.

Apple blossoms seem to me made of light and water. They have a full roundness like drops of water, and the iridescence of water. I expect to find drops of water in the curved, pink petals.

White dogwood, ghostlike in the woods, and cherry, white, and white birches with tender green leaves. We sat under a cliff of them and looked up dizzily to see feathery white birches along the edge of the cliff against that soft, blue, woolly sky.

Strawberries and cream, and we laughed at everything.

"My cup runneth over"!

I have woken up now two mornings (I have heard it through my sleep) to those three clear notes of a bird (clear as the drops one expects to find in an apple blossom)—the same ones I used to hear in Englewood in the sleeping porch from the elm by the gate, or in the evening.

I had a blissful morning. I sat in the window (*cut* from Miss Dunn) in the sun and looked out over my garden: the unkempt lush grass and the sweet-gum tree with elbowy boughs, crotchety and irregular. It is not yet out, bless it ("O Spring, grow slowly"!). Then the hedge, the little garden, iridescent narcissi still wet, tulips.

I watched people click back and forth over the sidewalk. Inside the field, two men made a great to-do about putting up a stick that had fallen down from the fence by the hedge. Back and forth they tramped over the thick grass with wire and post. It did seem *so* futile and ridiculous—in the sun, warm soft air—so serious of them to nail up that post. *Whom* are they trying to keep out? That garden—the grass, the gum tree—lies *so* open to me. It is mine. I consider it part of my room, a projection of it.

I sat in the sun and tried to patch up scraps of poems.

The chestnut candles are *almost* out. Looking at them was like being just on the edge of a precipice.

That flame dogwood all out, by College Hall. It is a miracle.

Today

8 A.M.   Ecstatic (sunshine and spring)

9 A.M.   Intense (writing)

164

10 A.M.	Energetic (poems good!) and happy
11 A.M.	Bored (in class)
12 M.	Lazy (looked at trees)
1 P.M.	Angry (potatoes, *"Willoughby dope,"*[1] and bread for lunch)
2 P.M.	Earnest and discouraged (writing over poems)
3 P.M.	Discouraged and *miserable* (poems *frightful!*)
4 P.M.	Coming up, relieved (*Wheely* liked "Lida"[2])
5 P.M.	Limp
6 P.M.	Amused at my absurdity!

We went by Emily Dickinson's house—red brick, firm stone steps; a thick, rather gloomy high hedge (of fir bushes) surrounded the house and garden. But I saw the lawn, and a scarlet quince bush blossomed like her.

Spring rain.

The bird (three-noted) *was* a thrush.

Reading Coleridge's *Biographia Literaria* and *Anima Poetae*. Terribly exciting!—like meeting a person with whom one can say, *"Touché!"*

I want to write something honest—*terribly* honest and sincere, something that I feel *terribly* and wholly like that feeling at Christmas of "conversion" from admiration of a smarty-smarty world. The

> "If ever I said, in grief or pride,
> I tired of honest things, I lied"
> [EDNA ST. VINCENT MILLAY]

feeling. Something as clear and as simple and as pure as . . . white and gold syringa.

[1] Chipped beef.

[2] A story sent to the Smith College magazine.

I have spent all day trying to form a story—that is, an incident, a turn of something that once happened. It is subjective, as usual, but not as petty and more sincere feeling than most of them.

Mrs. Curtiss' teaching and judgment—I find I have been counting too much on her praise, wanting it, working for it. That is a dishonest way to write, and insecure. But her praise or criticism *does* mean a lot to me and I find it shaping what I am trying to say. And I *do* like her and admire her tremendously.

Comfortable grooves that my mind turns to at night:

1—*"It would be nice to get the Jordan Prize, if . . ."* etc.

Line of attack: It wouldn't mean anything if you *did* get it. It couldn't change your writing for the better.

You are a fool. Don't let yourself be hurt. (All right, then, I'll think of something else—pleasant.)

2—*"Wouldn't it be nice if I were wrong about Colonel L.—if he liked me."*

Line of attack: Fool, fool, fool. You are completely and irretrievably opposed to him. You have nothing in common. You don't even sincerely care a damn for his world. You are just swept away by the force of his personality.

He wouldn't look at you—turned away when you spoke to him. You were just the kind of silly, adoring little schoolgirl that he turns and runs from.

If you think too much about it you won't be able to speak at all this summer, you will be so embarrassed. Remember.

(All right, I'll think about something else—pleasant. About writing—perhaps that's more my world.) *"Wouldn't it be nice if I got the Jordan Prize!"*

Ad infinitum!

It has rained for a week. The leaves are heavy, green, limp, about my window. Sky dull, smothering all around us. I feel like a fly in a green bottle.

Chestnut candles out, but I haven't yet seen them in the sun.

Madame Bianchi[1] talked about Emily Dickinson. A proud,

---

[1] Martha Dickinson Bianchi, Emily Dickinson's niece, editor of her poems, author of *The Life and Letters of Emily Dickinson.*

regal woman, her face drawn with pain and hard suffering. Embittered, disappointed, disillusioned about love in her own life, she still spoke with clear, unsullied peace and rapture, almost, of Emily's devotion.

A sophisticated woman, she spoke of Emily's clarity and simplicity.

Mrs. S.—beautiful, tired, having suffered; worldly, sophisticated, hard—lay back on her pillows with half-shut eyes and in her ashen voice said, "Did Madame Bianchi say anything about Emily's love affair? I, being worldly, feel certain that they were . . . a . . . *lovers*. I remember a poem, something—'Now I am lover-wife . . . I am crowned with life's highest joy'—surely that can only mean one thing."

I said nothing. Of course it only *does* mean one thing—*to Mrs. S.!*

That is *just like her:* her sophistication, her weary decadence, her experience; sees *too* much, *looks right through things* whose existence she denies.

She is wrong, *wrong, wrong!* She is fundamentally *wrong* about life. I, with my youth and inexperience and health—I know she is wrong. There *are* things she does not see.

There *is* spiritual beauty in people. There is devotion to truth and honesty and love and kindness.

She herself has *superb* courage. I am wrong to rage—her life has been so dreadful.

Mrs. S.: "I want R. to learn that one gets one's happiness not from people but from intellectual pursuits."

That's a lie.

Bastien and Bastienne in the President's garden at night.

Lanterns in the cool dark and a queer blue light thrown on statues here and there against the dark trees. A Paris-park-after-the-opera air about it. Wisteria falling down the white lighted pillars—the shadow of the flower clusters distinct, delicate.

A very romantic air about it, too: one could not see who the people were! Light on dresses (silk) and light on faces. But not people one knew, except Mrs. Curtiss sitting and smoking in her leisurely, regal manner. (But I thought of those frightful papers and shuddered.)

We have had over a week of rain. I feel like an old woman (at twenty-one!). I feel fat—fat physically and mentally. I have a corn! Think—a *corn*—a hideous, disfiguring *corn*. Kitchen gardens, pots and pans, nursemaids—I see myself as one of Nurse's feet, bulging and spreading out of an old shoe—that's me.

I will never, never dance or be thin and pretty and gay again!

These four years I have wasted so frightfully.

I am tired and sniffly—a cold—and too much to do; and I am going to Boston tomorrow and I shouldn't go. I will be miserable all weekend, thinking about work not done. I shouldn't be with nice people like Laura [Brandt]—I should hide somewhere and get over this.

Nobody comes for my laundry, and my shoes hurt, and the dresses from the cleaner's are too tight, and my teeth are *all* cavities.

The lilacs are faded. I detest dead flowers and throwing them away and the putrid, scummy water. It is almost better not to have them. I hate—it really hurts—to see them fade. I pretend they're not faded and give them cold baths and look the other way when I see them drooping. It's no good—they *always* fade! "Oh, woe! Woe! Woe!"

(I feel like Mr. Housman tonight! That *delicious* parody of Ezra Pound's.)

Boston

Boston and sunshine—gay with Laura.

Laughing, and airplanes in the sky, crowds and traffic and bright shops, and much, *much* to say.

V. for tea. He was tall and thin, and his cheeks caved in a little; tired.

It was a joy to see him.

He sat angularly in a chair, eyed us with half-shut eyes, and argued—teasing me all the time.

I want to write about the amazing *variety* and intensity of relationships with people—the many kinds, the subtle distinctions, the infiniteness, the richness, the excitement of them.

It was *completely* satisfying this time with Laura.

I would like to write about . . . that it is possible to be, in a way, *objectively in love*—that is, to be in love with a person—not seeing them, not particularly wanting to, not asking anything from them—just knowing that they *are,* and going to them in your mind as one goes to a hill or a field or a flowering tree, for worship and peace. I say "in love" because there is an intensity and divinity about such appreciation, different from friendship.

Nothing exists when I am driving a car except the road, the car, and the excitement of going fast and having to keep mind and eye alert, focused.

The most flaming apple tree, the most winged skies, are nothing—I see them if they are pointed out but I *feel* them no more than I *feel* a car pointed out if I am sitting looking at an orchard.

This is the eleventh day of rain or overcast. It is Monday, too, I missed breakfast and I am heavy and tired from the long, nervous drive to Jaffrey. I ate a digestive cracker that I had left on my window sill—it was damp and soft.

I feel damp and soft too—"damp souls of housemaids," T. S. Eliot said.

Will the sun *ever* come out and dry me out?

I found a little starling today. It couldn't fly. Some girls were trying to catch it, to put it out of the way of cats. I held out my old brown coat and it hobbled into it and I put my hands over it softly and picked it up. It didn't seem awfully scared or wild and frightened as some animals. It did not struggle. It cheeped and I found myself saying quite naturally, "All right, darling—just a minute."

I almost put it into a robin's nest!

Holiday, Decoration Day—a long day of intensive work on Petrarch, Humanism, Erasmus, etc., for Miss Dunn—*very satisfactory,* though only for me. It won't help for the exam.

Thunderstorm.

The robins on the fire escape.

At night Con's high, ecstatic voice over the telephone: "Oh, Anne—it's so *green!* It's so *green!* Mexico was *dry.* Oh, it's so fresh and *green!"*

It was real and good beyond words to hear her.

I am sitting in the sun on my window sill facing the garden. It is early—seven thirty. I woke at five thirty, for it is a clear, sunny, still day.

This morning is like something new-born.

Everything fresh—wet, gleaming, glinting; the tips of leaves wet, the slate roof, the grass bent over and brushed silver with rain and drops on the telegraph wires and drops themselves slanting off brightly from the tiles and single threads of spider webs—a suspicion of one glinting in a quivering silver line from one leaf to another.

It is still and trembling in its perfection and newness.

I feel as though it were a chicken just out!

It is so new and so whole and perfect, after all that two weeks' struggle of rain and overcast and cold.

It must have been like this the morning after the Flood stopped.

Birds are singing clear, sparkling notes.

Elizabeth Montagu Prize[1] for Mme d'Houdetot.[2]

Jordan Prize . . .

[1] Annual prize for the best essay on women of the eighteenth century or women depicted in the literature of that century.

[2] A paper by A. M. L.

Dieu!

Ecstatically dazed, overcome and happy, this morning. It was unreal.

Now I realize nothing is changed, and I didn't really deserve the Jordan Prize. I *know* just how good those petty little subjective things were—*not good enough.*

Mother, though—Mother! That makes me very happy.

I felt like a shaky bride going up the long aisle to get the medal.

The family are simply absurd about the prizes; in fact, everyone is—all the outsiders. You'd think I'd given birth to triplets.

Two prizes *sounds* so grand and *is* so absurd—I'm sure no one else tried for the Elizabeth Montagu one. I feel greedy and silly, as though I'd resurrected all the old prizes no one else cared about, and then sat back smugly on undeserved praise.

People are absurd and dear, complimenting me. Their *praise,* as such, means very little, but their love is *thrilling!*

Mother here a night and a day. I love her so, but this day made me sad again, as it was on the train.

She said, "A wonderful day. I have seen *So-and-So,* and *So-and-So,* and *So-and-So,* and Miss — for a second, and wasn't I lucky to run into Miss —, and then I went and saw about the house and called on Miss —, and I saw the school and talked with — and —." Oh, God—that isn't my idea of a wonderful day.

I would say, "What a glorious day—I only saw — *all day long.* I really talked to — alone"

or

"I sat in that field until it was part of me and I was part of it"

or

"I didn't hurry once—all day." But I haven't as much life as she has. I am smaller and swept along in her life.

Rain

Exams

Rain

Rain

Rain

Rain
Rain
Rain
Rain

Exams

Rain

Swan-necked tulips

Rain
Rain
Rain

Exams
Rain

Rain
Rain

Exams
Rain
Rain
Rain

The worst about leaving people is knowing that you *can* and *will* get along without them (though sometimes I believe, with Emily Dickinson,

"To the faithful, Absence is condensed presence— To the others —*there aren't any others!*")

To the dentist.

It does seem so discouragingly sad to me: rooms get dusty and clothes always need mending and flowers fade and teeth decay. It's always like that.

Colonel L. probably coming. Oh, dear—
I am perfectly happy.
Why do I have to see him again?

Commencement weekend

If anyone else says anything nice to me, or gives me anything . . . If I have to say anything nice to anyone else, I shall scream a long shrill scream.

My tongue cloys in my mouth for sweetness!

It is not restful, it is not *possible* to talk wholeheartedly to more than one person at a time. You can't really talk with a person unless you surrender to them, for the moment (all other talk is futile). You can't surrender to more than one person a moment.

Too many people, too many demands, too much to do; competent, busy, hurrying people—

It just isn't living at all.

All this insincerity—if I have to thank anyone again for praise I don't deserve—which means nothing, or for gifts I don't deserve—

Rush of getting away and back.
So tired.

North Haven, June 22nd

The new house![1]
unbelievably good and right for us—
delicious wood smells
white paint
familiar furniture and china
hot water
candles
coming home!

It is my birthday—twenty-two—and North Haven again. So much has happened since I was here last fall—

> Mexico
> Lindbergh
> P. married
> That frightful winter
> Frances
> Dwight
> College over.

Third day of rain, fog, cold.
  Colonel L. forced down.
  More fog—the fates against us.
  He's not coming. We feel dreary and discouraged.

[*North Haven, June, 1928*]

Sun out this afternoon. Con and I took a walk over a hill—we looked back and saw yellow daisies against the sky, daisy heads bobbing against the sky. Con and I talked. If I *never* in my life meet anyone else, I have been happier than anyone who ever lived in knowing her. It must be like being in love. I am never envious of her—her writing, her music, anything. I know how wonderful she is. Nothing is too good for her: great fame as a

---

[1] The Morrow summer home, newly constructed at Deacon Brown's Point, on the island of North Haven, Maine.

writer, great skill, airplaning! Colonel L. for a husband—nothing is too good!

My heart is light and full of joy. I should like to sing and sing.

Con said, "What irony of fate made strawberry leaves red!"

To Rockland, shopping. Where does Mother get all her energy from? My knees and back felt like jelly and I had to sit.

A frightful huge antique shop on the sea street. Fat, greasy-haired women flatter you with false bargains and dirty sallow-faced little children slide in and out of the old pieces. They run in and out of an old house—a fine, square, imposing old Maine house that faces the bay. They have littered the old lawn with bric-a-brac, steamer chairs, birdhouses, wicker tables.

I sat on the steps of the old house, looked down the stone path to the bay. Sea-gray flagstones, bordered by old-fashioned flowers: bleeding heart, columbine, bright red poppies, wide-petaled and blowy, and blue lupine. Beyond, the flat blue bay—the sun on it, the sun sliding up and down the white boat sides—and gulls perched on a high pulley of a dock, all faced the same way, like children in school. Then a motorcycle would go by the road and the gulls would all fly across, helter-skelter like blown scraps of paper, their white breasts catching the sunlight like the white boats.

I wished that I might paint. I tried to sort out the colors: harsh red poppies, rust-red pulleys on the wharves, yellow packing boxes on the wharves, reflected in the water. The wharves and wharf-houses were a dingy green. The smoke from some machine was a dingy earth color.

I tried to discover what made it so inexpressibly lovely. It was all reflected in the water, of course.

The brightness of the bay, the blue water, white boats, white gulls, packing boxes, pulleys, seen from the green shady lawn and between the black (in contrast) trunks of elms along the road.

Going home at sunset. The sea becomes sky at this time—so

smooth—and colors like a pigeon's throat (the ring of feathers around their necks—iridescent pink, green, blue, pearl).

Also the bright sides of the white boats are the brightest things there are at that time.

Sailing: that delicious sound—soft, soothing, slow—of the boat pushing through the water. It is lots of summer sounds together. The spray falling sounds like wind in the trees.

Elisabeth reads poetry in the evenings. People are embarrassed and sit staring uncomfortably at one spot, afraid to catch other people's eyes. It gets too personal and all suppressed. I feel as though the roof might pop off.

Elisabeth's beaux look mournfully at each other.

Anne escapes for ginger ale!

Elisabeth and X—Elisabeth falling in love again? It all seems a trifle familiar—this reading of her "special" poetry book, reading poetry all day long to each other and special stories and going off "on the point"—"Lovely, the hills breaking through the mist!" and "When X was a little boy, he told me . . ." Oh, these life histories! And they come in late to lunch, and stop talking when another person comes into the room.

I feel very old and grandmotherly and amused watching it, and a little cynical.

"And when X was *twelve* . . ." "Ah, yes, my dear—I know!"

Rather cynical about falling in love and—a little sad. The "Now-may-the-god-for-blasphemy-so-brave, punish-me-surely with-the-shaft-I-crave"[1] feeling.

I am getting very tired and cross about the beaux. I know it is horrible, but I can't seem to help it. I am sick to death of being the nice younger sister who gets out of the way, who talks sympathetically of the loved one, who sympathizes and concords with the slavish attention inevitably her due. And I am homesick for that warm glow that one feels—that spreads from you in all

[1] Edna St. Vincent Millay.

directions—when you are in the warm sympathetic company of someone who loves you extravagantly.

I want slavish, absurd attention too—I want to look up and find someone watching me. That makes you feel like a candle!

Then I want to sit and listen and have someone talk, tell me things—their life histories!—books they have read, things they have done—new worlds! Not to say anything—to listen and listen and be taught. And then to think,

> "O brave new world,
> That has such people in't."

Oh, it is petty and small, and I grow angry at every little well-known trick and then realize that I really am just the same—want just what she wants.

One frightful night when I sat by the window and wept for hours and contemplated with preposterous seriousness . . . But some calm came of it. After I had slashed down everything, the same things remained: islands in the fog of my emotions and thoughts.

How dearly I love Elisabeth—the clear flame of her. How little anything matters except that.

Very beautiful things outside of people—objective things: color, shape, shadow, line, touch and sight, sound of beautiful things. Losing oneself in these things, fusing oneself in them . . .

Then there are people who stand for clear, fine things—*more than beautiful*—good, true things. President Neilson's love and truth and honesty. Mrs. Neilson's faith, clarity, and sincerity. Humor—wonderful clarifying liquid humor in lots of people. Unselfishness and courage in Mother and Aunt Annie and Elisabeth. I could go on and on.

Then—*Constance.*

Also, I am beginning to think it does no good for me to think about my sins. They just get worse. Forget them in these other things.

The "non-self" is divine.

It then being early morning, I munched a damp digestive cracker and slept.

On the way to Holderness for Grandma's birthday. A long drive—Maine, New Hampshire. Half the day I mulled in my usual fashion over Elisabeth's beaux and what I shall do when Colonel L. comes. (He called up to say he would come, just when we had given up hope.) It has gotten to be a hideous nightmare to me—trying to combat that inevitable envy before it comes, knowing that it will come.

Then suddenly I was able to turn inside out and become completely absorbed in things I saw. I have been blind for weeks now, not looking out of myself at all. Then I suddenly looked up and saw the intensity of a great many things: that silver-white slashes of birches in the woods look like rain, that the after-the-rain coolness reminds me of the mist (cold mist) that came off the moss under the spring rocks in the Catskills, that a field of summer grass sometimes wears an extra bloom (like the bloom on autumn fruit), all the tips of the grasses are reddish.

The pale underside of leaves blown back in a coming storm. These pale faces against dark storm sky—never noticed them before.

Also, there is a kind of terrible beauty in a jaggedly torn branch, stripped off a tree by a storm. Beautiful as lightning and as knifelike, the sharp yellow-white inside bark.

It was joy to do this. One can get just as much exultation in losing oneself in a little thing as in a big thing.

It is nice to think how one can be recklessly lost in a daisy!

Then I made lists for myself of what made New England. I have forgotten now—gray stony fields and gray stone tumble-down walls, and elms, and bay windows with geraniums, and red barns and little fields and lilac bushes—and Queen Anne's lace along the dirt roads, and blue carts. I can't remember the rest.

I wonder if someone has written a poem reversing the Penelope story—someone who made a web at night and (in the cold light of morning and reason) unraveled it each day.

July 13th

Drove back from Holderness. I drove all morning—made very good time. But I drove at my own pleasure. That is, not too fast, steadily and carefully. I felt it was a kind of test. And Burke[1] said I did very well. I was happy and sang all the way.

Then from Brunswick. We had to make the boat. Burke drove Aunt Sue's[2] car—I, the *Memphis*.[3] He said we had to keep up a good clip. We went steadily for sixty miles at a speed—a steady speed—of forty-five to fifty miles around corners, up hills, past cars, bumping over bridges, tearing through towns, on a strange road—and I *mustn't* lose sight of Burke, *must* pass every car he passes, *must* make the hills he makes.

After the first five minutes I was green with fear—terrified. ("My God, *what* am I doing—Burke! Burke! *Stop!* I can't do this, I can't. The strain—I shall plunge into a fence. I haven't got the nerve, the strength. I shall go mad and run into a tree with just a weak cry and my hands over my eyes. God, why do they trust their lives to me? Oh, *Burke. Don't* pass that car—*not so fast,* Burke!) I was sick like that with panic for a moment. (Like a moment before, when, Freshman year, I found myself on the Northampton railroad platform—*alone.*) But I didn't say anything. I sat up very straight, sat forward and *clung* to the wheel, and my eyes glued on the back of that limousine ahead—things spinning and jumping and whirling on all sides of me. I did not even look at the speedometer. My eyes never left the road—I felt complete concentration. (And I did not get as tired as I did in the

[1] Alfred Burke, chauffeur of the Morrow family.

[2] Mrs. Charles Burnett, wife of classmate and friend of D. W. M.

[3] A station wagon named after the cruiser that brought Lindbergh home from France after his flight.

morning.) But that wheel was the only steady thing in the world. After that first moment, the panic left—it was only a second—and then "through the crust of fear" I just felt a kind of subdued exaltation. Myself and the machine under control. And it was a terrific test, and I *must* hold out. *If I could—if I could* . . . Then I could do many things!

I felt as though I were flying.

We got into Rockland. I began to sing, for the first time. I had done it. I felt terribly relieved (also all the passengers) and *much* older! As if I had walked through fire or leaped over a great chasm. I felt like an entirely different person. I had proved *it,* whatever it was! Burke beamed delightedly, said I did wonderfully, told Elisabeth I was an awfully good driver and certainly had "nerve," and what's more was careful, which most fast drivers aren't! Said I had lots of *nerve!* Imagine—no one has ever said that about me before! It is the most exciting praise I ever had, because *I,* only, know the coward I really am. But that I could hide it in sheer will power! *That* is thrilling.

I feel like a transatlantic flier—or a mail pilot!

(There was one moment when it rained and I couldn't see, and I thought it was all up.) How absurd this will sound in fifty years—to be afraid of driving a *car* at the *crawling* speed of forty-five miles an hour!

An airplane goes two hundred miles. Shall I ever drive one? Burke said he thought I'd make an aviator yet. (To Elisabeth.) But Burke doesn't know.

Still, I do feel like a recruit who has just earned his wings.

Letter from V.—a teasing, sparkling, rippling letter, shot through with understanding and humor and familiarity. Oh, it made me so happy and suddenly sure of myself. We can be natural with V. and *he likes* it! The people you can be absolutely sincere with—sincere to the truest you—are the ones I am happiest with.

———

The things that count most for me are: keeping in touch with the people I love; writing and reading and "appreciating," and keeping enough fit physically by exercise, sleep, etc., to really devote myself to doing these things.

Today and these two weeks have been spent on the secondaries: golf, eating (rather, dieting!), recovering, and being perfunctorily social. I am tired of seeing and hearing so many people.

Is it *always* going to be like this?

How *can* one be in love with so many people at the same time! At least I don't know what to call it—the possibility of being in love, perhaps, a kind of keen excitement that they are alive, an excitement that leads sometimes to exhilaration, sometimes to a kind of too-sensitiveness, sometimes embarrassment, and almost always shyness. There is V. and Colonel L. and a touch of it when I see A. C., though I don't know him at all, and the amazingness of L. A. No, it is not being in love, for there is Miss Sturm and Mrs. Neilson and President Neilson and sometimes Mr. Locke and Mrs. Curtiss.

Sometimes it is realizing an amazing "keenness" in someone. Sometimes it is the frightening—almost—breath-taking realization of one's nearness to a person, suddenly finding oneself terrifyingly near another person (in tastes, sympathies, etc.) *without* having progressed there together. They were going along there and so were you! How *could* you *not* have discovered them before (even though not introduced in this visible world of conventions)! As though you had gone along a road in the mist and never knew there was someone else there too.

When you finally *do* meet in the visible world—at a dinner table, say—you feel almost abashed. You know the same country. The intimacy is terrifying, and it is unconventional, and people cannot understand—you aren't *supposed* to know anyone that well. It is somehow indecent, and every quick "Oh, do *you* like that *too?*" is another path that you both know and you can't pretend you haven't been there before.

Lucia's Alan[1] said he thought trees were the most permanently satisfying things there were (in nature). I think so—

(They are so happy and so wonderful together that it gives one faith—like watching President and Mrs. Neilson.) Lucia is three times more beautiful than ever before, and so understanding.

She wears "the bloom."

Alan looks at her the way P. used to look at me.

As for Colonel L., it is something else, of course. Just sentimental hero-worship perhaps, and yet has nothing to do with the flight. Just "Here is the finest man I have ever met" (not the most brilliant or the "keenest" or most cultured or appreciative—those things hardly matter at all in thinking of him), just the *finest, clearest* man I ever imagined, and someone utterly opposite to me. So opposite that I don't exist at all for him or in his world.

V. is here. It is one of those times when you flower. As though you had been all plant and root for ages just taking in sustenance, and suddenly you can *give*—you bloom. I want to show V. all the books I have been reading—all discoveries. It is like setting out for a journey, not knowing exactly where you are going, with all the thrill of discovery ahead and yet no fear.

H.—tawny and vigorous, a courageous girl. A little too showy, and yet she and the "show" are quite distinct and you don't mind.

An Indian summer voice: She opened a new and exciting world—singing. It is such pleasure to be given a little power to control your voice, and so exciting to find how much more you can do, knowing something about it—more volume, more scope, more resonance.

Today, Aunt Alice called from N. Y. Colonel L. is going to see

[1] Lucia Norton Valentine and Alan Valentine, Dean of Men at Swarthmore College, later President of Rochester University.

Elisabeth in New York, and of course not coming up here. Elisabeth of course again.

It was like that sudden falling down you have in a dream—ka-plunk—and I have woken up.

But it is not so bad now. "When I was fearing it, it came." It was inevitable and now I feel almost reconciled. The tooth is pulled.

That dream is peacefully dead—speedy burial advised.

Con and I stayed awake hours, getting hysterical discussing the wedding (we feel it's inevitable now).

And the publicity—it would be a world joke and a world romance. It sounds like the *Saturday Evening Post*. It is too absurd. Think of what Will Rogers[1] would say! There would be cartoons about it and popular songs and a special number of *Life!*

It would be too *superb!* Think of Mrs. Lindbergh and Mother in the front pew! And Phil Love[2] for best man!

V. and Con and I are so happy. I wake happy every morning to remember that there is another day—a beautiful, clear, blue day; water sparkling, trees cut against the sky, grass fresh and clean, lots of white clouds like clothes on a line. Living is just like those days now.

And long talks—much too serious young talks.

It isn't the pleasure (very momentary) that one has sometimes talking with someone and bringing things to them and having them agree. V. doesn't listen that way, or take. He is there before you, with a new light, a new twist on it, arguing or questioning.

A walk in the rain—my old brown coat much too large, and rain against one's face. And a scramble over rocks, through the

[1] Will Rogers, 1879–1935, known as the "cowboy philosopher, had a great success in motion pictures, the radio, and with a newspaper column.

[2] Philip R. Love had been a cadet in Lindbergh's class at Brooks and Kelly Fields in Texas, 1924–25. Lindbergh chose him as one of the pilots for the St. Louis–Chicago air-mail route in 1926.

brambles—lost—and wild raspberries: "Five lovely ones—for *me!*"

Superb absurdities, laughing *delightedly* over them, like V.'s idea to plan out a dinner for guests who are hard to talk to. Give them squab (or lobster claws), artichokes, and corn on the cob, etc., etc.!

Then, too, V. does a strange thing for me. Courage and cowardice stand out more clearly in their bleak contrast. That is, I have a clearer sense of what, in my actions, is cowardly. Instead of slurring over something in my mind, I can see, "No, that is weak—that is cowardly," or, "No, that is mean and sneaking." A sharpening of my moral sense, it is, I guess.

I had not expected it this summer. And then, to have it given you. I didn't know life did such things. *". . . et on s'aperçoit que la vie n'est pas aussi triste qu'on l'avait jugée!"*[1] It is so like the letter—the French letter: *"Faire de beaux rêves, etc. Un sentiment d'amère réflexion est donc le résultat de cette première épreuve. Le cœur blessé dans son essence même, dans son premier élan, saigne et semble à jamais déchiré. Cependant on vit—et il faut aimer pour vivre encore; on aime avec crainte, avec défiance, et, peu à peu, on regarde autour de soi et on s'aperçoit que la vie n'est pas aussi triste qu'on l'avait jugée. Le cœur plus ferme, accepte les obstacles, les chagrins, les dégoûts même; sûr de lui, il les prévient, les combat, et les change quelquefois en biens. Plus résigné, il jouit mieux des jours heureux, les appelle avec plus d'ardeur, les prolonge avec plus de soin. Il en vient enfin à se dire:*

'Le mal n'est rien, puisque le bonheur existe.'

Laissez battre votre cœur, laissez vous aimer, laissez faire le destin. Il y a de beaux jours ici-bas!"[2]

---

[1] ". . . and you realize that life is not as sad as you judged it to be."

[2] "Dreaming beautiful dreams, etc. . . . . The outcome of this first test, then, is a sense of bitter thinking. Wounded in its first upsurge, in its very essence, the heart bleeds and appears torn for ever. And yet you live and you have to love in order to continue living; you love with apprehen-

Enter the M—'s, bright clear morning. Mr. M. with his fierce bulldog look; Mrs. M. clear-eyed, quick, seeing everything, knowing everything, and the searchlight of her penetrating humor on everything—hard and bright. With Mrs. M. I felt young, terribly, terribly young and rather ridiculous as though in the presence of someone who knew the world and I knew nothing. And yet I cannot keep my eyes off her and always listen to her. She is so charming. Mr. M., a courageous man, is quiet, listening, watching—I have never seen a more courageous, straightforward man.

It is a great joy to listen to Mrs. M. Her thoughts hit the mark like clean arrows—so sharp, so fine. (One ought to be able to get along with the mediocre people—it is not good to be always with the people who are like you.) She has courage and wit and perception and sympathy and tolerance and true sophistication—knowledge of the world, remarkable insight into relationships, and the intuition and eye of an artist.

I think she sees much further than I can see, but I see a little: that V. has much, much more exciting things, exciting worlds of power and work and beauty to break into. He enjoys just now exchanging perceptions, ideas, books with me. But he will go so far beyond, and so will I, and perhaps, after all, talking with two introspective girls, being attracted by their minds, is better than necking parties.

Tonight I sat and waited on the dock for the Fays and Lockes to come across to supper. It was very still and cool. Put-put-put in

---

sion, with defiance, and little by little, looking around you, you realize that life is not as sad as you had judged it to be. A steadier heart accepts the obstacles, the sorrows, the disgusts even; sure of itself, it anticipates them, fights them, and sometimes changes them into blessings. Having learned resignation, it enjoys the happy days more fully, expects them with greater ardor, prolongs them with greater care. Finally it reaches the point of telling itself: Suffering is nothing, since happiness exists. Allow your heart to beat, allow yourself to be loved, allow fate to take its course. There are lovely days on this earth." [Anonymous] the distance. Gulls side-slipping, turning. I sat in a corner—people went by and didn't notice me. A man below dipped his oars gently in the water and let them drip circles. Put-put-put—they were coming. I heard the scrape as the boat landed against the dock, and their chatter and broken phrases and the float creaking as they stepped on it. I did not get up from my shadow, I didn't move, a minute more and they would be upon me. I dreaded it as though I were standing on the edge of a pool, dreading the chill shock of jumping in.

"Why, Anne, my dear—"

One day to Rockland. Came back at night in mist: boats in harbor, great dim shadow skeletons (four-masters) with one faint gold light.

Mist around us, not close, but a circle of mist and stars above, and then the moon, a chill glow, a befuddled moon and, soft on the water, silver shavings—a cold unearthly light, and no sound but our motor, no sight of land or ship or light. Then on the other side suddenly we notice that vague arc of white light—deeper now. A great white arc—a moon rainbow! But it looked like the back of some fiery planet rising from the sea—just the bright light from its fiery side glowing over the edges.

But a cold, unearthly light—not a trace of fire in it, not a trace of gold or earth, just cold, back-of-the-moon light, as if we were under the sea, or far, far north (the feel of great planets, worlds, swinging round us).

An Ancient Mariner feeling, too:

> "We were the first that ever burst
> Into that silent sea."

Stopping dead in this unearthly light to listen for the bell buoy, the engine sputtering out, dying feebly. The chill, distant sound of the bell—slow—chill.

Then the moon brighter in a nest of iridescent rings! And the moonbow brighter at the ends.

Coming into vague headlands melting one behind another. The warm little gold lights on anchored ships and from the town—warm, earthy lights. All the boats turned the same way, silent, like dogs leashed.

I am convinced this summer that I must never let myself slip completely out of the stream. It is so easy to do, such a frightful temptation, to get along with just a few chosen people—or *the lack of them!* To cherish the lack of them to the exclusion of all other people. Never, *never* give in to it (Aunt Annie said). It gets harder and harder, and one is always glad when one breaks through the shell of solitariness, to find the stimulation of people—different people.

Then I have a firm realization, too, that one can give oneself out in a very exhilarating way—that one can go out almost physically into a field of green, glossy-leaved, shaking corn, or a birch gleaming unexpectedly white in green leaves, or even stones or the turn of a road.

It is a funny experience but quite definite and a great relief to find it so real. As real as losing oneself in music, or a person. It is as real a change as that "out-curve" in singing that H. showed me, or suddenly when the sun goes down being able to open eyes wide and look *out*.

Aunt Annie—very wonderful, alive, keen, quick, perceptive, young, appreciating everything—how has she kept herself that alive, that keen to see, hear, and feel everything? Her brown face, very sweet mouth, eyes bright and almost hard in their quickness to see the ridiculous—playing charades, her face mischievous and young under a silly hat and her feet on the rung of the chair.

"Will power has nothing to do with being happy." What did she mean by that?

And about not being married. "Listen to me—*you don't want to live half a life.*"

I want to be married, but I never, never will.

———

One night a moonlight picnic, a great wind and the sea stormy, a strange blue light on the tops of the waves, two red sparky fires, and on the bay the moon splinters, almost blue.

I went back to the house for things, and when I tried to find my way back to the beach, the fires, the people, I got lost for a while. I couldn't hear anything but the long breath of the sea and the wind. The moonlight made strange shadows of the pine trees. I floundered about in marshy ground with Daffin a little white ghost skidding along behind me. I had a sudden feeling that it was perhaps all a dream and I was walking in my sleep, that the picnic—red fires, sparks, people with half-lit faces bending over baskets, ginger ale bottles, laughter, snatches of songs, frying pans, driftwood—that it was all in my imagination. Or that, like Rip Van Winkle, I had slept a hundred years, and the picnic was swept away aeons ago.

Then around the curve the reassuring red glow of sparks between the trees.

Singing around the fire, the wind roaring.

Duncan [the boatman] not at the dock to take Bunny[1] across the Thoroughfare. I was cold. The moon was shining blue across the choppy water, the boats bobbing. No one around.

"*Row* across!"

I did not feel like it but tried to be cheerful. We started. The boat chopped up and down, wind blew, we sang. It was very exhilarating. The hard pull: the wind against one's face, moonlight in one's eyes. One could see everything clearly in the bright light of the moon—boats bobbing, with here and there a red light on the mast, the dark shadowed shore on the other side and a few lights. Bitta singing the high part of the Volga boat song.

We made no headway around the Point and decided to tie the boat and walk up to the Lockes' by the road. We left the boat chopping and chafing against the wharf and stole quietly up the gangplank, across someone's lawn, silver grass, shadows, around

[1] Bunny and "Bitta" [Laura] Fay, daughters of Professor Fay.

under an apple tree and a white house—still and bright and the light glistening on all the leaves—up a long grassy dip, the trees strange blue shadows.

"The Witches' Sabbath!" Bunny flapped her coat like wings.

Up the wood road—the sound of our feet pounded on the dirt. White bright birches gleaming, white flowers growing high by the side, and the bright leaves quivering, glinting, turning, and strange blue shadows from familiar things. The trees, a weather vane, weeds towered above us (we seemed much smaller) and quivered silver—and that distant long breath of the sea and wind (we were inland now). Everything with its breath caught, listening, and we were listening—no sound, no lights, just that thud of our feet thundering (it seemed) along the road.

A fruity smell as we passed a group of huddled apple trees. Coming back up that grassy dip again, past the glistening silver apple tree, little apples shining, and the white house shining, I felt as though I could not reach out my hand, it was so beautiful. I wanted to touch the shiny little apples, and yet I was afraid—as though that would break the spell, as though things would shatter around me if I did—all these "things" that were holding their breath to let me pass.

But I did! I had the feeling—which I have not had since I was much younger—of great ecstasy at seeing anything so beautiful, enough to make you catch your breath, as if you couldn't bear it. It was too much to bear that night.

When we got home safe to the fire, I felt as though I had been years away—another world, an ocean voyage.

And it seemed to me that it is terrifying how nearly one comes to missing such revelations. To think that chasm of beauty was so near, and I was timidly and safely just stepping on the edge. I did not want to go.

It is strange, but often one comes on them that way: a bad accident, and then reality so beautiful, so rare.

I remember getting the car stuck far from Northampton, and a great yellow moon rose—

My period of great activity for the year is over, I think. I saw more people and did more and felt more in a few days this autumn than I often do for a year.

I was almost like Mother in what I "got in."

[*Englewood*]
Wednesday morning

Colonel L. called me up.

He wanted Mother or Daddy or Elisabeth. But Jo said (like a scheming stepmother with an ugly-duckling daughter), *"Miss* Morrow is abroad but Miss *Anne* Morrow is here." At which he grunted and asked for me. But I wasn't home, and he called up again! There's glory for you.

I arrive on the midnight. Jo says, "Guess who called up yesterday?"

A.: "?"

J.: *"Charles Augustus L."*

.   .   .   .

J.: "He is going to call up at ten today."

(It was then 9:30. Something inside me turns over. But I can't realize it—too vague. Thought he had gone like "a dutiful bream.")

"Bzzzz . . ."

Jo (shuts the door with firm, quiet, and kind of "Now you've got to face it" voice): "There he is—for Miss Anne Morrow."

A. (hysterically): "Jo, I *can't*—I simply *can't*—*I can't speak to him.*"

J.: "You've *got* to, Anne. Go ahead—it won't be long."

A. (Sits in front of telephone, looking at it paralyzed, gulping, like standing in front of a glass of castor oil, wondering whether one *can* bridge the gulf and take it. Then takes up the telephone and very weakly and questioningly): "Hello-o?"

From far away, a low gray voice, abrupt and rather shy, and

words snapped off at the ends: "Hello. This is . . . Lindbergh himself."

A. (very weak and shy): "How—how do you do."

(A very audible grin on the other end, a shy laugh.)

C. (bolting out the words—shot out, all prepared, a definite statement he had to make, and _he made it,_ going straight to the point): "When I was south last winter I promised to take you up sometime here in the East. I called up to tell you I'd be very glad to arrange a flight, if you'd care to go . . . ?"

A. (Long "taken-aback" pause): "I—I'd love to. . . ."

C.: "Any time you say, at all."

A.: "But—you—you're very busy, aren't you?"

C.: "What's that?"

A.: _"You're very busy—aren't you?"_

(How dumb that sounded, _louder._)

C. (abruptly): "Not particularly."

Pause.

A.: "Well, I'm afraid I have to be away for . . . about five days . . . beginning today." (Disappointed.)

C. (always picking me up quickly, as though rather impatient to be off—naturally!): "Well, say sometime after Saturday?"

A.: (completely blurred and helplessly lost): "Is . . . is that five days after today?" (I was vaguely _sure_ it was Wednesday.)

C.: Much audible grinning.

A.: "Just a minute. Would you mind if I went and found out . . . I'm not sure when they'll let me out."

C.: "Certainly."

A.: "They say I won't be out till a week[1] (deciding I was too much bother and to give him a chance to get out), so I'm terribly afraid . . . that will be too late for you. You were _very_ kind to ask, and I'd love to go, but I'm afraid . . . ?"

C. (now definitely impatient but good-natured): "No, I'm going to be around for some time now, any time at all you say, next week—any time you say."

[1] A. M. L. was going to the hospital for a minor operation.

A. (*at last decided*): "I wonder—would it be too much bother if you called up in a week? I think I'll be all right then." (I certainly sounded like a lunatic or a jailbird: ". . . when they'll let me out"—"I'll be all right then," etc.!)

C.: "Certainly—ten o'clock next Wednesday?" (*Typical!* To the dot!)

A.: "That would be fine. . . ." (Pause. I *must* get in something about the family. He is talking to *them,* not me. *Desperately.*) "My father . . . will be very pleased that I've spoken to you—I'll tell him."

C. (Much audible grinning, a little embarrassed, trying to think of something to say. Then finally grasping on rock fact again): "Well—ten o'clock next Wednesday, then."

A.: "Thank you very much, Colonel Lindbergh."

TO C. C. M.   *The Presbyterian Hospital in the City of New York* [*October 8, 1928*] *Monday*

Darling—

It is very difficult somehow to write here, even though I have been here almost six days, I still feel so strange and lightheaded when I sit up. I can't do it for very long. Today I tried to walk a few steps and I felt like the light Princess when she became heavy! What uncontrollable things legs are! It is really quite nice now, for I do not feel sick or nauseated or in pain. I love lying in bed playing poetry games. This is a wonderful one for going to sleep: Say two lines, then take the last letter of the last line and begin another two with it! See! It is endless—idiot's delight. Only it is so difficult to find lines beginning with *E* and most lines end with it!

ex. 1 "The world is too much with us; late and soon,
       Getting and spending, we lay waste our power*S.*"

   2 "*S*ince there's no help, come, let us kiss and part!
       Nay, I have done, you get no more of m*E.*"

3 *"E*xultation is the going
   of an inland soul to se*A*."

4 *"A*ll small forgotten things that once meant yo*U"*—
   etc., etc.

Darling, I loved your sweet letter. You are a saint to be happy about Colonel L. But honestly it ought to be you—I don't even want it enough. But perhaps that's the hospital. I can't see how I can go up in a plane next week when it makes me dizzy now even to *sit* up! I will write you everything.

Won't you *please please* write me something about your subject[1] because it's my one clue to conversation. (We probably won't have any—he goes at it as though it were a business transaction or a doctor's pill that *He* has to take.) And if we do converse on "Miss Constance," he will ask questions. Safety in what kind of flying? Commercial? Professional? Amateur? Are you taking the stand that any or all of these *are* safe now, or are you pointing out improvements that will *make* them safe? Could you give me just a few points so I could see what lines your speech will take?

Also, of course you won't say a word to anyone about his calling up. I haven't even written Dwight because things leak out so abominably—even if you just mention a name casually, you know. It would be awful if this Elisabeth rumor blew up again. You know—you understand—

Also, do you think I could drive out there alone? I'd like to, but I think Jo wants to go. Now, *what* am I to do? *Damn!*

Also, would you like me to get a map of Lindbergh's flights for your wall? I don't want to send it and embarrass you if you don't want it.

Anyway, I have a foreboding that I won't get out and on my feet before it's too late and "the bird has flown." That would be typical of *them* to do, wouldn't it! Must rest now.

---

[1] C. C. M. was making a speech at school on "The Safety of Aviation."

TO C. C. M.   *The Presbyterian Hospital in the City of New York [October 8, 1928]*

Darling—

I forgot to say, please don't write Mother that I might go up with Colonel L. Because I'm afraid she might telegraph me not to go! And that would be *too awful.* I wrote her that he telephoned.

     Adios—

       Anne

Afterwards. It doesn't matter.

DIARY

Home! I sat in the sun on the steps after an ecstatic drive home. I feel as though I'd been shut up for years. The trees—oh, the trees are so crisp and beautiful, all gold, and the sky so blue and a sheen on everything from the sky—all blowy and dazzling. I sat on the steps and the afternoon was some kind of wine, a gold brown. Two chipmunks chased each other around the sweet-gum tree. The sky was warm, rich blue through the big oak.

I was warm and tired and deliciously convalescent—delicious to walk, to stretch languidly—sun in one's eyes, brown leaves on the grass and yellow maples.

Evening

The telephone bell has a horribly paralyzing effect when one expects someone exciting to call. It is like having a giant bee sting you—you can feel the sharp prick of pain and then just paralyzing numbness swells in a lump around you. Colonel L. called—having called at ten to find me in the hospital—at seven. Really I heard Emily say, "Yes, sir—yes," and my insides *pained* as they turned over, *ka-plunk,* inside me, and I felt faint. Upstairs, threw open the window—cold air good, felt choked. Looked at "castor oil," gulped, took it!

"Hello—hello."

"Hello, this is Lindbergh speaking."

And I burst into a flood of "Oh, Colonel Lindbergh, I am so

terribly sorry about this morning," and he laughed very kindly and good-naturedly. "Oh, don't be sorry."

A.: "You see, they didn't let me out of the hospital until this afternoon. I gave them my number there to give you. I didn't mean to be rude."

C. (very kindly, and laughing a little embarrassedly): "Oh, that's perfectly all right." (Then starting right in—a dive for business:) "I called up to see if you wanted to go on that flight. . . ."

Then suddenly I found that he was "coming out" to "talk over a few points" about it. It was so frightfully sudden, and just like him. It is so disconcerting for me to have someone against me who is *so* precise.

C.: "Well, about what time could I come?"

A.: "Tomorrow?"

C.: "Tomorrow—what time?"

A.: "Tomorrow, well . . . (I *hate* being beaten to the wall like this) *any time*—I'll be here all day. It really doesn't matter. Tomorrow afternoon. . . ."

C. (audible grins): "Well, *what time* tomorrow afternoon? Any time you say."

A. (cornered and beaten but still fighting!): "Well, any time after three?"

C.: "Well, tomorrow at four, shall we say?"

A.: "That will be fine."

C.: "I'll see you tomorrow, then." (Well, there wasn't any question as to *what day,* anyway! No self-respecting question or doubt could raise its head after such a bombardment.)

Then I was completely upset for the rest of the evening—frightfully excited. Now it is humorous again and I am the poised "woman of the world" (!) laughing amusedly at his naïve direct-ness—his obstinate clinging to facts, facts, facts. The small-boy simplicity. The way he looks at this—an apple he is handing me, a good little girl whose father has been nice to him. And like a small boy, action, *decided* action, follows thought at an amazing speed. There are no complications: "Good day for fishing." Off! Presto! Like that.

I can be amused, but oh, what happens to me when he is there on the telephone or in person—I am the swollen bee-bite.

Well, four o'clock tomorrow business with Colonel L. on subject of flight. He will rattle off the points, shake hands, and bolt. (How simple is life for the small boy.)

And I—thoroughly upset, sick with excitement, shy, awkward, adoring—trying to make my world meet his somewhere—a person I have only one thing in common with: youth.

Well, that's over. Colonel L. came. I had all the poise in the world. But he is so obviously doing it out of duty, it was humiliating. I feel so sorry for him, but not worshipful.

TO C. C. M.   *Englewood* [*October 12, 1928*]
Darling—
Colonel L. was late!!!!

Isn't that *superb!* I have never been so happy. You see, he called up again and said He'd like to "settle a few points" about the flight (doesn't that sound impressive!) and could he come out and talk to me about them? And *suddenly* I found myself planning to see him at four—today—here!! At three I took a fifteen-minute rest. At 3:45 I walked into the garden to read. (I knew that doorbell would make me *die* of paralysis.) At five minutes of four I was hysterically thinking over things to calm me: (1) "This isn't an operation or anything. It isn't any of those hideous things in the hospital. *Why, why, why* that feeling in your tummy?"

(2) This is all positive—it *can't* be a failure or wretched, because it's all to the good, an *extra;* it doesn't count.

(3) It is just a business arrangement.

(4) He is just talking to your father's daughter. You're not there at all, so you can't be embarrassed!

(5) (The last straw—I am *always* using this.) *"Anyway, you can't be more embarrassed or awkward or ridiculous than you were the last time,* so what's the dif? But 4—4:05—4:10— Then he telephoned. He is delayed—delayed, delayed. How joyful that he is delayed! (Sounds like a Gilbert and Sullivan chorus, doesn't it?) ⧖ He is held up and cross and apologetic. *Cheers!!* (cymbals)

And I am so relieved and poised for a while.

Darling, if you were only here then I would be happy and natural and we could enjoy it so, together. And it would be righter. Oh, *I want you here*—everything would be all right if you were here. *You* could talk to him and be un-self-conscious (you always are, apparently) and poised and intelligent, and he would be pleased and grin and not be abrupt and embarrassed and bored. I am sitting on the steps, facing the garden all tangled over and sprinkled with curled-up brown leaves. And I am looking at those two lovely big trees—"the married ones" I always called them because they stand together so nicely, protecting each other, one a little shorter than the other and more delicate—do you remember? *He*—the big oak—is touched with red and *she* is frail and lacy at the top; a cool, gold-green evening sky behind them.

I will finish this after he comes.

. . . .

Oh, Con, if *only* it had been you. Oh, it was *awful*—simply terrible—nothing that I expected. I feel so miserably unhappy and uncomfortable and angry—and flat. The only nice part for him or me was when I talked about you. Then we were both happy. I will tell you all about it.

He arrived—driven—and I walked out of the shrubbery and met the chauffeur asking for Mr. D. Morrow's place and He jumped out and was embarrassed to see me there, ready and waiting! Oh, it was *awful*. Strangely enough, *I* wasn't embarrassed at all but quite poised and cool during the whole thing—

only *very* unhappy—and we exchanged a few politenesses and apologies and so forth and then entered the house. Lord, he is tall!—I had forgotten—and thin and *fair,* so young-looking, not stern at all but quite sunny. (That sounds odd, but you know what I mean—his face quite sunburned, not tan, and he blushed quite a lot and his hair is so *fair,* and he grins such a lot.)

The first thing he said (in an abrupt, hard, direct way, as though a rebuke to me for being so forward—as though to say, "Don't think I have the slightest interest in *you* or any young girls") when he got inside the door was "Is Mrs. Graeme here? I'd like very much to see her." I said she would be down in a moment. Then he strolled, in that long amble, with one hand in pocket, and sat down in the Morris chair by the fire, and I think he started in on where I'd like to go—which I didn't know—and what kind of plane, and I said, "An open one!" and he said, "All right, an open plane." Then as to where we'd meet, and he bolted out suddenly, "Well, we can't go to any of the fields or we'd be engaged the next day" with an embarrassed laugh and his eyes wrinkled up and a little red. And I was so startled and laughed and blushed a little (I think) but *looked right at him* (it's better to do that when you're embarrassed) with an "I'm so sorry for you" look.

A.: "Oh, I know—I'm *so* sorry. That would be awful!" (I said it with such a long face, too! That was tactful of me.) Then he blushed a little more and with an almost hard humor said, "I've been engaged to two girls in one week and I haven't seen either of them."

A.: "Oh, I'm sorry—it's awful. Well, don't bother about me— I'll meet you anywhere you want."

So then he said we could use a field near the Guggenheims'.[1]

Then followed a long altercation. He said he would pick me

---

[1] Harry F. Guggenheim and his wife, Carol, close friends of C. A. L., who wrote most of *We* in their home at Port Washington, Long Island, 1927. He was President of the Daniel Guggenheim Fund for the Promotion of Aeronautics, 1926–30.

Popocatepetl

Ixtacihuatl

Charles A. Lindbergh, Mexico, Christmas, 1927

Anne Morrow
in Esmond Ovey's
garden,
Cuernavaca, Mexico,
Easter, 1928

Commencement, Smith College. Center, Anne Morrow, June, 1928

*Deacon Brown's Point, the Morrow summer home
in North Haven, Maine*

The Camden Hills from Deacon Brown's Point

Ambassador and Mrs. Morrow in Casa Mañana, Cuernavaca, 1928

Ambassador Morrow with Mexican potter.
George Rublee, background left

Garden and pool of Casa Mañana: seated, Mrs. Rublee,
Mrs. Morrow, Elisabeth Morrow, Herschel Johnson {U.S. Embassy},
George Rublee

*Charles Lindbergh and Anne Morrow in the cockpit of his
Curtiss Falcon biplane, before flying over Popocatepetl,
November, 1928*

Next Day Hill, Englewood, N. J.

PHOTO BROWN BROTHERS

Anne Morrow, 1928

up in the city. I said I could get out there myself—it would be easier and less embarrassing for him. He disagreed and then would look perfectly solemn and say, "Just whatever you'd like," and then when I'd try to get directions he would stubbornly get back to his "I *still* think the best thing would be for me to pick you up in the city." So I had to give in.

But *where* to meet? No apartment. We haggled over that. Oh, it was awful. I had the feeling all the time that it was the most *hideous* bother for him, he didn't want to go, it was embarrassing for him. He was just doing it out of a sense of duty and not disguising it a bit.

I can't remember the sequence, but when we were not talking business He asked immediately, "When is Elisabeth coming back?" (with a faint quaver in his glance, the engagement discussion still humming in his ears). So I told him all the news—where she was, where you were, where Dwight was—and added very sincerely, "I'm awfully sorry they're all away, that I'm the only one here." And he grinned very kindly.

He thought you were still in Mexico and was very amused at my saying, "How queer it was to be the head of the family, taking people to school." Then I said (relief in my mind to have something to please him)—

A.: "I think Con ought to have this instead of me—she is so much more intelligent about planes than I am."

His face *really* lit up—more than it had at all. *Honestly.* He looked so terribly pleased, really sunny. And I was so happy, I beamed. There, I had really touched him and he looked up quickly from the address he was writing, looked really interested and said, "Is she really?"

A.: "Yes, she really is—she has looked up quite a lot about it."

C. (very quickly): "I'll take her up sometime."

A.: "Well, she would *love* that. Didn't you make a speech lately? She wanted me to hear it."

C.: "No (smiling). I *read* a speech."

A.: "Well, she wanted me to put off everything to hear you, so I could give her points on it. You see, she is making a speech before the school, and she has decided to make it on *The Safety of Aviation.*"

C. He grinned delightedly. And then, with an ironical smile, *"The Safety of Aviation*—well, *I'm* not a very good one for *that* subject. Just what is she talking about—what points?" (*I knew* he'd say that. Why *didn't* you *write* me!)

A.: "I don't know. She might be persuaded to change the subject, if you . . ."

C.: "No (with great seriousness and respect), no, that's a 'vurry' good subject indeed—'vurry' good."

Then he said he would get some things from the Guggenheim Foundation: "That is just their subject. I'll have them for you Monday."

Oh, yes, and he wanted to know how technical—"technical or otherwise?"

I said you could stand it quite technical but I didn't think the school could.

He asked me when I was going to Mexico and I sighed not very audibly and he grinned and said, "What's the matter—aren't you anxious to go?" And I explained that I didn't like the things I would *have* to do.

"Have to do?" with a grin, and then, getting it, "Oh—going to receptions and that?" and I nodded and he grinned, and I added that I was afraid I couldn't be as rude as I wanted to be.

"Rude?"

"Yes, I can't say *no* if I don't want to see people."

"You can't say that you don't want to see them!" (He seemed to find that very amusing. He threw back his head and grinned.)

Then I went off into a discussion of how I didn't bother much generally with people I didn't want to see. He sat bored and startled, not getting it at all.

He made some very intelligent remarks about Daddy down in Mexico.

Then I went to get the delaying Jo—"Yes indeed, I'd like vurry much to see her." So Jo came down and I went out for ginger ale and came back. He asked about Mexico. Jo said of me, "She doesn't want to go very much."

C.: "Well, I must say I would feel the same way if I had to be there for vurry long—though (with a worried and swift glance at me) it is vurry enjoyable for a short period." (Almost slipped up *there*, old boy!)

"But it's a *whole year*," I said.

He smiled. "That's not vurry long."

Jo: "And you break it at Christmas."

A.: "Yes" (beaming).

C.: "Oh, you're coming up for Christmas." (He looked very pleased.)

He asked a lot of questions about E., calling her "Elisabeth": when she was coming back, was she going down to Mexico, would she be there all winter? I think, Con—I really do—that our mad dreams that night are not so astray!

Then he got nervous—said he had to be back for a 7:15 dinner. (His coat doesn't fit him any better—the wrist watch shows way up his wrist.) I said calmly (mistaking the time), "You'll be late." (*That* was tactful, too.) He blushed a little. "Not *as* late, this time." A.: "You'd better run. It *is* an awful trip." He said the "not at alls" and got up awkwardly to leave. To me: "Well, glad to have seen you again" and went out, a little bewildered, giving that funny sort of salute wave from the porch to both of us standing in the door—I behind Jo. Now, if you think that was anything wonderful, you don't know the half of it, dearie.

I can't explain how hideously I felt. Lord, that man is cold—he is the coolest man I've ever met. I just felt terribly unhappy that he had to go through with this "flight." It was so obvious that he was embarrassed, that he was bored, that it was a frightful lot of trouble for him to sneak around and plan it—and all for *duty's sake*. He didn't want me in the first place. He called up Elisabeth.

It's always that on-his-guard attitude. ("Don't think I like you at all. It's just a piece of duty.")

I feel terribly sorry for him—that he's in for me—and yet on the other hand a little insulted: I'm not used to being treated like a spoonful of medicine that's got to be taken!

My only consolation was in having complete control of myself: that was gratifying. I felt perfectly poised and perfectly natural and could talk perfectly naturally. I didn't stutter or blush or choke, the way I invariably did in Mexico. It was much better than Mexico. But then why, why, why did he treat me like an ugly sea parasite with tentacles reaching out for him?

Do you remember Katherine Mansfield's saying in a letter, "Why do you treat me as though I had gotten in a family way and was driving round to your front door for you to make an honest woman of me?" *I* don't want to marry him—God forbid.

I don't even want to go up in the plane. I hate people making a terrific fuss to do something for me, when it's just out of duty. I don't *like* taking things that way.

I wish he'd act as though I *liked* aviation. I don't dare show how much I do for fear of his seeing those *tentacles*.

I'd like to listen to him on aviation. That is the most interesting thing now to me about him—not the personality that people worship.

Oh, God—what a jolly ride we'll have out to Long Island Monday afternoon.

New York, October 14, 1928

Dearest Con—

Today is Sunday. I wonder what you did. I wonder if you have lots of those trees that are big and have those almost square leaves that turn bright gold. Each leaf is distinct. It really looks like a tree covered with gold coins.

Laura and Jo and M. R. and I went to Irene Bordoni's *Paris* the other night. Some awfully good songs—one called "Let's do it—let's fall in love." *Millions* of verses all going something like this:

> Japs do it
> Croats do it,
> Up in Lapland little Lapps do it,
> Let's do it—
> *Let's fall in love!*
> Finns do it,
> Swedes do it (??),
> In Lithuania little *Letts* do it,
> Let's do it
> *Let's fall in love!*

It was rather crude in spots but quite gay and a relief. Then Laura, Jo, and I went to a concert. Have you ever noticed the man with the cymbals? He is so funny, especially when he tries to still the excited cymbal: he hugs it to him in a frightened manner as if trying to hush a naughty baby. My thoughts turned to the cymbal player this afternoon. I wondered how one knew that one had a genius for cymbals—as a child, I mean. Do you think as a child he clashed kettle tops together, or as a waiter in a hotel tried his hand at clapping soup tureen covers against plates? And where does he practice! Can you see him clashing those disks all alone by the hour in the bathtub?

I'll have really exciting things tomorrow. You *Pill*—why haven't you written me something about your subject? What am I to say to him tomorrow? It made him so happy and it was the only thing he liked—talking about you. Well, imagine me tomorrow in light gray riding trousers, an old leather coat, town hat and street slippers, meeting Colonel L. in the Blisses' apartment! "And *this* is that attractive Morrow girl!" Oh, dear—I'm not frightened of him any more, but I *hate* bothering him. I wish he knew it.

TO C.C.M. The Westbury Hotel, New York [October 16th?]
Started, the night of the flight—

I am in such a daze that I don't know whether I can write clearly. Two impressions stand out clearly:

I. Flying *is practically* possible for you and Elisabeth and me!!!

II. Colonel L. is the kindest man alive *and* approachable, *and* we *are* going to see him, casually or not, but *certainly* in the future. He *really does* like us!

The whole thing is so unbelievable it seems like a dream. I shall try to remember.

Well, I met him at the Blisses' apartment at 11:30 A.M. in *your* riding trousers, Mother's woolen shirt, my street hat and shoes, and enormous thick gray golf stockings of Daddy's stretching my shoes to busting point. Also my red leather coat. Gosh, what a mess I looked. I thought boots would be too clumsy, and I had only high-heeled shoes to wear over those *hideous* gray stockings. Also, I carried (not wore) the leather coat and put on—to hide everything—Mother's blue Burberry. I was quite sick with fear and misery. He arrived and *roared* when I showed him the lack of boots and the high-heeled shoes. He said the boots would have helped to weigh me down if I had to jump. "But I hope we don't have to use it!" with a grin. About bringing me back: "I'll bring her back" to Jo.

A. (with great sincerity): "Now *really*, please don't let me be any more bother than is necessary."

C. (with a slight twinkle, looking straight at me): "It's no bother at all." (Do you remember the way his voice goes up at the end of a sentence? A sort of slurring it over and then a rise on the "all." I'll imitate it for you sometime! "It's no bother at all. I have to come into town, anyway."

A. (still insisting): "But it's been a lot of trouble already, getting a parachute and lunch. Really, you don't have to worry about me—I don't have to have lunch."

C. (*broad* grin, throwing back his head with that short laugh): "Well, *I* find it more convenient *myself*" (to have some). Then, turning to me: "Well, any time you're ready?" We were in the Blisses' elevator hall. I said, "This doesn't seem quite right—Con and Elisabeth ought to be here."

C.: "Well, I'll take her up sometime, and your sister Elisabeth too."

A.: "That would be lovely—only I'd like to see them having such a good time." He smiled appreciatively.

We got into his car, a new Franklin sedan—very nice, black I think, with a lion (quite a small silver one—I mean not a Bronx Zoo one!) sitting on the radiator. *He* was driving. He put on his hat, turned down in front. Also he had a bright, beautiful blue tie! (In the elevator I told him how nice it was to be doing anything I wanted to so much and have it all right. I told about going up in Northampton. He grinned and hoped I had permission this time!)

Con, I simply can't get through this whole day—it is too much. I don't think I can remember or write down everything.

He said we were going up in a small "De Havilland Moth"— the kind that Lady Somebody flew to South Africa. I hoped it wasn't more trouble getting an open plane? He said, No, it showed very good judgment. He was tired of his closed plane and liked an open one. We took *ages* getting out of the city. He didn't know the one-way streets or traffic laws and kept asking me, and was very funny about it. Nobody—hardly *anyone*— recognized him. Once or twice they looked at him queerly. Once in a jam a toughie walked up to the window, shouting and putting out his hand: "Hello, Colonel—*I recognized* you!" Colonel L. looked *hard* ahead of him and pushed up the window. "That's *that*," he said in a firm, hard voice. I remarked that they didn't do it as much as I expected, and he said, No, with great relief.

I talked somewhat about you, your speech, how you were really going to fly, and whether he thought we could. He said, as though he didn't quite believe it but *extremely* pleased (like a man who has a beloved mongrel petted!), *"You* want to learn to fly?"

A.: "Yes, we all want to. Con will, I think—she's clearheaded and steady—and Elisabeth will too, she's got *nerve.*"

C. (dryly): "And you haven't?"

A. (a trifle startled—he *never* says what you expect): "I don't know—I've never been tested." (And I thanked him *mentally* for such an unexpected nice thing as saying that.) Then we went into a long discussion as to how much of a mechanical-understanding mind one needed to have. He was a *dear,* and said you needn't understand all about the engine etc. Also I said I disapproved of amateur flying (that it isn't like driving a car, that you can pick up and drive once in six weeks). You ought to fly a lot, it seemed to me, to have it safe or worthwhile. He agreed more or less on that.

I said I didn't think planes were made yet so that any old fool could fly.

C. (with a twinkle): "I hardly think that's necessary!"

There was a great deal more (this discussion went on intermittently all day) about how long it would take us to learn, etc., etc., and was *most* reassuring! He asked me about my going up in Northampton and I told him all about it: why I wanted to go, I knew it was foolish but I thought maybe . . . though I couldn't tell what kind of pilot he was I could tell by asking questions.

C. (interrupting, very amused): "Whether he had *sense?*"

A.: "But he sounded like a careful man, and I found out afterwards he was."

C. (ironically, as though he thought I was a fool but didn't mind): "How do you know?"

A.: "Well, I found out . . ."

C. (ironically again): "How do you know?"

A.: "Well, it was a new plane . . ."

C.: *"That* doesn't mean anything—they can fix that up."

A.: "And he'd been flying three years."

C. looked at me in amused pity. *"Front* cockpit?"

A.: "Yes."

C. (with an ironical smile): "*Crash* cockpit."

A.: "*Anyhow* . . ." (I launched into how much I liked it, why I wanted to see that country etc., etc. Geology motive, you know.)

C.: "Sure, it's fine *now.*"

A. (stubbornly): "But *he looked* careful. He wasn't a young man."

C. (grinned): "That doesn't make any difference." He went on explaining. I was squashed. "I feel very silly."

C.: "You needn't. We all do it—most of us. How long were you up in Northampton?"

A. (quietly): "Oh, I went up three times."

C. (laughing with a "You're-hopeless" laugh): "Worse and worse!"

A. (after some silence): "You won't tell, will you?"

C.: "What?"

A.: "About my going up in Northampton. I wouldn't do it now, knowing how strongly they feel against it. They didn't want Elisabeth to. You won't tell?"

C.: "Certainly not." Then with a grin: "But I'll tell about this time." I told him that Elisabeth went with me once and he shook his head and smiled again that "You're-hopeless" smile.

(Good heavens—I have *just* gotten us over the 59th Street bridge. Do you want to hear all this? I am too exhausted to write any more now and all the best is ahead. I'll go on in the morning.)

I said I'd broken a good many rules in college and he laughed. "Oh, they're *made* to break—school rules. You're all through school?"

"Yes. I am so glad."

"Should think you would be!"

Somewhere in here we were talking about my getting a job— teaching, perhaps—but I didn't think I could.

"And why not?"

"Well, I don't think I'm quick enough, in the first place, and then it seems to me so many useless things are taught. I think a great many of the things I learned were useless."

"And they probably were. I'm sure a great many of the things I learned were."

"I should be thinking, 'Why should *I* be sitting up here dictating to them? Do *I* know any better than *they* do?' Children see things quite clearly sometimes."

He smiled.

He talked about the Zeppelin: thought they arranged the publicity wrong, made it sound like a practical proposition, ought to have been satisfied looking at it as an experiment. Transatlantic flying will not be practical for a long time.

I asked if it didn't also do *harm* to aviation.

C.: "No, I don't think so. I think differently about that than most people. I don't think anything is going to stop the people that want to fly from flying. To have someone else crack up isn't going to stop them. And nothing is going to push it forward much faster than it's going."

I made a mild protest—not much. Then I said what I was *dying* to tell him: that I felt there were still a great many people like us—"Elisabeth, Con, and me" before Christmas—and I explained exactly how we felt, *perfectly frankly.* I was dying to explain, and *I did,* how we had never been interested in aviation, never been interested in anything scientific, never touched anything as modern as that. We had seen planes but never realized that world *practically.*

"Never been up?"

"No," and I went on to say that when we were in that atmosphere of planes coming and going—conversation about it, practical plans about it, etc., etc.—how very exciting and tremendous it was for us. You see, I wanted to explain that *we were* terribly interested in *it* and not just silly girls excited by *him,* and *why* it was that we were so thrilled at Christmas—having a new, unexpected world open. I wanted him to understand our enthusiasm and not have it embarrass him. And he *really* did. I don't remember what he said but he nodded very sympathetically and seemed pleased. I was so grateful and I felt so at ease. *Now* he understood! It was like building a firm platform to stand on: He understands, we needn't think he will take our enthusiasm in the wrong sense!

Again, when I spoke of how grateful I was about this, "You're terribly nice to let me have this. I would rather do it than . . . anything I can think of."

C.: "Well, I ought to be—I've been promising it to you for almost a year now. It's about time. And I said I'd get up to North Haven, but I couldn't—the Western trip." (He hurried over this, a little embarrassed.)

A. (*very* quickly and casually): "Oh, there was *everything* to keep you. Besides, I shouldn't think it would be very good flying country—it's so foggy."

He nodded and asked about landing fields. I described the two-hundred-yard field running up from the water. He said that would be long enough for some planes. He said he was trying to get a Loening amphibian but didn't know if there were a place to tie up.

Another time he volunteered, "My, that trip was uninteresting after Mexico. That is (with a grin) I didn't want to leave—I enjoyed it very much." (Isn't that nice! He just volunteered it, and it was so sincere—he *really* liked Mexico. There's a tribute for you, Mother and Daddy.) He said the flying was interesting, "And the most interesting parts have never been told," and he described flying over mountain colonies of Indians way up in the hills. No one has ever been there. They had probably never seen a white man, to say nothing of a plane. He shook his head and grinned, remembering it. The Mexicans never flew over there— no chance of landing or coming out alive. I asked him about the different difficulties of the trip. He said it got awfully monotonous: too much entertainment. He said he wanted to fly through

South America sometime. I said Elisabeth and I were going by boat, and we talked about that. He said he wanted to come down to Mexico next winter again (!). I said, quite casually pleasant, "That would be wonderful."

C.: "Do you think your father and mother would come back with me? They have to come back anyway."

A. (cautious): "I . . . *should think* they would."

C. (grinning): "But you wouldn't like to answer for them?"

A.: "Well, I guess Daddy would go with *you*. . . ."

C. (interrupting—ironical): "If he went with anyone? So many people say that, and I don't understand it." (Some friend said to him, "I don't understand it. A man flies alone in a single-motored plane over the Atlantic, and he gets the reputation of being *conservative!*")

A.: "Well, I don't think you're quite fair about that. Daddy wouldn't mean it that way. I think he just respects you and your judgment."

He looked rather pleased and didn't say anything; smiled a little, looking down.

Oh, dear, I have so *much* more to say and it is impossible, I can't. I'll have to wait till I see you.

I want to tell you how amazingly at home he is at the swell Guggenheim place (gatehouses and towers and lawns and peacocks!), pushing open the great carved door without knocking, picking up his mail casually, introducing me with the most complete poise, strolling into the baronial living room (Madonnas in all the niches, etc.) with a jovial "How's *Kip?*" Carrying on a delighted conversation with a young married Guggenheim (very sophisticated) about some practical joke played on the unfortunate Kip.

I can't go into that lunch. I never expected to go there for lunch, and you can't imagine my feelings at being ushered in—in my riding trousers, leather coat (which I couldn't remove and I boiled in it), and street shoes and gray golf stockings and street hat! Oh, it was priceless—I and the Madonnas! It was quite nice, though, feeling as awkward as I did, to know him better than the others. You know the feeling: I was an *absolute* stranger to *them* and that made me feel more at home with him, and it was rather nice to have to turn to *him* for all plans and suggestions.

Besides, I can't explain to you, Con, what a change had come in my attitude—just from that hour ride out. I discovered that I could be *perfectly* natural with him, say anything to him, that I wasn't *a bit* afraid of him or even worshipful any more. That Norse god has just gone. I can't understand why I saw what I did before. He's just *terribly* kind and absolutely natural, and (it seems so strange to say it of him but it expresses what I feel so ·well—the casualness and the normalcy of my feelings): "He's rather a dear."

Oh, I drove his car part way. He asked me if I wanted to and I *did* want to, so I just said so! That's the way he makes me feel. Isn't that amazing. He said driving a car helped in driving a plane, and that there were dual controls in the *Moth* and *I could try today!*

The Guggenheims and I had quite a lot of "silent communion" after He left to get the plane, though they horrified me with tales of "Slim's" practical jokes. (They all call him "Slim.")

He went to Roosevelt Field, got the plane, and I waited in a field back of the Guggenheims'. Soon a silver-winged biplane slid over the trees, circled round, and skimmed down. He got out, his blue tie flapping.

C.: "Do you want to try this?" with a grin—the parachute. It is like a pillow of lead thumping against your behind. It fastens like a diaper and overalls, and it thumps against you as you stagger forward.

C.: "That *hat* won't do." He put it in the plane and gave me a brown helmet and goggles, told me about the parachute, "And (with a grin) *don't* jump unless I tell you to." I staggered into the seat. With perfect gravity, not paying any attention to my protests, he told me, "You pull this to go up, push it to go down.

The rudder works this way. Also, in turning, you have to push the stick this way. Now, when I point up (he was to be in the front cockpit) go up; when I do this, go down; *this,* straight ahead. When I do this (he threw both his hands out) the controls are all yours (twinkle), and when I do *this* (he tapped his hand on his helmeted head) let go of *everything* (grin)." Well, I was so afraid that I couldn't think. I didn't *want* this forced upon me, I didn't want him to see how dumb I was.

I can't describe the flying—it was too glorious. Only when he threw his hands out, I was too terrified to look down, and then, finding that the things actually worked, I stopped being afraid. Only it was so funny—I couldn't keep in a straight line. There are tremendous forces in the air that one doesn't realize. It was like an unwieldy and stubborn elephant. It *would* go to the left and I was pushing the *right* rudder (not very hard, evidently!). "No, no, no!" I plead with it. "Don't do that." Then, "Oh, well, all right—I'll go that way if you want." So we twisted back and forth. I tried to go *either* up *or* down the coast (quite a leeway, don't you think!). I tried to restrain its east and west tendencies, and then I found that once really started in one direction it was liable to take the bit in its teeth and just keep going around in a circle. I was hysterical, it was so funny—I couldn't be frightened. Besides, of course, he had the stick in his knees and could work the rudder with his feet! And he was a dear and nodded firmly and slowly at anything I did (as though I had done it on purpose!) and kept pointing down when I wanted to climb up perpendicularly. Oh, I was such a fool. I kept thinking of you: how calm you would have been, how good at it.

It was such a relief when he tapped his head and turned around and grinned. (The noise and wind were terrific, of course.) We landed in a cornfield, just skidding over a fence. I was very humble and embarrassed and amused. He said with a rather quizzical smile, "Did you use the rudder at all?" (*There!* There's a comment on my flying for you! "Did you use the steering gear at all!"—that's what it amounted to.) It was quite a problem to get out of the field. He explained it to me: he had to fly *under* some wires and *over* a fence. Just before we started, he turned around and said with a broad grin, *"I'll* take off, this time!"

We turned a loop and a "tight corkscrew" (?) and I almost burst. It is a sickening feeling. I tried the controls again and it went a little better. It *is* possible. I have held those things in my hands and I know it *is* possible, and I think we *will* do it.

I can't tell you everything. But after it was over, driving back was such fun. He doesn't mind enthusiasm—airplane enthusiasm —and it was *so* easy to talk to him. He talked about publicity, too, saying he couldn't go anywhere over the country without being watched, then adding to my "It's rotten," "Well, it's got to be taken. As long as it's coming to me. I've got to put up with it."

A.: "Does it keep you from much?"

C.: "Nothing that I really want to do—I just do it anyway. I don't believe in letting publicity shape your life for you." (Imagine his saying that—talking about it!) And then again on this subject he said, grinning, "If ever you get into a crowd and they start mauling you, just kick their shins—they don't know who's doing it!"

And when we were discussing the difficulties of Mexican social life he interrupted my "The worst of it is . . ." with

C.: "This business of having to make conversation—I just never do it, myself. These people—women, generally, it is with me—who sit down and reel off conversation . . ." He shook his head and went on to tell about the silly questions people ask him.

I spoke of how the crowds in Mexico frightened me and he said (*just* our point—it amazed me), "Oh, they weren't bad, but you wondered what they would be like *angry."*

A. (excited): *"Exactly!* That's exactly what I meant!" (Imagine being able to say that to Colonel L.—almost a *"touché."*) Oh, so much more—of the difficulties of life in Mexico, of girls getting jobs, of people going to college (he was *most* intelligent on the subject), on how I couldn't take up flying as a profession because books and reading and writing and teaching would be more of my world.

Then he got absolutely lost. After a while I said, "Is this the right road?"

C. (with a perfectly happy-go-lucky grin): "How should *I* know!" (That delighted me! He's not so practical—not so hopelessly practical.) He said he was glad his mother went—said she needed a change; good for her to go into a new place, surroundings and people (very keen of him, I think), and we discussed Daddy's jumping into politics—very courageous, he thinks.

Oh, this was funny. He said with a twinkle, "What will *your father* say to my letting you have the controls? I leave it entirely in your hands to clear me."

A.: "I don't know that I'll tell. Anyway (casually), I think he thinks you have pretty good sense."

"Thank you!" he said in a mock-insulted tone—very amused.

Do you see what fun it was and is going to be! We are going to see him again and he's just like any boy, only nicer, not a bit awe-inspiring, not really very thrilling, just *nice,* easy to talk to, natural, kind—and a dear.

My, but he has changed, though: the ease, the poise of centuries of luxury, with which he pressed the bell at the Guggenheims' for the maid to show me a room to change my clothes in.

He suggested that he would take Jo (and me too—*if I wanted to go*) on a short trip down the coast, just to Lakewood, N. J., some afternoon!

. . . .

Dear Con—

So much has happened since I started this. Jo and I went this afternoon to the *Teterboro Airport,* near Paterson. Flew to Lakewood and back—heavenly. I can't write. Just the flying. No talking, of course. I am too tired to write any more. Somehow it

has leaked out, though, and will I am afraid be in the papers
tomorrow. I feel like Diana, absolutely crushed and furious. It
means the end of everything for all of us for a while, for Daddy
won't let us see him if it means publicity, so Mother said in a
telephone call yesterday. The *Times* has been calling up. Isn't it
disgusting? I feel furiously, bitterly angry and tired. And I dread
tomorrow. And I feel so miserably, for I have spoiled things for
you. *He* doesn't mind the publicity. He said so, laughing, to me:
"Don't worry about *my* publicity. It's coming to me, anyway. I've
got to take it, but I don't want it to be embarrassing for you." But
Daddy is rabid on the subject and won't let him do this again for
us, if it means publicity. It is too wretchedly unfair if it keeps you
and Elisabeth from a flight. Oh, the *brutes*. How can people be
such brutes! "He" says he has some books and papers for "Constance" (grinning sweetly).

> When morning gilds the sky
> My heart doth wakening cry
> Someday we'll learn to fly!

Sunday [*October 21, 1928*]

Dearest Con—

I am so tired. I have some clippings for you and some books and
magazines that Colonel L. brought. I read him your letter and he
said he would send you some more things and asked for your
address, so I tore off part of your letter and gave it to him. He
squinted up his eyes and said, "Does she write a whole letter that
way?"

I want so much to talk to you about him. He is so much
sweeter than we thought and understands almost everything you
give him a chance to understand.

It is gratifying to have such a wonderful person *not dislike* you,
for he has been very kind about going up and everything, but very
upsetting, as at Christmas, to be face to face with a person who
you think is about as wonderful as anyone could be, and is the

embodiment *of what you aren't* in every respect. Oh, I wish I belonged to that world of action and nonintrospection—that superb, objective, vigorous world of his and Elisabeth's.

He is going to Mexico to hunt with Sandy MacNab. He said he would come to Mexico City. I want to see him again, but it is foolish and upsetting.

Oh, my dear, my dear, I feel so alone tonight. I wish you were here. You are so far away, and I feel so far away I feel as though I were going away for good.

Con, don't tell *anyone* about my seeing Colonel L., will you—not even Mother. Don't say anything.

The Westbury Hotel, New York [*October 26, 1928*]

Dear Con—

What do you think? All the worst anyone ever thought of me has been conclusively proved: *I missed the train to Mexico*—"Ta tee ta ta ta ta" (sing to "O-oh-say-can-you-see"!)! Yes, I really did. My trunks are now speeding to St. Louis while I and my three bags, two boxes of records, one box of china, golf clubs and victrola are left behind. Isn't it too awful. We looked at the slip of the ticket which said 6:45 St. Louis (the *St. Louis* train—*not* the New York one). Richard, Jo, and I arrived at the station at 6:30. The train had left at 6:05. I couldn't believe it, I couldn't bear it—I wanted to fly. It is the *flattest* feeling. So Richard took us to a theater and out to an enchanting Russian place Jo will take you to—or I will at Christmas—*much* better than the Samarkand. A beautiful woman sang—*just for me!*—so sweetly, and we smiled at each other, and I loved her.

There is nothing that I feel like doing except writing you about Teterboro. (I can't walk the streets—a might-have-been!)

Teterboro.

Well, our first mistake was to ask a taxi man where Teterboro was. He smirked and said, "You want the field!" and I said elaborately casually, "Oh, it's all right, Jo, *she'll* meet us there."

I drove the *Memphis!* I was determined *not* to make him wait, and we got there a whole hour early and decided to motor around. Suddenly at quarter past one (I was to meet him at two) I had "that sinking feeling"—I left my helmet and goggles behind. (Did I tell you that he handed over the helmet and goggles to me—"Your first helmet"?) I *couldn't* tell him I had forgotten them. We rushed back. I never have gone so fast—we broke every rule there was and hit every bump. It takes a half hour to get back to Englewood. I wanted to do it in twenty minutes, and we were only ten minutes late—arrived 2:10—in those Hackensack flats. Several big hangars, lots of cars, a few planes. I looked around nervously as we drove in. There *He* was standing against the hangar. Do you remember how bright his face is—young and ruddy—and those clear bright eyes that do not seem his or any man's, but as though many bright skies and clear horizons were behind them? I don't think he saw us. We jumped out, looked around, a few curious people smiled at us. An adoring little boy said to me with great pride, *"Lindbergh* is on the other side of the hangar." We ran through—Jo ahead. He bowed, hardly looked at us, and we started for the plane. A slinky reporter pattered after him. *He* was polite but curt. "What is your destination, Colonel Lindbergh?"

C.: "Indefinite—*as always.*"

Rep.: "What general direction are you headed?"

C.: "Up."

(Don't you love it! "Up"!—"Which way is Ireland?")

It was his new plane—a silver monoplane, dark blue plush inside, long cabin behind, two seats behind him where we sat. The stick has a swell handle—amber stone of some kind.

A. (first words spoken to him): "It's my fault we were late."

C.: "You're not late—got here within ten minutes of the time."

A.: "I went back for my helmet."

C. (grin): "You don't need it."

A.: "I didn't know. I thought I'd bring it anyway."

We started—you know the feeling. We went up very steeply. It was superb. He looked as though he were enjoying some huge joke. Jo noticed that, too. He didn't wear a hat. Do you remember what *long* curling lashes he has? A kind of amused glint underneath them. The noise was terrific but you could hear if you shouted. We couldn't even shout in the open plane.

He shouted to Jo, pointing out the altimeter, the speedometer (relative to the air), and a meter that shows how fast you are going up or down. He said we were going down the coast and *over the city!* It is *superb.* You must do it. The shadows of the buildings look so strange and futuristic, and the small squat ferries like ladybugs paddling back and forth, and smoke like raveled thread. It took us only a minute to get over the city from Teterboro. I thought of our many long ferry rides back and forth. The light on the river was beautiful. We were going up and up all the time—then the clouds—we were going through mist, then up again and suddenly we were on a huge plateau of clouds— yes—and they *really look* like clouds too, piled up, and cottony, and here was a hole and far down you could see a patch of water and minute docks. Those clouds—it was the most exciting feeling, like being on the moon. One time we were flying "blind," mist on all sides of us (I thought of his transatlantic flight), then we would break into a sunny plateau. Once I saw ahead two mammoth clouds, gray and rolling, towering like waves straight in front of us. There was a dark crack in between—a tunnel, almost. Nearer, *nearer, nearer* toward the towering banks we dove, then *zoom, right through the tunnel!* We gasped with excitement and pleasure. He said we had to go down—"Too much head wind"—and we plunged at 160 miles an hour, down, down, down.

Then we were going down the coast. I looked at his map. You can really tell the inlets and bays and peninsulas. It is terribly satisfying. To the left of us, just sea—little waves and spray thrown back. I thought again of his flight. I don't see how he told which way the wind was blowing from the waves. We went towards Lakehurst. He circled about it—a huge hangar and thousands of cars, and two small "dragonflies" side by side alight by it.

Coming back, we met two planes! That was one of the most exciting things about it—a fellow traveler! It was so thrilling, as though we were two great commanding hawks, understanding and respecting each other. Almost a silent greeting went between us, because of course we knew he noticed us. We went home inland, sometimes flying very low, skimming over the tops of trees and fields, men at work over haystacks, horses plowing. By the way, the colors on the trees are lovely from above.

I kept thinking of that poem:

> "Today I want the sky,
> The tops of the high hills
> Above the last man's house,
> His hedges and his cows,
> Where, if I will, I look
> Down even on sheep and rook," etc.
> [EDWARD THOMAS]

I saw hawks among the trees, but we were above them!

We went around the city to Long Island and landed on a little field (the one he landed on before). He stopped the motor and turned around to speak to us. Isn't it *ridiculous*—to have to go to a deserted field on *Long Island* so that we could talk quietly and make arrangements! He said he would draw the crowd (if any) by taxying up the field. He said he'd like to take me up in a "Jenny" (I was just thinking, Well, this is over, I won't see him again. It's over—it's been a dream, this week—better to realize it. I can come back to earth and get along without things like this. Better to.) Then Jo (afraid he might get careless about publicity) said something about "only you will be very careful not to let it out . . . Mr. Morrow . . . etc." He looked straight at her with that amused glint in his eyes and said, "Are you asking me a question or *telling* me something?" It was awfully funny. Then he looked up, saw two planes heading toward us (evidently they recognized his plane), and said, "Well, we'd better move on or we'll have company here in a moment."

Then we went up the river. (I get the geography of the city, Long Island, and New Jersey *so* clearly now.) It was about 4:30 and the light on the water was so beautiful, and the bridges (to Long Island, 59th Street, etc.) spanning the gold and the sunset behind them, gold. It was superbly beautiful. I was so happy, and I sat up straight. I saw the hospital by the new Hudson River bridge and shouted to Jo. He turned and I said joyfully, *"The hospital!"*

C.: "Yes, I think it is"—not particularly interested. "Do you know *what* hospital?"

A. (wanting to say, "It's *my* hospital"): "The new Medical Center, the one I was in." He grinned but showed no signs of sympathy.

Then very quickly we landed. Jo and I ran (over a newly planted grass plot) like . . . well, like Daffin when his one idea is to get away, for the car, and rushed off. I could hardly think. Looking back, I saw the silver plane rise and head off for Long Island.

We arrived home and found reporters, telephone calls, etc. They had found out nothing, but, it being in New Jersey, they just *guessed Morrow*. We told them Elisabeth was abroad, and a Mexican paper came out with this item, at the bottom of headlines about "Lone Eagle no longer lonely—Courts Elisabeth Morrow": "Inquiries at the Morrow home brought forth the news that Miss Morrow had been up with Colonel L. and was going again." The damned *liars!* No one *ever* said that. And Mother and Daddy (absolutely *crazy*—I never thought of having to ask *them* to keep still about it) told all the staff that it wasn't Elisabeth, it was me. It makes me cry with rage. I have never before been angry at Mother or Daddy, but really that does seem so insane of them, so *mad*. What *were* they thinking of? What sheer insanity, to make a joke about it—*with all the Embassy staff,* of all people. It would have been so easy just to say, "Elisa-beth is abroad. I don't understand this at all. It is just absurd—Elisabeth is abroad." But to say *on purpose*—to tell an Embassy staff, so it's all over Mexico City, to blab out, "It wasn't Elisabeth, it was Anne—isn't it funny."

He probably was teased and met by reporters, and if I *should* see him in Mexico . . . When we just about *killed* ourselves keeping it quiet here and nothing came out definitely. *Have they lost their senses completely?*

Well, I certainly have lost my temper and sense of proportion, but honestly, Con, wouldn't you have been mad?

Well, when he called up again we were insane with the twitches: every time a bell rang I hid—I have never been so shaky and sick. I felt like a deer, hunted by smiling, smirking, sure-of-themselves, relentless hunters. Jo told him she was afraid of the telephone's "being tapped," so he said he'd come out—for supper.

He came in his Franklin. He said he didn't care about the house being upside down.[1] We talked about the various people he has been engaged to (!) including Elisabeth. (Oh, he is very keen and very clever.) We didn't say a thing but he said with that quizzical smile, "Wasn't there a rumor about my being engaged to Elisabeth—when I was out West?" (*"Wasn't* there a rumor"! He is canny.) He had the books for you, and I got the letter and was reading it aloud and He insisted on reading it over my shoulder, which embarrassed me because some of the begin-ning was about Donald Keyhoe's book.[2] I don't think he saw that, though.

And we laughed about the reports, especially Jo—"Two young and beautiful American girls"—and Colonel L. said to Jo (imag-

---

[1] The Morrows were moving out of the old house in Englewood into newly built Next Day Hill.

[2] *Flying with Lindbergh* (1928), by Donald E. Keyhoe, former Marine pilot, special aide assigned to C. A. L. during his U. S. tour with the *Spirit of St. Louis.*

ine *this* from *him*), "The only incorrect statement there is that you're *American*," with a twinkle.

He told us more about his Central American trip, and He and I argued vs. Jo when she said, "Why do we want to speed things up?"

"It means you will have more time in the places you like."

Also we argued at supper about Al Smith. I told about Dwight (voting for Al Smith). He said to me, grinning, "Your father is voting for Hoover and *he*'s pretty right about things" and also—with a delicious laughing grin—"*Terrible!* These sons voting against their fathers!"

After supper we drove for miles and miles in the Franklin, in *dense* fog. It is so much easier to talk in a car: the engine purrs and fills in the spaces. It was quite amazing, it is so easy to talk to him—and very exciting—discovering that, although he is in a different world, *he* is not so very different and it is very exciting finding points of contact. He has amazing sensitivity of understanding. I told him, apropos of lying newspapers, that it was a shame the way they had made an entirely different person out of him.

"A sort of Santa Claus," he said, laughing.

I laughed. "You know, we didn't want to meet you at all before Mexico."

"I can quite understand that."

And I told him (he was amused and curious to know: "Well, what *did* you think of me?") our impression of him—the stern Norse god.

"Well, maybe I *am* stern."

"Yes, you probably *are*, but you're very kind."

We talked about the restless, confused feeling of not knowing what you can or ought to do after college. He understood beautifully and said he could remember how he felt.

"But *you* knew what *you* wanted to do."

"Yes, but I didn't know *how* I was going to do it," and he told

me how he earned money by stunt walking etc. and I pretended I
didn't remember it all from the book!

He talked about it so naturally. "I was crazy about it" (flying).
"It's fascinating (from the man who doesn't use adjectives!) to
grow up with a new development like that, watch its growth."

And, strangely enough, he talked about *aviation* in a way I
never dreamed he could, as though it were an end for greater
things. "The thing that interests me now is breaking up the
prejudices between nations, linking them up through aviation."
And I don't think he'll stay forever at that job. He talked about
Americans, especially New Yorkers, getting too interested in
their business, losing all sense of proportion.

I also talked to him about writing. (He asked me what I
wanted to do.) I don't know if it was just luck, but he was
amazingly understanding about it and said (!), "I *wish* I could
write." I was amazed and had to ask *"Why?"* and it was all very
interesting.

I talked about you too—how Miss Sturm said you were the
kind of person we were going to make in the future: someone *on
top* of the circumstances, not ruled by them.

He smiled and said in a very grandfatherly tone, "Well, you
simply can't let circumstances shape your life—you couldn't live,
you'd just be crushed if you did."

I told him, too—apropos of whether we were really interested
in aviation—how upsetting to all our world of books and introspection that new world of action and science was, how small it
made me feel.

C.: "Yes, aviation *does* make you feel like that."

(Now I wouldn't have expected him to see *that*.)

Then at home. He standing by the fireplace, very sunny-
looking and laughing, even his hair laughing (Jo said)—it *does*,
you know.

And in the pantry (ginger ale), to Him, *"You* can crack the ice
if you want." And digestives: "Do you remember these?" "I

should say I do." He was so jovial and natural, and not so different. (Oh! I forgot to tell you, I told him I was frightened of him in Mexico. He grinned. "Did you think I'd *bite?*") I have suddenly had an *awful* thought. Suppose someone should open this letter. Wouldn't it be awful. I'd suspect a reporter of anything. I think I shall mark it "from Mrs. Graeme."

Darling, you won't repeat or mention to anyone anything, will you—not to Elisabeth, even, or anyone. I have told you so much, but even to have any of us talking about him among ourselves is a dangerous idea.

Write me who are your best friends now and if you've been to any concerts. Forgive this for being so full of me, but when I get started writing about an experience, I have to finish it.

TO E. R. M.   *Englewood* [*October 26, 1928*]
Darling—
Your heavenly letter about Paris and all this dreadful news about the bronchial pneumonia are just reaching me now, just before I go to Mexico.

Oh, dear—how miserable to be ill in London. In a "nursing home," were you? That sounds too depressing for speech. Don't come home before you can. And *don't* rush around in New York madly. Either rest (?) in this sarcophagus in Englewood or come to Cuernavaca and sit in the sun.

Oh, I want so terribly to see you and tell you about plans for Christmas, about Dwight and Con, but most of all I want to talk to you about the Great God Boyd,[1] who is no longer a god— *much* nicer and more approachable than we thought, and really quite a dear! *And he likes us!* And *loved* Mexico, and we will see him again. Jo will tell you about it. He called up for Mother,

---

[1] "Robert Boyd" used as a cover name for C. A. L., because of a story in the *Saturday Evening Post* the hero of which, Robert Boyd, was evidently drawn from him.

Daddy, or you and somehow got me, which was entirely unexpected, and I felt like a pig and an ugly duckling. You should have been here. He asked when you were coming, and all about *all* of us, and will take you up too.

Oh, I must talk to you about him. I can't say it all now. But for God's sake don't tell a soul—it *always* gets out.

Do come soon—I need you badly. Please get well.

> [*On the train to Mexico*]
> 25 *after 4* P.M. [*October 27, 1928*]

Dear Con—

I have slept so much that I don't know what day it is. It was Sunday before my nap. We have suddenly gotten very warm—almost to Austin.

The first night I read Keyhoe all through at lightning speed. I think he (Keyhoe) has quite a lot of perception. I think the description of his smile (p. 85) is awfully good: "as though he were embarrassed at having been led out of his gravity for a moment." And that picture on the front gives me a regular loop-the-loop feeling—it is so sudden and superb.

I think the description of *blind flying* is superb. It gives me a wonderful picture. I like the part about seeing a map come "alive." I felt that, going from Teterboro. Then somewhere Keyhoe says that Colonel L. never describes his feelings, but *if he did* one would find him an unusually sensitive person—far more sensitive than most. Do you know, I think that's true. He is amazingly "aware" of all sorts of things, but he has no desire—as we have—to express anything and he's been too busy to talk to anyone, except along with action, which, of course, means aviation.

The reason I think he is so sensitive is not only the things he is "aware" of (he described a place somewhere in the West by saying that you could believe you were on the moon) but he understands such fine distinctions. I don't know *why* I trust them to him—probably the fascination of seeing how much he will take. Because of course when he doesn't understand he says, "Exactly what do you mean by that?" Only he *does* get them—about our being an introspective, bookish family, of how distant that world seemed from the new one we discovered at Christmas, whether it was true that it was just the differences in physique that make different temperaments, i.e., that a rather sickly man turns from the world of action to one of contemplation, introspection, artistic things.

He said, "I have often noticed that. But I don't think it's *always* true. Take yourself, for instance . . ."

He asked me what kind of writing I liked to do, and I found myself telling him that I thought the trouble with modern writing was that it was written from the top down, not from the bottom up, not from feeling *into* expression. People did not write because they *had* to say something and they did not let the feeling influence the form, as they should. To my utter astonishment, he nodded gravely and said with warm approval, "That's *exactly* the trouble," and went on to put it more clumsily, but he *got* it! Now what in hell does he know about it? He never opens a book, does he? How that separates him from our world! It is hideous to think about—a hideous chasm. Do you ever think we could bridge it and get to know him well? Oh, I am afraid—terribly afraid. I do not want to see him again. It is terribly upsetting, liking someone so utterly opposed to you. What *do* you think, Con? It is a problem, for he *does* like us and *is* going to see us again. How are we going to accept him? How far in can he get? Do write me what you think. Also, I told him you did not understand the earth inductor compass. *Wide* grin: "I don't know that I can explain it myself. It's very difficult to explain." Then followed a *lucid,* compact sentence or two shot out like bullets that I couldn't *possibly* repeat. Also, he said jovially in answer to me, once, "I'm *not* being polite. I don't believe in being polite!" Which is nice.

1928

Embassy of the United States of America
[*Mexico City, November 5, 1928*]

Dearest Con—

I have just come back from Cuernavaca, which is heavenly. I thought of you all the time. It didn't seem right that you shouldn't be there. I feel as though I had been here weeks and it isn't a week yet. Mother, Daddy, and Allan Dawson[1] met the train. Mother and Daddy asked thousands of questions, all about you and Dwight. Three honks at the gate and then up the red carpet! There were tuberoses in the hall.

Daffin came wriggling out of the door. He was very clean and fluffy. He wasn't quite sure he remembered me but he has since warmed up! Sabino said a long speech to me in Spanish and Miguel bowed and said another! Your room has new bright curtains which were drawn and a bright red Mexican chest, and there were red carnations on the bureau.

I went to bed wanting you so badly (do you remember how we talked the first night?), and Daffin seemed to know, for I said miserably, "Oh, Daffin, Daffin, where's *Con?*" and he (contrary to all rules!) jumped up on the bed and licked me comfortingly!

I had my first Spanish lesson with a Mme Constantine who has pale straight hair and pale blue eyes that peer through *very* thick glasses. She is very nice and I *love* Spanish.

In the afternoon there was a reception. Such funny people came: a large, fat, odious, garrulous schoolteacher who asked me if I was "Mr. Lindbergh's girl." I said, *infuriated,* "I haven't *seen* Colonel Lindbergh for a *long* time (it *seems* like a long time, anyway), and that was all a lie in the papers. My sister is abroad!"

Dear Mr. Beck[2] came and asked me to ride the next morning.

That night I went to a dance. Allan D. is an *angel*—so considerate, understanding, keen, and interesting. The club was

[1] Third Secretary of the U. S. Embassy.
[2] Eman Beck, long-time resident of Mexico City, friend of D. W. M. His daughter Susanna was a friend of A. M. L.

awfully pretty, but it seemed so flat to me. I do not like talking casually to people—it does not interest me—and most of them are unwilling to talk at all seriously. Oh, I can't flirt and I don't want to, and nobody here rouses the slightest spark in me.

I like Sue Beck. I have an instinctive warm feeling about her.

The next morning I rode with Mr. Beck. I rode a little bay polo pony. I love it. I am going to ride every morning I can.

I meant to tell you about Cuernavaca.[1] It is much roomier than Mr. Ovey's and not so theatrical—more satisfying. You eat in an arched porch—very much the same—on red brick tiles, looking out on a green court and down a terrace to a second court, in which are *two beautiful* bougainvillaea trees. You look down an arched walk that leads to our bedrooms. There are little candles lighting up the arches, and a lovely vine runs up by the door arch, and the light makes it very beautiful—double, with its black shadow. Two lovely old French people (an old couple who keep house there) served us supper in Mexican crockery, and the crickets sang! Daddy is *delicious* about it—pulling at your arm all day long to show with delight pots or an arch or tiles or where he is making a *further* garden, or watching the cement being put in the swimming pool, or dragging you up to the *Mirador* to show off the mountains. "He *owns* those mountains!" Allan D. remarked with a twinkle. So Daddy putters around, saying a hundred times a day, "Now, isn't this nice—don't you think this is going to be a nice place? And *look here, Anne* . . ." etc. Mother and I *longed* for you.

Dear Con, this has been a dull letter because there has been no glow about it. Somehow I did not enjoy writing it although I wanted to tell you things. But you will understand, and I will write you again. If Boyd writes you, *please* tell me about it, won't you? I have just heard that he won't be here until Friday or Saturday, and I thought it would be Wednesday.

[1] Referring to Casa Mañana, a house Ambassador and Mrs. Morrow had bought and made over for weekends in Cuernavaca.

I feel the way one did at North Haven when, at 6 P.M., Binns said to you, "No, Miss Anne, supper is not until seven thirty."

[*Cuernavaca, November 19, 1928*]

Con darling,

We are in Cuernavaca again—last week seems so long ago—Grandma and Aunt Annie, and Robert Boyd. I hear that Mother wrote you about his arrival and salute. How we *longed* for you, that moment. I don't really know how much I can say—I shall ask Mother before I send this. They[1] telegraphed that they would arrive not later than six, and precisely at six we heard the roar of the motor and rushed out: a biplane circled low over the Embassy with a great roar. We were out on the steps weak with excitement, then it made for the field. About half an hour later I heard the shouts up the street. Mother went out to meet them. I stayed in my room until called. Sandy MacNab and he looked extremely dirty and camplike, and he looked very sunny.

He went with me and Allan to the Becks' dinner dance. Crowds of adoring fifteen- and sixteen-year-old girls tittered around him, and from time to time he was left with one very energetic vamp. I was sitting right opposite talking to a very subtle, sophisticated, charming man (during the dancing) and I would watch the silences fall and then see her turn desperately to a statue of Cupid armed, and make comments, or an old Mexican silver plate. (It was like that conversation game!) Then Allan and I would form a defensive league, get some man to go up to him, or I would talk to him a moment while someone snitched the vamp for a dance. He stayed very patiently until twelve. I was having, for once, a wonderful time in my new Raquel red petally dress with Allan, whom I talked to about Elisabeth. Also with Fred Hibbard,[2]

[1] Colonels Lindbergh and MacNab had been on a hunting trip in northern Mexico.

[2] Frederick Hibbard, Second Secretary of the U. S. Embassy.

who delights me, with a violet-eyed little Englishman who makes shoes and dances divinely and has not one brain in his head; talking to an awfully nice Scotchman, sort of rough and kind.

To Cuernavaca in the morning. He and Daddy talked about cows all the way down, and agriculture and irrigation, and I sat in the middle and wagged my head between one and the other—like a little dog, ears cocked and uncomprehending.

Do write me. I love your letters. They are the best in the world. I sat in the sun and read on the Embassy steps—Daffin with me.

Daffin has given me two flea bites! More later.

Mrs. R. is *quite mad*, isn't she? But scarlet! Her hair caught on fire the other day from a cigarette—not at all surprising; her hair is always a last year's birds nest, don't you think?

Embassy of the United States of America
[Mexico City, November, 1928]

Con, darling.

I am sitting on the Embassy steps with Daffin's nose on my blotter. Isabel[1] is arranging calla lilies on the porch. I want to see you so badly.

It is awfully hard to write you about Boyd. I shall have to wait and see you. There is, of course, a great deal to tell. There was the day he came. I wrote you about that, and the party that night, and then Cuernavaca the next morning. That was rather agonizing because it is so hard to talk nicely when there are so many people around, smirking and fussing, and watching: old Jean running in and out with cups to stick in the cupboard (dried from lunch) all afternoon. Someone scrubbing in the open sink all afternoon; a steady stream of chauffeur, cook, kitchen maid, small boys carrying water, small girls with chickens, back and forth at the back end of the court where we were sitting; several Mexican gardeners with large hats pruning trees, watering the grass, etc.; and the constant sound of slip-slap—feet on the stone

---

[1] Mrs. Morrow's personal maid.

walks—of dishes being washed, of towels being flapped, oven doors shut, etc., etc., and inarticulate Mexican sounds.

It made us *horribly* restless.

Then Monday we came back. Sandy MacNab is *so* funny about him—he acts as though he *owned* C. Just bursting with pride and as though C. didn't want to see anyone but Sandy and was just being polite about the Embassy family. Sandy acts as though he were doing C. a great favor every time he takes him away from us, which is a joke! In a voice that pats C. on the back and Mother on the head (if you get what I mean!) Sandy says, "Have you any plans for *us* today, Mrs. Morrow?" It makes me *boil!* And C. looks at us and says seriously, *"I will be back this afternoon as soon as I can."*

Then there was a huge dinner Monday night for Portes Gil[1] (referred to for weeks as "The Portes Gil dinner"). *All* the Ambassadors and of course Estrada[2] and Montes de Oca[3] (I *love* his name) etc. Of course they all spoke Spanish and nothing else. Do you know what is *the most* terrible feeling in the world, like being caught on a rock and the tide coming in on all sides? Being left alone with someone who speaks nothing but Spanish! And you have already said, *"Tengo mucho gusto de conocer a usted"* and *"No hablo español—dos lecciones solamente."* Then you sink back and drown in your mutual silence and good will.

Anyway, I sat next to Fred [Hibbard] and said not a word to the Mexican on my left. A man sang very sentimentally (though quite a lovely voice) *Manon* and some Spanish. But somehow there was no heart in it and a dripping song, "I love you," which Fred said he wanted sung at his wedding, funeral, and birth of his twins! But C. and I both disliked the man. Then one day we went to the pyramids, C. driving. He has a funny Texas hat he wears for disguise.

---

[1] Emilio Portes Gil, the newly elected President of Mexico.

[2] Genaro Estrada, Foreign Minister.

[3] Luis Montes de Oca, Minister of Finance.

(Of course, this letter was started weeks and weeks ago—at least, somewhere in the recent unapproachable past. C. has just left, so I must write furiously to forget that he is not here.)

I have told you about the Portes Gil dinner. Oh, I forgot to say that we had such *grand* dishes, superb fairy-tale dishes, almost the kind one boasted about in "London Bridge Is Falling Down" —do you remember? "Will you have a chocolate ice-cream castle or an orange-ade fountain?" The crowning dish was a palm tree of hardened syrup sheltering a pyramid of ice cream! Somehow doesn't it seem ridiculously childish, and amusing! No one dared snap off a leaf of the palm, though C. said when we talked about it later and discovered it was a kind of cookie, "That never gets by me again!"

I want to tell you about flying, though. It seems so long ago—a little over a week. You could not see the mountains. He took up Aunt Annie and Mr. and Mrs. Sills, and then (last) it was my turn. A Curtiss Falcon it is, a biplane with a positive stagger (is that correct?) and a dihedral (?). (I've forgotten what all these things mean. Have *you* got *Everybody's Aviation Guide?*) Anyway, the wings are painted orange and the fuselage blue. Rather a small plane, two cockpits—one behind the other—and dual controls.

Never have I had such a wonderful feeling of escape as we left the ground—that crowd of inquisitive, quick-eyed watchers suddenly below us, dropped below, little black things looking foolishly up. The huge hangars dwindling to matchboxes, the line of poplars a few feathers bending in the wind. And then ahead, out of the mist, the mountains—our equals! Then I don't remember what things looked like for a while because he waved his hands above his head with a grin to me, which meant apparently (!) that the controls were all mine! It was much easier than in New York and I wasn't as frightened and I could make the plane obey me! And I could follow his directions much more easily, though I had formed the bad habit of grasping the "stick" with both hands when one hand is needed for the throttle. It is instinctive to do that, though—like grabbing the pommel of a Western saddle when your horse shies!

When he tapped his head we were up against the mountains and I could breathe again and turn around: a long valley behind, flat and not populated (comparatively), with those burst bubbles of old volcanic hills in distinct lines, and ahead, unbelievably white and mammoth, the great snow slopes of Popo. Below us, thick pine forests, green gorges, and green hills, very like the mountains around Geneva—*not a bit* tropical. You looked down and there was no sign of life: no towns, no houses, just still green firs. Then we came to the edge of the old lava flow, where the liquid soot (it looked like that) had stopped. The straight firs sprang up. The line was very clearly marked. Above the line there was no growth at all, just that soot-appearing lava flow, up for a great distance, then as we came up closer and higher I could make out the rough black rock with jagged fissures in it—then *snow!*

We circled around to the right and I could see a great reddish flow (hard, of course). Then, Con, and this seemed the most amazing (almost): you know how we inevitably think of those mountains as being the end of the world—the lip of the cup, so to speak? Well, at one breath-taking instant I saw *beyond!* Plains, hills, and far, far on the *new* horizon *another* snow-capped peak! The far side of Popo is just one sheet of snow. At first we were only about two thirds up the side of the peak, about where the lava met the snow; we circled up on the windward side, up to seventeen thousand feet! I did not realize that I was cold. I was sitting up straight—singing! But the large fur mittens he handed me were comfortable! I had no idea of the *size* of the mountain. There was nothing to measure by. I got a shock of realization to see our shadow, a small dragonfly, black against the *mammoth* stretches of snow.

Oh, that marvelous stillness, that superb icy immobility of the mountain. We seemed so impertinent—as though, like that boy who tried to drive the sun, we had gone out of our bounds, arrogantly had gone into a sphere not ours. And looking down I had a stupendous feeling of the chasm—the *immeasurable* chasm in between *us* and *it*. I talked to C. about it afterwards and he understood and translated it a good deal more lucidly. It is the realization of the terrific time and effort and daring it would take to get to the snows on that peak any other way, and we got there in about twenty minutes (I think—to the base, at least). It is the realization, too, of what would happen if we stopped. It is the contrast of being so perilously near and so impossibly far away at the same time. I have had the feeling looking down a terrific ski jump at people at the bottom who have made the leap. *Here* I was, *there* they were, a few instants of time between us, and yet—! My Lord, the *chasm!* The chasm between us and that white, unapproachable, sublime peak was like the chasm between life and death.

As I say, we spiraled up. The crater faces away from Mexico City. We went *over* it—an enormous crater (in diameter), strata of rock (grayish brown) going round, and below, *snow*. In the center a *small* crater—sooty black rock. (It did not look liquid and you could not see *any* depth. I expected to see all the way down, like the core hole of a baked apple, to burning red coals!) The black rock was smoking—lots of little threads of smoke. The next time we turned we dove in slightly and zoomed up out! The smell of sulphur was very strong. (I know, now, why aviators are inarticulate. The bare facts alone are transferrable; anything else is just so much froth on the surface of the realities.)

Then we continued *around* the peak, pointing now toward Mexico City. On the leeward side it was terribly bumpy. (Do you remember those *gliding* diagrams?) Then we started to go down. Con, we dove down ravines at the most stupendous speed, down *through* ravines, green cliffs on both sides of us, and I could not see how we could dive through the crevice ahead. That, to me, was almost the greatest pleasure of all. I can't describe it. Perhaps a trout leaping down cascades has that feeling, going toward the sea. Imagine playing with mountains and gorges that way! I can understand how he loves it. But how he can be so dexterous and maneuver that plane, I can't conceive of.

I noticed in the green gorges what I thought were streams, then I saw they were huge serpents of lava which had pushed the trees aside. We skirted over the forests at the bottom of Ixta (which is not nearly as imposing or interesting). There people were cutting wood and, in places, planting. We went over a small lumber-mill town. We saw logs floating down a sluice from the mountain.

Then I had the controls again, and remember no more!

We went over an old blown-out volcano, and there was corn planted in it! The symbolism of that appeals very much to me.

There are miles and miles of mirror—water—marked off in squares—flooded flat fields, perhaps.

Then over the field, that small black mass of people, and we had to come down. How could they bother us? It seemed so impossible.

Dear Con, I have not written or talked to anyone about this. It did not get out—although Mother's flight did—so please don't tell anyone about it unless you *know* it won't go any further. It would be meat for reporters. And for heaven's sake don't say *anything* about my having the controls, as that would get him into serious trouble.

I have much, much more to tell you about C. but I guess you are weary of my handwriting and I will write again about that. You see he has been here for two weeks, and I only went flying once, and I have seen him and been with him a great deal of the time. He is a very absorbing person so that I have thought and lived nothing else for two weeks, and I can hardly look back or forward, I can hardly talk about him because I am still a little blind, "As one sees red suns everywhere from looking at the sun." (Do you remember *Cyrano?*[1]) It is especially difficult as he has not been an aviator or a hero during that time and it is extremely

[1] *Cyrano de Bergerac,* play by Edmond Rostand.

difficult when people speak of him to reconcile *that person* with the one we know.

He wants to look over and correct or add to your speech if you want him to. If you could have an outline or something done by Christmas vacation, we will see him sometime then and you can talk to him.

TO C. C. M.   *Embassy of the United States of America*
[Mexico City, November, 1928]

Sweet Coz,

I have just sent you a mammoth letter, but I think it went by pouch. Here is some information that may help your speech. When does your vacation start? We get home, I think, on the 9th. If it isn't for ten days or so after that perhaps I could come up and see you.

I wanted to tell you, too, how amusing Fred was about our second weekend in Cuernavaca, with C. there. You know what fun Fred is—gay and talks a lot. Well, it did seem that weekend—with Daddy exhausted, Mother distracted, I also, C. as usual—that Fred was talking *all* the time: a continual, bright, and not very profound fountain. You know how disconcerting that immobile, tolerant unconcern of C.'s is. Fred described him as a rock over which the waves of conversation broke in vain, not making the slightest impression. He also, after an exhausting weekend (three meals a day for three days) of this, admitted in a whisper to me that he felt like a bad little boy reprimanded for his noise by "that Viking Silence," which phrase, of course, is *perfect.* Only that does not seem half as typical as the very "little-boy" manner when he is with us alone—having dinner in the study, throwing nuts up and catching them in his mouth, getting some extra dessert for me (I, who was ashamed to ask for another helping) on *his* plate and making a speedy exchange, Sabino catching us at it and hobbling out with his mouth twitching!

He seemed so much younger than the others then, and he is

much less sophisticated, and yet he does seem bigger, stronger, and, ultimately, more complete. I wonder if you would agree, if you heard him talk or saw his view of the world of action, and of books. (He is introspective enough to look at both clearly and decide what he wants.) I am wild to have you see him again and to have a long "hash" with you.

I am going to learn the *jarabe*.[1]

Amo, amas, amat—

(Why is the verb *to love* always regular in any language!)

> *Embassy of the United States of America*
> [*Mexico City, late November, 1928*]

Elisabeth darling[2]—

A week from tomorrow evening we leave for home. That means we arrive the ninth. It seems about two years since I saw you—at least that much. Will we *ever* get caught up? Though I have accomplished nothing here. For a week I studied Spanish, but there are so many distractions—receptions come round like Physics lab. afternoons (both on Wednesday afternoon too!).

We have just talked to you. Darling, it was so short and I could not say anything. Anyway, you have come into reality again when you have seemed unreally far away.

I will try to talk to Mother about your not being there [in Englewood]. It is all right, and don't take any chances about it. Don't do too much about the party,[3] and don't try to seem stronger or more energetic than you are. That is fatal. The trouble is that in trying not to frighten Mother they have evi-

---

[1] A Mexican dance.

[2] E. R. M. was recuperating in the house of friends of the family, the Leffingwells, on Long Island. Russell Leffingwell was a partner of J. P. Morgan & Co.

[3] A housewarming party planned for the new house in Englewood, Next Day Hill. It took place on December 31, '28, and was attended by 960 people.

dently not put things very strongly and have given rather a false impression of a comparatively slight illness—*which it certainly couldn't have been.* A great deal of the fault of such a false impression is on *this* side, of course. You know that Mother is a phenomenally strong person and cannot comprehend illnesses or the impossibility of *instantaneous* recoveries. An instantaneous recovery seems normal to her when, of course, to most people it is an impossibility.

Only, darling, don't let her have too much of a shock when she sees you. That would be very hard for her to bear. If you are terribly thin and weak, not able to walk around much, *do* tell her so *before* she sees you. Telegraph her, if necessary, but don't let her get too much of a shock at seeing you or having Jo meet her with surprising news about you.

Oh, please, please don't pretend or try to be stronger than you are for anybody's sake. Don't try to do things. Don't do the things Mother asks if it is going to tire or excite you. Let the party go hang—it doesn't matter. Don't let Con and Dwight tire you. Darling, I know how courageous you are and how you always put the best face on things, and are cheerful and active beyond what you can do. For heaven's sake *don't,* this time. *Pretend you're sicker than you are.* Don't do *anything.*

I think it's quite natural you should be weak and have no resistance. I don't see *how* you could take that trip so soon. It seems pretty suicidal to me. And if you are comfortable and quiet there at the Leffingwells', *of course,* stay. It will be hectic at Christmas and you *can't* be quiet when Mother feels energetic. You *couldn't* be quiet in that new house considering the Christmas season and Dwight and Con, home for the first time, and the new house and considering Mother's temperament and yours. I think it's much better for you to be out at the Leffingwells'. I would love to come out and be with you. Don't even worry about Christmas. We can go to Nassau together, anyway, and have a rest there.

I have a great deal to write you about Boyd, more than you can think possible. You see, he was here for two weeks and saw practically no one else and did very little of what one generally considers his sole business and interest. In fact, it is very hard to think of him in that light at all. He is much more like us than you could imagine. He is not stern or abrupt or feelingless, and he is not divine or all-powerful or Godlike. Also, he is appreciative of all the essentials in our world. He is amazingly understanding—sees far outside of his world, even into ours. He is terribly young and crude in many small ways (the books he's read, and liking to play tricks) and quite seerlike in tremendous outlooks. Sometimes he will say something that wrenches terribly, that "Yes, he liked poetry: when he was a boy he read Robert W. Service"! (that just hurt *terribly*) or once (when I had been accusing him of never reading a book) when we were laughing about *Ramona,* he said something about the story not being much and then turned to me with a half-boastful and a half-pleading look as if to say, *"There,* I've read a book!"

He argues *superbly* with Daddy and listens stonily to a frivolous and charming conversationalist.

He is amazingly gentle and thoughtful and sympathetic, and yet cruelly relentless, sometimes, probing your thoughts.

He has a rapier sense of the absurdities in people, and couldn't possibly appreciate Fred Hibbard or the *New Yorker.*

I can't write any more. As you can see, I am completely turned upside down, completely overwhelmed, completely upset. He is the biggest, most absorbing person I've ever met, and he doesn't seem to touch my life anywhere, really. ("Essentials" don't seem to touch you personally—they are cold peaks. It's the near-essentials that warm one's heart.) Well, for two weeks or a month I've thought of nothing else, so I'm in a complete coma now. I can't even remember him. I thought I knew him very well (as well as one can know someone at the other pole), and now I think, Who is this person I have been so absorbed in? All my feelings are numbed. I only know that I can't look ahead: there isn't a thing in the world I want to do—ever. I wish I could sleep for the rest of my life. As for looking back, it is all unreal. There is no past—it doesn't matter.

I probably *shall* sleep for the rest of my life if my conduct since his departure is any indication. I sleep till twelve every morning, and take naps in the afternoon!

Well, I wanted to break the news to you that a maniac is coming home. You'd better ask the doctor about my seeing you, although at present it is the one straw the camel bites at. (How's that for Daddy's game of proverbs!) Darling, I can look ahead to that—just seeing you, having you read French poetry to me and tell me about Paris and all the charming people like Mrs. Grenfell,[1] and the book about your children that you are going to write.

We won't think about anything else. I have lots of things to laugh with you about—nobody laughs so beautifully as you.

Christmas will be nice (though the intimate party at night makes me curdle—just because I love all those people so and have forgotten them so completely). Mother thinks Boyd might come, but don't say anything. We'll see him sometime at Christmas anyway.

Dearest, *where* is our convent!

Well, I must dress for a Diplomatic Dinner. This life is so unreal—I don't know what my real smile is and what my party one, what my real feelings are and what the superficial ones.

Boyd's main inconsistency, of course, is liking me. It's not inconsistent of him to like you—which he does (said you were a *"very* unusual girl" and said he liked you and liked talking to you). By the way, he speaks of us as Elisabeth, Anne, etc.

I am *terribly* sorry about the publicity, as so much is my fault, but he is *very* sweet about it—talks it all over, laughs, etc. Says (*private*) that he will try to take some girls up in Washington to split publicity.

---

[1] Wife of Edward Charles Grenfell, head of Morgan, Grenfell & Co., London.

Embassy of the United States of America
[Mexico City, November 30, 1928]

Dearest Elisabeth,

We thought so of you on Thanksgiving Day. (You know, last Thanksgiving we were in Amherst and it rained horribly and we tried different churches, and then that evening we had supper in my room, and smuggled Dwight up the stairs!)

We went to a service in a little Union Church. A choir of Main Street bonnets sang atrociously and so forth.

Then Daddy spoke. He was very wonderful. He defined Thanksgiving Day, starting from the personal, home-family rejoicing and feasting day, going back to old "Thanksgivings," saying that men are judged by their "Thanksgivings." One man has brought hisses upon his name for generations because of his *thanksgiving*—the Pharisee ("Thank God I am not as other men"). Then he led up to what our Thanksgiving in a foreign land should be: "Thank God we are *like* other men." Only it was not preachy or obvious, done very subtly and beautifully, Daddy with his mouth compressed, his eyes earnest and far-seeing, leaning forward to speak with force what he was feeling.

That night we had a long table covered with pumpkins: dinner for the staff. I sat next to a Mr. Whitney[1] (a friend of Sandy's) who knows Boyd quite well. I had a divine evening pretending I *didn't,* and leading him on, by disparaging comments, to praise Boyd—e.g., "People say that . . ." etc.

Adios, dearest. We'll be home a week from tomorrow!

TO C. A. L.   *December 1, [1928]*
Dear C,

My grandmother was very touched and pleased that you should have remembered forgetting the package, and your taking the trouble to replace it. It was very thoughtful and kind of you, and we all thank you.

[1] Cornelius Vanderbilt Whitney.

I don't see how you thought of it anyway on your modern hunting trip or had time for packages or anything else.

I laughed and laughed about it—only it couldn't have been very restful. When do you get caught up—camel-fashion?

To write about what is happening is to write . . . nothing. Or very nearly. I have written three letters about things—a dinner, lunches, a ball, receptions, cocktail parties, etc.—and it all sounded like an evening of the kind of conversation you forget.

This life is still so terribly unreal that I have not woken up yet, even though riding and sunshine give me short intervals of sanity. We all eat too much and sleep too little and smile too much. It will be good to get home and find out who I am.

Yesterday was very exciting—the inauguration of Portes Gil. A holiday, of course. We drove through the streets lined with guards for miles (at least quite a distance to the Stadium). Looking down a side street you could see workmen, crowds of men and women, running, without disorder or noise, to the Stadium. Inside (you know that building where the school children danced) it was jammed—a bright-colored crowd, with red parasols and pennants and people selling oranges and every once in a while a shower of white papers, like a flock of birds, in some sections (men throwing lottery tickets around). All around the top (so that looking up you saw them outlined against bright blue sky) at regular intervals were stationed soldiers. And above them, at regular intervals, flags were blowing. They were triangular-shaped—pennants. They were bright and looked like so many flames. The diplomatic people sat in the middle on a platform in front of the stage where Portes Gil and Calles, etc., sat.

You know it was funny: the crowd *looked* so bright and acted so somberly; there was very little cheering, no disorder, no wild American enthusiasm. And yet you respected them for it. You felt great respect for the solemnity and seriousness of the occasion. It had the dignity of a person who has suffered.

Portes Gil gave a short, compact, serious speech, not one appealing to enthusiasm. Thoughtful, serious, and very convinc-

ing (I read it afterwards in English). There was absolute quiet—
few interruptions and little applause. (But the complete and
serious attention of those thousands of people of all classes was
very impressive.) He spoke using some sort of sounding horn, of
course.

There were some enthusiastic shouts for Calles when he stood
up and raised his hand.

Then the band played the Mexican anthem; there was no
shouting, no crowding. That tune is very moving, I think, but
not at all happy. It is minor in tone, somber and stern, like the
occasion.

I can see Calles embracing Portes Gil, patting him on the back;
the tears were rolling down his face.

You felt really impressed by the seriousness of it, *convinced* of
the sincerity of the people, *convinced* that they should be respected. I felt proud to have witnessed it, and proud of my father.

Sandy is back. I saw him at a ball, bright and shiny in his
immaculate uniform with lots of gold braid. I couldn't believe
he'd ever had a serape on! Also, I sat next to a "Somebody"
Whitney who flies and volunteered a good deal of conversation
about you. He was quite nice and quite interesting.

I am so sick of this life. I would give anything for a little of the
humdrum of college. At least I knew what I was doing and what
I wanted to do, then. I feel fed on pastry and I'd like some brown
bread. Going home will be a relief.

Thank you.

Anne

TO C. C. M.   *Embassy of the United States of America*
                            [*Mexico City, December 2, 1928*]

Sweet Coz—
It is Sunday afternoon—Thanksgiving Sunday afternoon—and
you, perhaps, are going back to school, which is the most horrible
of all feelings. I can remember with complete vividness going

back on that four o'clock, cold, miserable, getting each minute further away.

I ride every morning with the Becks (except for the two weeks Boyd was here—they mercifully and tolerantly took my tissue-paper excuses of "being tired," "busy," etc.!). Sometimes we ride for two hours or so, out towards *Los Remedios,* across the corn-fields and the cactus rows, down through Barranca's. But usually we go the same way: up the Paseo and out along the edge of the fields of some hacienda, cantering under those plumy eucalyptus trees (blue in the morning light), a long row of them shading a road.

I am very happy, riding. The rest of the day is terribly unreal and restless: either lunches or receptions or dinners, or else just sitting around here waiting. It is so unbearable: "Only half past five, two hours till supper—*two* hours and too tired to do any-thing, too lazy to take off my coat, even, and too cold . . ." (It is so terribly cold most of the time.) I take a hot bath—that takes up about twenty minutes—and then perhaps a nap. That is so delicious. My big idea is: not to think, just *not to think at all.* As a result I am in one of my "sunken-island" moods again.

It's due to our friend Boyd, of course. When he was with us I was so absorbed in him that I completely forgot everyone else in the world—*literally. College*—never was. *College friends*—did not exist. *Reading*—a rather small part of life, after all. People I could sparkle intimately with—gone. A whole world of sparkle and scarlet and appreciation of small things, just swallowed up in the sea, lost. No looking back, no looking forward, just this amazing, overwhelming, and extremely forceful man. And now that he's gone all those things remain true—*with no compensation.*

I can't read or write or get absorbed in my old world of appreciation. Nobody interests me (though I've met charming people and talked pleasurably with them). He's taken every resource away from me and has not left—himself. Because I can't even remember him. I'm perfectly numb and dazed—I don't even want particularly to see him again, I don't miss him, it wasn't real enough—it is impossible to believe. When he isn't around, he doesn't exist. I don't know what I am feeling, *really*. There is nothing in the world I want to do. It doesn't help to think dazedly, "Who *is* this man, anyway? I can't *really* like him. It is a dream and a mistake. We are utterly opposed. He likes you, but it isn't the real you. You don't like him anyway—you don't even miss him."

Just this devastating discontent, and in the meantime Grandma sentimentalizing over him and watching me. I'll see him in Englewood, I think, but *à quoi bon?* Oh, dear, this isn't half as easy or as much fun as the *Saturday Evening Post* readers might suppose. And it hurts so to have Allan and Fred carelessly laugh about him—his lack of sense of humor, his practical jokes, his one-track mind. Oh, it is cruel, and I have to laugh too. So you see it is best to ride and take baths and naps and not think at all.

Boyd said that you *never get over* that feeling of serenity and sense of proportion that   gives you. Also that he can hardly bear to sit and watch a sunset—he wants to follow it and be part of it. We got a letter from him the other day telling among other things about a mad ride in a car at night, after which ride, he said, he was prepared himself to write an article on "The Safety of Aviation"! How is yours?

En route [to New York], Pullman Private Car
First day [December, 1928]

Dear Con—

I have just finished *Orlando*.[1] That has taken up three fourths of the day! At 4:30 I finished it and had a long orangeade, with a maraschino cherry. That means about two hours till supper.

I haven't, for a month or more, read a whole book *through*, and it was very absorbing—not exciting but absorbing: you merged into it, so that when you walk out of it you still have bits

[1] Novel by Virginia Woolf.

of it sticking to you. You live through a thin veil of it for a while—the way, sometimes, you live half a morning through the veil of last night's dream.

Of course it is beautifully written, more beautifully and more carefully than any of the others and, in a sense, in a more orderly fashion. The comparisons, the similes, the descriptions are beautiful and satisfying. Orlando himself—herself—delights me. I think it is beautifully done, so that it is *all of one piece*—consistent and convincing and consecutive (and that I think is a triumph). But didn't it seem to you to lack economy—to be *too* rich, too full and too rich to have the clarity that the others have? Not half as many clicks, not that crystal understanding of relationships, and not, somehow, the vision—not a kind of burning core in the center that *To the Lighthouse* had.

I probably didn't understand it. There are parts I know I didn't get, near the end. I think it gives you a wonderful understanding of *her* (V. Woolf), of her sensitivity—too much of it, almost to madness.

Didn't you *love* "He called her a melon, a pineapple, an olive tree, an emerald, and a fox in the snow—did not know whether he had heard her, tasted her, seen her, or all three together"!

Also the description of his and Sasha's conversation "of a face; of a feather," etc.—p. 45. I think of exceeding beauty the paragraph on p. 67, beginning, "But if sleep it was . . . events that . . . are brushed with a dark wing which rubs their harshness off and gilds them, even the ugliest, and basest, with a lustre, an incandescence . . ."

There is lots and lots of delicate humor in it, too. "A fine gentleman like that, they said, had no need of books. Let him leave books, they said, to the palsied and the dying" (Boyd's idea!).

She treats time well, all through: "the discrepancy between time on the clock and time in the mind" and how old people really are.

Oh, I love the description of Orlando on p. 124 best: "the

power to stir the fancy and rivet the eye which . . . a power . . . mysterious . . . compounded of beauty, birth, and some rarer gift, which we may call glamour and have done with it. A million candles . . . burnt in him without his being at the trouble of lighting a single one."

Her analyses of the sexes is pretty good, I think, and very amusing.

A lovely sentence, illuminating and true, a crystal sentence, is: "High battlements of thought; habits that had seemed durable as stone went down like shadows at the touch of another mind and left a naked sky and fresh stars twinkling in it."

TO E. R. M.   *Last letter from the old house*
                                 [Englewood, late 1928]

Darling—

I know this house will be a horrible shock to you. But isn't it dear? I don't think I shall ever be in it again, and I have gone over all the rooms (just now), thinking mostly of you—you and me in the nursery with the blue roses screen; and you and me in the guestroom with measles, playing with beads; and again, the night before Con was born—the Boy Scout parade.

Then your room: your books and pictures that are the richness and— (Well, what am I trying to say? They warm me to look at them, as though I heard you talk.)

Then Mother's room: Sunday School on the sofa, and tugging at that sticky bureau drawer to get a handkerchief. Dwight's room: you sitting up with him, ill.

Then I ran through the garden, down that path—there were cinders, smelling of leaves burned—under the arbor. (Do you remember our stunts?) And where the pear tree was, and the syringa bush, and the sandbox, and that dogwood tree whose red berries we used to play store with. And Austin[1] took them all

---

[1] Austin Lamont, son of Thomas W. Lamont. Later a doctor and teacher of medicine.

away from us one day to tease us. Then the garden, looking back at those two big trees. I said to Con I always think of them as "the married ones." They are so strong, one a little shorter than the other, looking up, as if for support. I love that straight oak that is protecting (*He,* of course). But they are both so strong and independent. The elm, too, is beautiful from the steps. Then the lilac bushes by the door, and the great green door that slams to with such a joyous, satisfying "Everybody home" sound.

Oh, darling, darling, we will always be together, won't we?—woven together by all that and for a hundred other new and growing reasons, because we are two independent people, interested in each other. We will, won't we, whatever happens?

[*Undated*]

Dear Corliss,[1]

I meant to write from New York to thank you for the Philosophical Poets. Elisabeth and I were so pleased and flattered to think that you and Margaret[2] thought we could understand it! When I get to Mexico I intend to get away in complete privacy (if I have to get into a bath and lock the door to do it) and read it.

Corliss, it was so nice to see you again. I would have liked to have a long talk with you and would like to now. Apparently I am going to marry Charles Lindbergh. It must seem hysterically funny to you as it did to me, when I consider my opinions on marriage. "A safe marriage," "things in common," "liking the same things," "a quiet life," etc., etc. All those things which I am apparently going against. But they seem to have lost their meaning, or have other definitions. Isn't it funny—*why does* one marry, anyway? I didn't expect or want anything like this. I think probably that was the trouble. It must be fatal to decide on the kind of man you *don't* want to marry and the kind of life you

[1] Corliss Lamont.

[2] Wife of Corliss Lamont.

don't want to lead. You determinedly turn your back on it, set out in the opposite direction—and come bang up against it, in true *Alice in the Looking Glass* fashion. And there he is—darn it all—the great Western strong-man-open-spaces type and a life of relentless action! But after all, what am I going to do about it? After all, there he is and I've got to go. I wish I could hurry up and get it over with soon. This horrible, fantastic, absurd publicity and thousands of people telling me how lucky and happy I am.

Corliss, if you write me and wish me conventional happiness, I will *never* forgive you. Don't wish me happiness—I don't expect to be happy, but it's gotten beyond that, somehow. Wish me courage and strength and a sense of humor—I will need them all.

Funny, my writing to you this way. But I could not write you a conventional "He-is-just-fine" letter. I feel as if I knew you so well. Corliss, you will not show this or quote it to anyone, will you? It would be awful if it got into the papers—as everything seems to. I don't mind if you tell Margaret, for I trust her and like her.

I can't leave this with an utterly frivolous picture of him. He is so much more than that. But talking about a person is almost always futile. Just reserve your opinions, Corliss, until you meet him. Newspaper accounts, casual acquaintance opinions, friendly articles about him are so utterly wrong.

He has vision and a sense of humor and extraordinarily nice eyes!

And that is enough to say now.

INDEX

Index

coming back - up that grassy
dip again - past the glistening
silver apple tree - & little
apples shining - & the white
house shining - I felt as
though I could not reach out
my hand - it was so beautiful.
I wanted to touch the shiny
little apples - and yet I was
afraid - as though that would
break the spell - as though
things would shatter around me
if I did - All these "things"
that were holding their breath
to let me pass.
   But I did!